CANON LAW
for
RELIGIOUS WOMEN

CANON LAW
for
RELIGIOUS WOMEN

BY

Louis G. Fanfani, O.P.

Doctor of Canon Law
Master of Sacred Theology

AND

Kevin D. O'Rourke, O.P.

Lector of Sacred Theology
Doctor of Canon Law

THE PRIORY PRESS • DUBUQUE, IOWA

Revisores Ordinis: Patrick M. J. Clancy, O.P., J.C.D., S.T.M., Joseph J. Hagen, O.P., J.C.D., S.T.M.

Imprimi potest: Joannes E. Marr, O.P., S.T.M., Prior Provincialis

Nihil obstat: Patrick M. J. Clancy, O.P., J.C.D., S.T.M., Censor Librorum

Imprimatur: ✠ Leo Binz, Archiepiscopus Dubuquensis, die 28 a Februarii, 1961

First Printing

DEDICATED

TO THE MEMORY

OF

MY MOTHER AND FATHER

Kevin D. O'Rourke, O.P.

PREFACE

Since the time of Christ, the Church has encouraged her members to detach themselves from the world and follow the invitation of the divine Savior to practice the counsels of perfections as well as the Commandments. Through the centuries, untold numbers have answered the challenge of Christ and have shown their love for God by embracing this more perfect form of life. From the lonely hermits in the Egyptian desert, to the monks and friars of the Middle Ages, to the many modern religious communities of men and women, the religious state has evolved. This has been an evolution that has perfected rather than destroyed the original attempts at religious life. The goal of one who joins a community of religious today is the same as that which led the ancient hermits into the desert—union with God through charity; a charity perfected and nourished by the practice of the counsels of Christ.

As the religious state has evolved and been perfected, so too has the legislation of the Church concerning it. The Church's purpose in making laws concerning the religious state and in exercising vigilance over it is not to limit the religious state in any way. Well does the Church realize that the progress and growth of religious life is intimately connected with the fulfillment of her divine mission. Rather, by legislating for the religious state, the Church, through her motherly solicitude, strives to foster the growth of religious congregations and orders and to enable the individual members of these institutes to grow in charity in a more certain and orderly way. Using the divine and human wisdom at her disposal, the Church, through her laws for religious, seeks to remove temptations and obstacles to virtue from the paths of those who have chosen this higher form of life. In so doing, the Church wishes to make it easier for religious to attain that union with God which they so earnestly seek. Well might we echo the words of St. Paul when discussing the purpose of the Church's laws for religious: "The end of the law is love."

But before the law of the Church can serve as a guide to greater love of God, it must first be known. Before an orderly religious life can be led the legislation of the Church concerning it must be understood. Just as one making a journey must know the route he intends to travel, so too, one who enters the religious life should know the road map that the Church has provided to lead her children to the goal of this life. In short, the laws of the Church must be understood before they can be applied to the life of the individual religious.

While lecturing at the Institute of Spiritual Theology in River Forest, Illinois, in 1953 and 1954, and at the Institute of Spirituality, held at Notre Dame University, in 1953, 1954 and 1955, we observed with pleasure and edification the intense effort on the part of sisters and nuns in the United States to know and understand the laws of the Church and to obey them with loving obedience. The present volume should aid greatly in this endeavor. By means of its well ordered and clear explanations of the law for religious women, it should aid sisters and nuns to know what is expected of them and thus make it easier for them to travel the road to perfection.

Let us be quick to note that this is not a book reserved for the few who have already studied canon law. Those who never had a course in this discipline will find much to help them in this book. In any discussion of law, it is necessary to use technical terms, but when technical terms are used in this book the author quickly defines them in simple and clear language. Some laws are more difficult to understand than others, but when difficult laws are treated in this book the author usually offers an apt example which makes the application of the law easier to understand. Thus, religious who are comparitively unacquainted with canon law should benefit from this book as well as those who are well versed in it.

The author of this work, Father Louis Fanfani, is no stranger to the canonical problems of religious women. For years he served as a counsulter for the Sacred Congregation of Religious, and he also founded a community of religious women in Rome. He brought to the task therefore, a deep knowledge of the mind and the law of the Church concerning religious women, as well as a thorough understanding of the practical problems that religious superiors and subjects must face every day. But Father Fanfani's qualifications were not all intellectual; his deep charity—we might even say holiness—also rendered him emminently capable of writing a book which touches so closely, even though indirectly, upon the spiritual life. It is with pleasure, therefore, that we greet this revision of Father Fanfani's work carried out by Father Kevin O'Rourke. May it aid nuns and sisters to a better understanding of the laws which Holy Mother Church has designed to aid them in saving their own souls and the souls of others.

Very Rev. Paul Philippe, O.P., S.T.M.,
Secretary of the Sacred Congregation of Religious

FOREWORD

When Father Louis Fanfani wrote *Il Diritto delle Religiose*, of which this work is a translation and revision, it was his purpose to provide an accurate, orderly and understandable commentary on the laws of the Church for religious women. It is clear that he was eminently successful in fufilling his purpose since his original work has seen four editions and has been translated into three languages. Ordinarily, one rendering a work of such reknown into another language, does well not to change or substitute anything in the original text. While this is usually true, it was not possible to follow such a procedure in preparing *Il Diritto delle Religiose* for usage by English-speaking religious. Fr. Fanfani made the last revision of his work in 1953, and in the ensuing period, several important instructions and responses affecting the laws for religious women have been issued by the Holy See. These documents have not only necessitated several additions to the original text, but they have also made it necessary to omit certain sections and to rewrite entirely others which were no longer wholly accurate.

Other changes were necessary due to the fact that a book written originally for European religious is usually not rendered useful for English-speaking religious by means of a mere literal translation. Some adaptations must be made. Were Fr. Fanfani alive today, we feel that he would agree that, although the laws of the Church are the same for religious women all over the world, the practical difficulties encountered in observing and applying them differ greatly from one country to another. Thus, some particular law need not be explained at length to religious who will seldom be affected by it; but in another country, where social circumstances and the national mentality are different, the same law might be much more pertinent and thus a more thorough explanation of it would be necessary. In addition to these textual changes and additions, minor changes have been made in the enumeration and division of the chapters and paragraphs so that the text will be easier to follow.

Although these many revisions have changed the text and order of the original commentary to some extent, the motive of this work is the same as that which prompted the one from which it is derived. This book, too, is designed to provide an accurate, orderly and understandable commentary on the laws of the Church affecting religious women. Where it succeeds in its purpose, the credit must go to Father Fanfani; where it fails, it is the fault of the present writer.

The references cited and their meaning also need a word of explanation. To avoid encumbering the text with footnotes, the references to the various canons of the Code of Canon Law and to the documents of the Church have been inserted in the text immediately following the matter to which they correspond. When a canon is cited it does not mean that a strictly literal, word-for-word translation of it has been given. Rather, it signifies that the sense of the canon in question is contained in the foregoing section. In this way, we have sought to retain the accuracy of expression of the original canon while eliminating, insofar as the matter permits, some of the clauses and constructions which sometimes lead to misunderstanding or confusion. When documents of the Holy See are cited (for example, responses of the Pontifical Commission for the Interpretation of the Code), the date of the document is provided. Thus, anyone wishing to find a complete English translation of the original document may do so by consulting the Chronological Index of the *Canon Law Digest* (T. Bouscaren, S.J., and J. O'Conner, S.J.; Milwaukee: The Bruce Publishing Co., 4 Vols. and Supplement).

A work of this nature is not completed without the help and advice of many people. Therefore, no attempt will be made to enumerate all those to whom my deepest gratitude is due. Special thanks, however, must be given to the Very Reverend Alexius J. Driscoll, O.P., S.T.M., Santa Sabina, Rome, at whose suggestion the work was undertaken and whose help, especially in the initial stages of the preparation, was invaluable; and to the Reverend Bernard O'Riley, O.P., Dubuque, Iowa, who patiently prepared the manuscript for publication.

Kevin D. O'Rourke, O.P., J.C.D.
Feast of the Purification

CONTENTS

PART ONE
GENERAL IDEAS

PART TWO
ERECTION AND SUPPRESSION OF RELIGIOUS INSTITUTES, PROVINCES AND HOUSES

PART THREE

GOVERNMENT OF RELIGIOUS WOMEN

PART FOUR

SELECTION OF SUPERIORS

PART FIVE

CONFESSORS AND CHAPLAINS

PART SIX

TEMPORAL GOODS

PART SEVEN

ADMISSION INTO RELIGION

PART EIGHT

OBLIGATIONS OF RELIGIOUS WOMEN

xix

PART NINE

PRIVILEGES OF RELIGIOUS

PART TEN

DIVINE WORSHIP

PART ELEVEN

SCHOOLS AND MISSIONS

PART TWELVE

TRANSFER TO ANOTHER RELIGIOUS INSTITUTE OR CLASS

PART THIRTEEN

DEPARTURE FROM THE RELIGIOUS LIFE

PART FOURTEEN
NON-RELIGIOUS STATES OF PERFECTION

Abbreviations Used in This Work

A.A.S. — *Acta Apostolicae Sedis*
Ap. Const. — Apostolic Constitution
C.L.D. — *Canon Law Digest*
P.C.I. — Pontifical Commission for the Interpretation of the Code
S.C. Bishops and Regulars — Sacred Congregation of Bishops and Regulars
S.C.Indulg. — Sacred Congregation of Indulgences
S.C. Prop. — Sacred Congregation for the Propagation of the Faith
S.C.Rel. — Sacred Congregation of Religious
S.C.Rites — Sacred Congregation of Rites

PART ONE

GENERAL IDEAS

THE RELIGIOUS STATE
AND RELIGIOUS INSTITUTES

1. Nature of the Religious State

The religious state is defined in the Code of Canon Law as: **A permanent manner of community life by which the faithful undertake to observe, not only the ordinary precepts, but also the evangelical counsels, by means of the vows of obedience, chastity and poverty** (c. 487).

A manner of community life. Some theologians have questioned the necessity of community life as an essential element of the religious state. It is evident from the above definition, however, that today, according to Church Law, there can be no true religious state without some form of life in common; nor can one of the faithful be called a true religious unless he or she embraces some type of community life.

To fulfill this requirement of community life in the religious state, must the members of an institute live in the same house, or, as it is

3

usually expressed, must they dwell under the same roof? Before the publication of Pope Pius XII's Apostolic Constitution on Secular Institutes, *Provida Mater Ecclesia* (February 2, 1947), this point was debatable. Now however, all doubt concerning this matter is dispelled and the response to the above question must be in the affirmative. This follows from the words of the aforementioned Constitution which states that one of the differences between a secular institute and a religious institute is that the latter imposes upon its members community life under the same roof. Secular institutes on the other hand do not impose this form of community life (cf. Art. II of the above Constitution).

In which the faithful. Hence unbaptized persons, and heretics are excluded from the religious state (cf. *infra,* n. 114).

A *permanent manner of living in common,* that is, permanently, in an enduring manner, as the etymology of the Latin word *status* (state), which is derived from *stare* (to stand firm, to endure, to persevere) implies. The existing law for religious does not demand absolute but only relative permanence. Temporal vows which must be periodically renewed, are therefore sufficient to constitute one a true religious. However, the permanence which the religious state demands excludes the intention, at the time the vows are professed, to leave religious life at a later time.

Not only the ordinary precepts. Ordinary precepts are those which all the faithful are bound to observe, that is, the Commandments of God and of the Church.

But also the evangelical counsels, that is, those recommendations of the Gospel which, if practiced faithfully, will lead souls to a higher degree of perfection. The practice of the counsels, unlike the practice of the Commandments, is not absolutely required for the attainment of eternal life. This distinction between precepts and evangelical counsels is clearly illustrated in the Gospel of St. Matthew (19:21), and in other places in the Gospels.

By means of the vows of obedience, chastity and poverty. Obedience, chastity and poverty are not the only evangelical counsels, but the Code expressly mentions them to stress the fact that today they are considered by the Church as essential elements of the religious state. Later on we shall discuss these three counsels in detail. For the present it will suffice to point out that in the true religious state, the observance of these counsels must be ensured by profession of vows; for it is the vows which, implying as they do a strict obligation in conscience to fulfill a promise made to God, give to the religious state the stability demanded by its very nature.

It follows, therefore, that in the juridical concept of the religious state formulated by the Church, three things are required: (1) the practice of Christian or evangelical perfection; (2) the three vows of poverty, chastity and obedience; (3) some form of community life embraced in a permanent manner.

Hence, considered in itself, the religious state is, objectively speaking, more perfect than that state of life which merely requires the observance of the Commandments of God and of the Church. Rightly, therefore, in the words of the Code, the religious state "must be held in honor by all" (c. 487). Nevertheless, in practice, each individual should embrace the state to which he or she feels that he has been called by God; by corresponding faithfully to the graces of that state, he or she will attain perfection in the sight of God.

2. NATURE OF A RELIGIOUS INSTITUTE

A religious institute, in the sense in which we now speak of it, is defined as: **A society approved by legitimate ecclesiastical authority, whose members, in accord with the particular laws of their institute, profess public vows, whether perpetual or temporary, and by these means strive for evangelical perfection.**

A society, that is, a group of several persons working together for the same end and employing the same means to attain that end. There must be a note of stability in a religious society, and this is assured by the profession of vows.

Approved by legitimate ecclesiastical authority. In the past, not all authors have admitted that the approval of the Church is of its very nature an essential requirement for a religious institute. It is clear, however, from the present legislation of the Church, that no association can lay claim to the dignity of a true religious institute without the positive approval of competent ecclesiastical authority (cf. *infra*, n. 8).

Whose members profess public vows. A vow is said to be public when it is accepted in the name of the Church by a lawful ecclesiastical superior; if this formal acceptance by the Church is lacking, the vow is private (c. 1308, par. 1; cf. *infra*, n. 143). The profession of public vows is the formal element which distinguishes the religious institute from secular institutes and institutes of the common life.

Whether perpetual or temporary. From these words it is evident that it makes no difference, as far as the essence of the religious state is concerned, whether the vows are made in perpetuity or only for a definite length of time. All that is required is that they be public, and, if they are temporary, that they be renewed after a fixed time (c. 488, n. 1). Likewise, from this viewpoint, it makes no difference whether the vows are simple or solemn as long as they are true vows of religion.

In accordance with the particular laws of their institute. Profession of the three vows of poverty, chastity and obedience is absolutely necessary for every religious institute. Without these vows there is no religious state. However, except in those things which pertain to the very essence of the vows, all religious institutes are not bound to the practice of the vows in the same manner. Consequently, each institute needs its own particular laws to determine the observances which are proper to it, and also the manner of practicing the vows. These laws are known as the rule or the constitutions.

And whose members by these means [the vows], *strive for evangelical perfection.* Spiritual perfection, says St. Thomas, can be obtained in the present life in two ways: "First, by removing from man's affections whatever is contrary to charity, such as mortal sin . . . secondly, by removing from man's affections, not only whatever is contrary to charity, but also whatever hinders the mind's affections from being directed entirely to God" *(Summa,* II-II, q. 184, a. 2). Religious, by observing the three vows of religion, tend to perfection in this second manner. The perfection for which they strive is called evangelical because it is proposed to us by our Savior in the Gospel *(Evangelium):* "If thou wilt be perfect, go, sell what thou hast, and give to the poor . . . and come, follow me" (Matt. 19:21).

Hence, it follows that *five things are required for a religious institute* properly so called; namely, that the members: (1) live in a society or community; (2) approved by legitimate ecclesiastical authority; (3) with the intention of striving for evangelical perfection; (4) by means of the three public vows of poverty, chastity and obedience; and, (5) professed according to the rule of the particular institute.

If even one of these elements is lacking, an association may be a confraternity, a pious union, a sodality, or a secular institute, but not a religious institute strictly so called; that is, one in which the members are religious in the juridical sense of the word.

The practice of evangelical perfection is still possible even though one or another of the above elements is lacking. There are innumerable souls who offer and consecrate themselves to God and strive to scale the heights of perfection, and yet do not enter a religious institute properly so called. These souls possess the religious life in substance and if, after the manner of religious, they lead some type of community life, then in a broad sense they can be considered as being in the religious state. However, they are not religious in the strict canonical sense of the word, nor can their institute be called a religious institute or a religious order.

3. FORMS OF RELIGIOUS INSTITUTES

Religious societies, whether they are organizations of men or of women, are differentiated in the following manner.

A. According to the nature of its vows

According to the *nature of its vows*, an institute is either an order, a religious congregation, a pious society or a secular institute.

A religious order is an institute in which the members, in virtue of their rule, profess solemn vows (c. 488, n. 2).

In virtue of their rule, that is, when their rule and constitutions prescribe profession of solemn vows. It is not necessary, however, that all of the members actually profess solemn vows; an institute is an order if only some of the members do so.

A religious congregation is an institute in which the members profess only perpetual or temporary simple vows (c. 488, n. 2).

Simple vows. In a congregation, solemn vows may not be taken by any of the members even though they may wish to do so.

A pious society is an association whose members lead a community life after the manner of religious, under the government of superiors and according to approved constitutions, but without being bound by the usual three public vows of religion (c. 673, par. 1).

Without public vows, that is, without vows accepted in the name of the Church by a legitimate ecclesiastical superior (c. 1308, par. 1).

There is no reason why vows, even the three vows of religion, may not be taken privately in pious societies. Indeed, the members of these societies frequently follow this praiseworthy custom. However, like the vows taken by any other members of the faithful, they are only private vows, or, as they are usually called, vows of devotion.

Secular institutes are clerical or lay societies, whose members, moved by a desire of acquiring Christian perfection and of engaging fully in the apostolate, profess the evangelical counsels, even though remaining the world (cf. Ap. Const. *Provida Mater Ecclesia,* Feb. 2, 1947, Art. I). Members of these institutes do not take public vows nor is it required that they live in common "under the same roof" as religious do.

Profess the evangelical counsels. This is especially true of the counsel of perfect chastity, and hence, those who are married may not become members, in the strict sense, of secular institutes *(ibid.,* Art III, par. 2, n. 1). Some secular institutes, however, have "auxiliary" members who are married.

Moved by the desire of acquiring Christian perfection. As we have pointed out above, it is obligatory for all religious to strive for perfection, but it does not follow that those who remain in the world may not do so also. Our Savior said to all: "You therefore are to be perfect, even as your heavenly Father is perfect" (Matt. 5:48).

And of engaging fully in the apostolate. Consequently, secular institutes of a purely contemplative nature, may not be established. The apostolate under one form or another is an essential requisite in these institutes *(ibid.,* Art. I).

Even though remaining in the world. The members, therefore, do not wear any special type of clothing, sometimes retain their secular occupations, and do not have the obligation of leading a community life such as religious lead *(ibid.,* Art. II, n. 1).

B. According to the kind of approbation

According to the *kind of approbation* it has received, an organization is either an institute of pontifical approval or an institute of diocesan approval.

An institute of pontifical approval is one which has obtained from the Apostolic See either approval or at least a decree of praise *(decretum laudis)* (c. 488, n. 3).

In approving religious institutes, the first formal decree which raises the institute to pontifical approval is called the "decree of praise." In this decree, the purpose of the founder, the ends of the institute and the results already achieved are commended. But the Holy See does not render a final decision as to the merits of the organization, nor does it have any intention, by reason of the decree, of absolutely approving the institute. It is only after renewed petitions have been made by the interested parties, and after proof of the genuine utility of the new religious institute for the Church and for souls has been established, that the Holy See grants absolute approval to a religious institute (cf. *infra*, n. 10). This explains the distinction made above between "a decree of approval" and a "decree of praise," and it also explains why it is said that before a religious organization can become an institute of papal approval it must receive at least a decree of praise from the Apostolic See.

An institute of diocesan approval is one which has been approved by the local Ordinary, but has not yet obtained any commendation from the Holy See (c. 488, n. 3).

How and when a local Ordinary can give his approval to a religious institute will be explained later (n. 8). But note that, although a religious congregation may in the course of time establish houses in several dioceses, it remains an institute of diocesan approval, entirely subject to the jurisdiction of the Ordinaries, until it has obtained the approval of the Holy See, or at least until it has received a decree of praise (c. 492, par. 2).

C. According to the authority on which it depends

According to the *authority* upon which it depends, a religious institute is either exempt or non-exempt.

An exempt religious institute is one which is not subject to the local Ordinary except in those cases which are expressly mentioned in canon law (c. 488, n. 2). Hence not only institutes of solemn vows, but also institutes of simple vows may enjoy exemption, the extent of the privilege being dependent upon the good pleasure of the Sovereign Pontiff.

A non-exempt religious institute is one which, in conformity with the common law and the legitimately approved constitutions of each

institute, is subject in all things to the jurisdiction of the local Ordinary.

D. *According to its ministry*

According to its *ministry*, a religious institute is either clerical or lay.

A clerical institute is one in which a majority of the members are priests (c. 488, n. 4).

A lay institute is one in which the members usually are not elevated to the priesthood, and hence if one or another of its members is a priest, it is by way of exception or by a reason of a dispensation (c. 488, n. 4).

Religious institutes for women are thus necessarily and always lay institutes; those for men, on the other hand, are both lay or clerical according to the aims and provisions of their rules. The Benedictines, Franciscans, Dominicans and others are clerical institutes because many, indeed the majority, of their members become priests. The Brothers of St. John of God or the Christian Brothers, on the other hand, are lay institutes even though one or another of their members may perhaps be elevated to the priesthood. The great majority, in fact all or almost all, of the members of these institutes are destined to remain in the lay state.

E. *According to the manner of life led*

According to the *manner of life* led by its members, a religious institute is contemplative, active or mixed.

In **contemplative institutes** the members apply themselves principally, under one form or another, to prayer and contemplation.

Principally, because, since it is not possible in the present life to devote oneself continuously to prayer and contemplation, it has always been the custom even in institutes of a purely contemplative type to prescribe for the members, over and above the usual domestic duties, some daily manual labor.

The members of **active institutes** have as their special end the performance of works of mercy (such as the instruction of children or adults), the care of the sick or the direction of souls.

In **mixed institutes,** the members devote themselves to both contemplation and action; not as to two independent parts of their life, but rather as two elements which permeate and mutually aid one another; exterior action being vivified by contemplation, and contemplation taking on new vigor and life from action. The Dominican and Franciscan Orders are examples of mixed institutes.

In the *Summa Theologiae* (II-II, q. 188, a. 6), St. Thomas asks whether the contemplative life or the active life is the more perfect. In effect, he answers as follows:

Considered in itself, the contemplative life is without doubt more perfect than the active, because the former has God himself as its direct object while the latter is ordained to God through the medium of one's neighbor; and actions which tend directly to God are certainly more perfect than those which do so only indirectly.

In particular cases, however, because of the pressing demands of daily living, circumstances may render the active life preferable to the contemplative. Our neighbor has many needs which can be fulfilled only by those who, being free from family ties and consecrated to God, have the necessary time and spiritual drive to care for them. For example, the care of orphans and the aged is fittingly provided by religious because such people would be otherwise neglected.

The mixed life is more excellent than either the contemplative or active forms of religious life. "Just as it is better to illuminate than merely to shine, so it is more perfect to give to others the fruits of contemplation than merely to contemplate": and thus it was that our Lord and the apostles embraced a type of mixed religious life.

4. RELIGIOUS

In canon law **the term religious designates all those who have pronounced vows in any religious institute** (c. 488, n. 7). St. Thomas points out that although all those who worship God may be called religious, in a wide sense, "only they are designated religious in a special sense who consecrate their whole life to divine worship, by withdrawing from worldly affairs through the profession of vows; in the same sense the term contemplative is applied, not to those who contemplate, but to those who devote their whole life to contemplation" (*ibid.*, q. 81, a. 5).

The distinctive characteristic of religious properly so-called is that they have professed vows in an approved institute. Nevertheless, novices, although they have not yet professed vows in such an institute, enjoy all the privileges and spiritual favors granted to their institute (c. 567, par. 1; c. 614), and hence under this aspect they are to be considered as religious. It is doubtful, however, whether the same may be said of postulants, even though they have been formally accepted by an institute.

5. KINDS OF RELIGIOUS

A. *Religious are either regulars or religious with simple vows*

Regulars are religious who pronounce vows in an Order. The vows which are professed may be solemn or simple, perpetual or temporary; as long as they affiliate one to an Order they constitute the religious a regular (c. 488, n. 7). Regulars are divided into *mendicants* and *non-mendicants*. Mendicants in the wide sense are those who belong to Orders which at one time lived on the alms gained from door to door begging. Mendicants in the strict sense, "in name and in fact," are those who belong to Orders which prohibit the holding of property in common by provinces, or at least by certain houses, of the institute. Thus, to be a mendicant in the strict sense in the present day, one need not collect alms from door to door. Today, only the Friars Minor of the Strict Observance, the Capuchins, and by reason of their professed houses, the Society of Jesus, are mendicants in the strict sense of the word (cf. c. 621, par. 1).

Religious with simple vows are those who pronounce vows in a religious congregation (c. 488, n. 7). As we have pointed out above (n. 3, A), in a religious congregation the vows are always simple, even when they are perpetual.

B. *Religious women are either nuns or sisters*

Nuns, for example, cloistered Benedictines or Dominicans, are not the only religious women with solemn vows; also those religious women whose vows are normally solemn but who, by a disposition of the Holy See, in certain localities profess only simple vows, are nuns. These religious are to be considered nuns in the strict sense of the word unless it appears otherwise from the nature of the case or from the context of the law (c. 488, n. 7). Women religious of solemn vows in Belgium and France belong to this latter category. In these countries, since the days of the great Napoleonic revolution, even those religious who should in virtue of their rule profess solemn vows, profess only simple vows; nevertheless they are to be considered true nuns, and they possess all of the rights and duties of nuns (S.C. Rel., June 23, 1923). With the special permission of the Holy See they may now also make solemn profession of vows as long as they can and are willing to observe all of the prescriptions regarding the papal cloister. The Holy See easily grants this permission and it encourages monasteries to ask for it; in fact, "unless there are grave reasons to the contrary, nuns without solemn vows should take steps to return to them" (cf. Ap. Const. *Sponsa Christ.*, November 21, 1950, Art. III, par. 2).

Sisters, in the juridical sense of the word, are religious women with simple vows; that is, religious who pronounce vows in an institute in which only simple vows are permitted and prescribed by the rule (c. 488, n. 7).

Although in popular usuage the terms *religious women, nuns* and *sisters* are employed interchangeably, in the legislation of the Church these names refer to definitely distinct classes of persons. *Religious women* is a generic term which applies equally to nuns and sisters. The titles *nun* and *sister,* on the other hand, are specific terms which apply only to definite classes of religious, as was pointed out above.

It follows then, that what is said in Church law relative to religious women applies equally to nuns and sisters. On the other hand, what is said of sisters does not apply to nuns, and what is said of nuns does not apply to sisters, unless the legislator expressly states that what is said of one applies also to the other.

6. Evolution of the Religious State

It is almost universally admitted that the religious life owes its origin to our Lord himself, but all do not agree as to the manner in which he established it. Some maintain that he did so directly, by determining even its concrete form; others hold that he did so indirectly, by defining only its essential elements, such as the evangelical counsels, but leaving the practical work of organization to the apostles and their successors. One thing is certain, however: from the very first days of the Christian era there were men and women who under one form or another embraced the religious state. Some even maintain that the apostles themselves, after the ascension of Christ into heaven, lived as religious, and that the religious state should be considered as something indispensable, or touching upon the indispensable, in the very life of the Church. Hence they say that although sanctity, which is a characteristic note of the Church, can certainly be attained even outside of the religious state, nevertheless the splendor of sanctity seems to demand that there exist a special state of life in which evangelical perfection, or sanctity, may be practiced as a profession. This would well account for the special solicitude with which the Church has always regarded the religious state and it would also explain why the Code of Canon Law declares that the religious state is a form of life which should be held in great honor and reverence by the faithful (c. 487).

Although the religious state is one and divine in its origin, it does not follow that it has existed under just one form throughout the centuries. There have been in the past and there are today a multiplicity of ways approved by the Church in which the faithful can fulfill their vocation to the religious life. With the birth of Christianity, saintly virgins and ascetics individually embraced the religious life by practicing the counsels and leading the life of perfection. Then came the monks who, in the third or fourth century in the East and in the sixth century in the West, developed the religious state more fully by living not only in conformity with the counsels but also according to a special rule which guided them along the road to perfection. In the East, St. Paul the hermit (234-247) and St. Anthony (251-350) founded the anchorites, and St. Pachomius (292-348) originated the cenobitical form of monastic life. In the West, St. Benedict (480-543) was the Father of all the various forms of monasticism in the Latin Church.

The sanctification of the monks, however, is a life of perfection and holiness which is followed in itself and for itself. Hence the sanctification of others through the sacerdotal ministry was not envisioned as a part of this form of religious life. Monasticism, past and present, represents the contemplative form of religious life in the Church. Not until the eleventh century did the religious state begin to be united to the sacerdotal ministry and the apostolate for the salvation and sanctification of others. There arose first the Canons Regular, a form of religious life which was both canonical and ministerial. Its full development came in the thirteenth century at the time of St. Dominic and St. Francis, in the institution of the Religious Orders properly so called. To the apostolate, which was an essential part of their religious life, the Orders added an element which the monks did not possess—the federation of several convents into provinces and the union of several provinces under the authority of one supreme superior. As a result, instead of monks (from *monos*, single, alone), the members were called *fratres* (brothers).

A few centuries later, perhaps in place of or at least in addition to the Canons Regular, several institutes of Clerks Regular were founded; for example, the Somaschi, the Clerks Regular of the Pious Schools, the Barnabites, the Theatines, and the Jesuits. Their purpose was to devote themselves to the priestly ministry in all its fullness. To accomplish this they set aside monastic observances, without, however, depriving themselves of the aids of the religious life.

In the sixteenth, and especially in the seventeenth century, the religious families which are known in the Church today as Religious Congregations were established. These societies often lack several of the traditional aspects of the more ancient types of religious life; for example, monastic observances, the choral recitation of the office. Nevertheless, they preserve a sufficient number of the elements of the religious life (perpetual or temporary vows, community life, the practice of evangelical perfection according to a particular rule) so that they are religious properly so called, and are recognized by the Church as such (c. 488, n. 2).

About the same time that the religious congregations were founded there were also established associations of priests or of laymen whose members live in community after the manner of religious but without vows, or at least without public vows. The Oratorians of St. Philip Neri and the Congregation of the Mission of St. Vincent de Paul (known in the United States as the Vincentians) are examples of such associations. These institutes are recognized by the Church as Associations or Societies whose members lead a community life after the manner of religious, but they are not religious institutes in the strict sense of the word (c. 673).

There are, therefore, several kinds of religious institutes—Orders, Congregations, and Pious Societies—and to these have been added in recent years the Secular Institutes which were approved by His Holiness, Pope Pius XII in the Apostolic Constitution *Provida Mater*

Ecclesia of February 2, 1947. Members of these institutes do not take public vows nor do they lead a religious community life; nevertheless, they imitate religious at least in spirit by striving for Christian perfection and devoting themselves in an entirely modern manner to the Christian apostolate.

In recalling the history of the religious life we must not forget that women also have felt the desire, and have quickly grasped the value, of imitating men religious by embracing the religious state and by living according to a rule which, although adapted to their status as women, has been usually inspired by the rule of one of the great Orders. Thus, in centuries past, nuns such as the Benedictines, Dominicans and Franciscans came into existence. Today, they are countless numbers of other institutes of women which, whether united to the ancient Orders or not, daily flourish ever more abundantly and usefully in the fertile garden of the Church as Religious Congregations, Pious Unions, or Secular Institutes.

PART TWO

ERECTION AND SUPPRESSION OF RELIGIOUS INSTITUTES, PROVINCES AND HOUSES

I

ERECTION AND SUPPRESSION OF RELIGIOUS INSTITUTES

7. ERECTION OF A RELIGIOUS INSTITUTE

The foundation of a new religious institute may be proposed to competent ecclesiastical authority by any member of the faithful, provided he or she is called by God to do so.

Called by God. If a divine call is required in order that one may lawfully embrace the religious life in an institute which has already been founded and approved, for all the more reason is a divine call necessary for the work of organizing and selecting a new form of religious life capable of effectively leading souls to the practice of evangelical perfection. Without this divine call one would be building on sand. In this case the words which St. Paul addresses to priests may well be applied: "And no man takes the honor to himself; he takes it who is called by God, as Aaron was" (Heb. 5:4).

A religious institute is truly and canonically founded, however,

19

only when it is approved by the Church. This is evident from the Code of Canon Law (c. 488, n. 1) which expressly states that a religious institute is a "society approved by legitimate ecclesiastical authority . . . " (cf. also *supra*, n. 2).

8. APPROVAL OF A NEW RELIGIOUS INSTITUTE

A. The power of bishops

Besides the Sovereign Pontiff, to whom all ecclesiastical institutions are subject (c. 218, par. 1), residential bishops also can establish and approve new religious congregations for their own dioceses, whether these congregations be institutes of men or of women (c. 492, par. 1). This power does not extend to the vicar capitular or to the vicar general of a diocese.

Religious congregations. These words of the Code refer to institutes of simple vows; hence the approval of new religious institutes of solemn vows, that is, religious orders, is beyond the jurisdiction of bishops. Approval of such institutes, whether they be orders of men or of women, since it is a "major work," is reserved to the Holy See (c. 220). The approbation of the Apostolic See is also required for the founding of monasteries of nuns even if the members adopt a rule which has already been approved (cf. *infra*, n. 18).

For their own dioceses. A bishop has no jurisdiction outside of his own diocese. Hence a religious congregation of diocesan approval cannot establish houses in another diocese without the consent of both Ordinaries; namely, the Ordinary of the place where the motherhouse of the congregation is situated and the Ordinary of the place where the congregation wishes to establish the new house (c. 495, par. 1).

B. Bishops must consult the Holy See

Bishops, however, may not establish religious congregations in their respective dioceses, or permit them to be established, without first consulting the Apostolic See (c. 492, par. 1).

The manner in which recourse to the Holy See is to be taken in this matter, as well as other matters pertaining to the approval of religious institutes, was determined by the *Motu Proprio* of Pope Pius X on July 15, 1906, by the "Norms for Approving New Religious Congregations," promulgated by the Sacred Congregation of Religious on March 6, 1921, and by other recent documents.* Relative to the approval of new religious institutes by bishops, the following legislation is contained in the *Norms* (Chap. I, nn. 3-5):

> As often as any bishop, in conformity with canon 492, paragraph 1, shall deem it opportune to establish a new religious congregation of simple vows, *re adhuc integra* [that is, before making any definite commitments], he is to have recourse to the Sacred Congregation of Religious and is to give it all the information that is necessary in order that the Sacred Congregation will be in a position to judge whether it is opportune to establish the new foundation. He will especially make known: the identity and qualities of the founder [of the new institute]; the reason for his decision to establish a new foundation; . . . the name or title of the congregation which is to be founded; the form, color and material of the habit which the novices and professed will wear; the number and kinds of works which the congregation intends to undertake; the economic means the congregation will use to provide for its livelihood; whether in the diocese there are already similar institutes and, if so, in what type of work they are engaged.
>
> When the permission [of the Sacred Congregation] has been obtained, there is nothing further to prohibit the bishop from establishing the new institute. It will remain, however, a congregation of diocesan approval . . . until it shall have received approval or at least a decree of praise (cf. *supra,* n. 3, B).

It appears from what has been seen above, however, that the information which must be submitted to the Holy See before an institute may be approved by a bishop, presupposes that the end of the institute, the means it will use to attain the end, the type of work which it intends to undertake, and other important factors, are already well defined. Now, it is a fact of daily experience that no institution is per-

---

* In 1953 the Sacred Congregation of Religious issued another instruction in regard to the approval of religious congregations, societies, and secular institutes. In the main, the instruction of 1953 does not differ greatly from the *Norms* of 1921, insofar as religious institutes are concerned. Since the differences are slight, and because the text of the 1953 instruction is not readily available to all, we have chosen to describe the procedure of approval as it is outlined in the *Norms.* The reader should consult the local Ordinary or the Vicar for Religious if more detailed information is required.

fect when it is first established; and in the present instance, it is not possible to have sufficient evidence of the utility and solidity of religious institutions unless they are first tried out. It is our opinion, therefore, that although a bishop, in virtue of canon 492, cannot *definitively* approve a new religious institute, even within the limits of his own diocese, without first having had recourse to Rome in the manner explained above, nevertheless, before submitting the matter to the Holy See he may permit the institute to be tried out so as to determine whether it has the stability and importance which it should possess if it is to be truly useful. By proceeding in this manner, the bishop would not be approving the new institute; and if he acts with prudence, much less would he be prejudging the success of the project. He would merely permit a trial of the institute to be made and he would avoid the danger of encouraging valueless projects and of presenting useless cases to the Holy See (cf. S. C. Rel. *Instructio*, Mar. 19, 1948).

C. *Tertiaries must be affiliated with the First Order*

In order to establish a new congregation or institute of tertiaries who are to live in community, besides obtaining the approval of the bishop, it is also required that the members be affiliated with the First Order by the superior general of the Order (c. 492, par. 1). For example, if a new religious congregation should wish to become affiliated with the Dominican Third Order, besides obtaining the approval of the local Ordinary, it would also be necessary that the Dominican Master General grant the congregation affiliation with the Order of St. Dominic.

The Code of Canon Law does not explain the nature and implications of this affiliation. It seems to us that on the part of the superior general, it consists in his official recognition of the new institute as a true congregation belonging to the Third Order Regular to which it has sought admittance; for example, to the Dominican or Franciscan Third Order Regular. On the part of the new institute, affiliation consists in the acceptance of the rule of the Order. The rule must be embraced at least in all of its fundamental aspects, but it may be modified and adapted to the ends of the new congregation.

Religious congregations which are affiliated with a Third Order remain entirely subject to the jurisdiction of the bishops or the Holy

See. The superior general of the First Order, except in virtue of a special privilege, may not become involved in any way in the direction of such congregations (c. 500, par. 3). This is not true, however, of a Third Order Secular.

9. IMPLICATIONS OF APPROVAL

A. Implications of Pontifical Approval

Canonical approval of a religious institute by the Sovereign Pontiff or by the diocesan bishop principally implies three things:

1) The authentic testimony of the Church that the religious institute is proper and lawful and that it is useful for those who wish to acquire perfection (*Conditae a Christo*, Pope Leo XIII, Dec. 8, 1900, n. 1).

2) The granting of power to the superiors of the institute to receive, in the name of the Church, the vows of those who wish to become members of the institute (c. 488; c. 1308, par. 1).

3) The recognition of the institute as a moral person, that is to say, a moral entity, capable of enjoying all of the rights and of contracting all of the obligations which belong to institutions of this kind in virtue of common or particular ecclesiastical law (c. 100).

B. Precautions given by Pope Leo XIII

Because of these important effects of approval, the following precautions are prescribed in the Bull *Conditae a Christo* of Leo XIII (nn. 1-3):

1) Bishops, before approving a new religious institute, must make sure that there is nothing in its constitutions which is contrary to faith, approved customs, canon law or pontifical decrees, and that everything is in keeping with the purpose of the new institute.

2) Bishops rather than found or approve a new community, shall as often as possible make use of some community which is already established and whose purpose is in conformity with the end desired.

C. Approval or disapproval of Congregations

In the *Norms* of the Sacred Congregation of Religious (to which we have referred above, n. 8, B, footnote), the second chapter treats of "Congregations which in no way whatsoever, or with great caution, are to be commended and approved." In this chapter we read:

> Except perhaps in missionary countries, no (religious) congregation shall be commended or approved, which instead of having a well defined and special purpose, seeks rather to undertake all types of works of piety and charity, even those which are most disparate (*ibid.*, n. 13).

> Great caution should also be observed in approving congregations that live solely on alms which are begged from door to door. And if they are approved, exact observance of canons 622, 623, and 624, which prescribe the norms to be followed by religious who solicit alms, should be insisted upon (*ibid.*, n. 14).

> Nor shall approval be readily given to new religious congregations of sisters, especially those with perpetual vows, which have as an end the care of the sick of both sexes in private homes both day and night, or the doing of daily domestic work in the homes of workers and of the poor. If, however, occasionally and for just reasons, it seems opportune that approval should be given, conditions and safeguards, by which the sisters will be protected from all possible danger, shall be prudently prescribed in the constitutions (*ibid.*, n. 15).

> Likewise, approbation will not readily be granted (by the Holy See) to communities of sisters which have for their special work: (1) the opening, in their own houses, of rest homes and hospices for both men and women; (2) the opening of rooming houses for priests; (3) teaching in schools for young men, or, teaching in so-called mixed schools in which there are both young boys and young girls (*ibid.*, n. 16).

> Still less readily will approval be given to those congregations which have as an end the direct care of new-born infants or of mothers in confinement in maternity homes, or similar works of charity which do not seem too becoming for those who are consecrated to God and who are clothed in the religious habit (*ibid.*, n. 17).

10. PROCEDURE OF THE HOLY SEE

A. *Approval of Religious Orders*

Approval of religious orders, that is, institutes with solemn vows, is reserved exclusively to the Sovereign Pontiff, as was pointed out above (n. 8). In present day legislation there are no determined norms regulating the procedure to be followed in granting approval to these institutes.

B. *Approval of Religious Institutes*

Relative to the approval of religious institutes with simple vows, on the other hand, the "New Norms" (cf. *supra* n. 8), in Chapter I, "Of the Different Degrees of Approval of Religious Congregations," state the following:

> When a suitable interval of time has elapsed since the establishment of the first foundation [which has been approved by the bishop in the manner explained above, n. 8, B], if the institute shall have expanded sufficiently and shall have given proofs of piety, religious observance and spiritual worth, all of which must be verified by testimonial letters from the Ordinaries of the dioceses in which the institute has one or more houses, the *decretum laudis* [decree of praise] shall be granted (*ibid.*, n. 7).
>
> [The decree of praise] is the first act by which the Holy See interests itself in the work of the new institute in such a way that it ceases to be merely diocesan. In this decree the Sacred Congregation . . . after giving an introductory account of the founding of the institute, its purpose, name, vows, form of government and the authority of its superior general, concludes with these words: "The Most Holy Father N. . . . having examined the letters of recommendation of the bishops of the dioceses in which houses of the institute in question are located, in virtue of the present decree praises and recommends the same institute to the fullest extent and recognizes it as a religious congregation of simple vows under the authority of a superior general, always without prejudice to the jurisdiction of the Ordinaries, in accordance with the prescriptions of the sacred canons" (*ibid.*, n. 6).

To obtain the decree of praise for institutes of women, it is necessary to present to the Sacred Congregation of Religious:

1) A petition addressed to the Sovereign Pontiff, signed by the superior general and her assistants or councillors (*ibid.*, n. 8, a).

2) Testimonial letters from the Ordinaries, as pointed out above. These letters must be sent sealed and their contents must be kept secret (*ibid.*, n. 8, b).

3) A description of the institute signed by the superior general and her assistants or councillors, and confirmed as authentic and true by the Ordinary of the place where the principal house is located. This account should make known "not only the origin of the congregation and the name of the founder and his or her outstanding qualities, but also the personal, disciplinary, material and economic condition of the congregation, and all of the necessary information pertaining

to the novitiate, the novices and postulants, both in regard to their number and to their training" (*ibid.*, n. 8, c).

4) The constitutions, examined and approved by the bishop, composed in Latin or Italian or French, and published in printed form (*ibid.*, n. 8, d).

5) A decree of the Sacred Congregation of Religious, March 31, 1919, also prescribes "that there be submitted for examination and revision by this same Sacred Congregation all books containing customs, usages and similar things and which are entitled *Directories, Customs* and so on . . . and also books containing prayers which are peculiar to the institute and are customarily recited in common."

6) Finally, to obtain a decree of praise for tertiaries living in community it is also necessary to present the document proving that affiliation with the First Order has been obtained from the superior general of the Order, in conformity with canon 492, n. 1 (*ibid.*, n. 8, e).

The decree of final pontifical approval will be granted only if: [after receiving the decree of praise] a sufficiently long period of trial has demonstrated that the institute possesses stability; that the constitutions are well adapted to the end of the institute and that they have been faithfully observed; that the form of government is good; that the members are diligent in preserving discipline in the bonds of charity within the institute, and zealous in fulfilling all of the external works which are proper to the institute (*ibid.*, n. 9).

These conditions are to be verified, first, from the report on the state of the congregation which, in the form described above (3), is to be presented by the superior general when the petition for final approval is submitted; secondly, from newly written and sealed letters of recommendation from the Ordinaries of the dioceses in which houses of the institute are located; and finally, from the corrected text of the constitutions which is to be presented anew to the Sacred Congregation (*ibid.*, n. 10).

This procedure in approving new religious institutes is not so binding that every new institute must necessarily pass through all of these various stages. "At times, although rarely, final approval is granted without a previous decree of praise. This can happen when an institute, presented for the first time to the Sacred Congregation, is already so well established in all respects, that a further deferment of approval would seem to be without purpose" (*ibid.*, n. 12).

11. NAME AND HABIT

Neither the name nor the habit of another institute may be taken by a new religious institute (c. 492, par. 3). Hence "if new religious congregations take the title of congregations which have already been approved, they must make some addition to the title so that the distinction between them will be sufficiently clear" (*Norms,* n. 27).

The habit and name of every new religious institute should reflect the gravity, poverty and modesty which befits those who wish to make profession of evangelical perfection. "Hence names of religious congregations which are too contrived or artificial, or names which express or refer to forms of devotions not approved by the Holy See, are to be avoided" *(ibid.,* n. 28).

The **title of name** of an institute may be taken from some attribute of God (for example, The Congregation of Divine Providence); from some mystery of our religion (for example, The Congregation of the Adorers of the Blessed Sacrament); from some feast of our Lord, the Blessed Virgin or the saints; or from the special end of the congregation, and so forth *(ibid.,* n. 26).

In regard to the **habit,** the use of silk, gold or silver, with the exception perhaps of a small cross or medal, shall be avoided. In some institutes the religious are given a small ring as a symbol of their mystical espousal with Christ. This custom is praiseworthy as long as the gold or silver ring is simple, and without ornaments or precious stones. If possible, a picture of the habit should be sent to the Holy See with the request for approval. Once approved neither the name nor the habit may be changed without permission of the approving power, that is, the bishop or the Holy See. Recently the Holy See has encouraged institutes of religious women to change their habits if they are too cumbersome or difficult to wear; requests for change in design have been granted to many communities.

12. SUPPRESSION OF A RELIGIOUS INSTITUTE

A religious institute, even if it is diocesan, once it is licitly established, cannot be suppressed except by the Holy See. This provision must be observed even if the institute possesses only one house (c. 493). Hence, bishops no longer have the faculty granted to them in the *Motu proprio* of Pope Pius X (July 15, 1906), of suppressing diocesan congregations.

When a religious institute is suppressed, it is reserved to the Holy See to dispose of the property belonging to the institute, but without prejudice to the wishes of the donors of the property (c. 493). Hence the temporal goods of an institute which has been suppressed may not be divided among the members of the institute, nor given to others, even with the consent of the bishop. The goods must be given over to the Holy See which, taking into account the will of the donors, will dispose of the property in the manner which seems best to it. If a community is suppressed the goods of the individual religious, such as the dowry of goods merely administered by the community for the religious, must be returned to her, in accord with the law (c. 551, par. 1; c. 569, par. 1 and 2).

The suppression of an institute can come about as the result of a union or fusion with another institute; but even this may not be done without the approval of the Holy See.

II

ERECTION AND SUPPRESSION
OF A PROVINCE

13. NATURE OF A PROVINCE

A province, as understood here, **is the union under one superior of several religious houses so that they form a part of a religious institute** (c. 488, n. 6). The superior referred to here is not the superior general; the union of all houses of the same institute under a superior general constitutes an order or religious congregation, and not a province. The religious institute of which a province is said to form a part is an order or congregation.

Superiors of a province are major superiors (c. 488, n. 8), whether they be called provincials, assistants or visitors (cf. *infra*, n. 38).

Every province can become a moral person, that is, as long as it is lawfully established, it can become recognized as a legal entity, in conformity with canon 100.

14. Division of an Institute into Provinces

When a religious organization is an **institute of pontifical approval,** it pertains exclusively to the Apostolic See to divide it into provinces, to unite existing provinces or otherwise modify their boundaries, and to establish new provinces (c. 494, par. 1).

If, on the other hand, the religious society is an **institute of diocesan approval,** to divide it into provinces, to unite it with another province or to modify its boundaries falls within the jurisdiction of the superior general in accordance with the prescriptions of the institute's constitutions, or of the bishops to whom the institute is subject.

15. Suppression of Provinces

If a religious organization is an **institute of pontifical approval,** the suppression of one or more of its provinces belongs exclusively to the Apostolic See (c. 494, par. 1). If, however, it is an **institute of diocesan approval,** this power is possessed by the superior general, or by the bishops to whom the institute is subject, as was said above relative to the establishment of a new province.

When a province has been suppressed, the right of disposing of its property (the laws of justice and the wishes of the donors being safeguarded) belongs to the general chapter, or, outside of the time of the chapter, to the superior general with her council, unless the constitutions determine otherwise (c. 494, par. 2).

III

ERECTION OR SUPPRESSION OF A RELIGIOUS HOUSE

16. NATURE OF A RELIGIOUS HOUSE

In a material sense, **a religious house** is the place where several members of the same institute habitually reside; in a formal sense, **it is the association of several members of the same institute who dwell together as a community.** A religious house may have one of several names—abbey, hermitage, convent, monastery, college, conservatory, and so forth.

Every lawfully established religious house is a moral person, that is, it is a legal entity with rights and duties (c. 100).

17. KINDS OF RELIGIOUS HOUSES

A. Formal or non-formal

A religious house, whether of men or women, may be either a formal house or a non-formal house. **A formal house** is one in which

31

at least six professed religious reside; and if it is a house of a clerical institute, at least four of the professed religious must be priests (c. 488, n. 5).

A **non-formal house** is one to which less than six professed religious are habitually assigned. When the house is erected, at least three religious must be assigned there; otherwise it cannot be considered a moral person (c. 100, par. 2).

Professed religious. Hence novices, and with greater reason, postulants, are not to be included when computing the six religious. On the other hand, even in institutes in which solemn vows are taken, those in simple vows are to be included when computing the requisite number.

B. Independent or Dependent

A house or monastery is **independent,** or *sui iuris,* when it is independent of other houses or is not subject to superiors other than those of the house itself.

A house is **dependent,** or *non sui iuris,* when it is subject not only to local superiors but also to other superiors of the institute; for example, when it is also subject to the provincial or to the mother general.

C. Motherhouse, Principal House, Filial House

A **motherhouse,** considered historically, is the house where the order or congregation had its beginning. In a juridical sense it is the house where the superior general habitually resides. It is also called the general curia (cf. c. 495).

A **principal house** is a convent that has, as branches or divisions, one or several small houses which are subject to it in all things.

A **filial house** is one which is not autonomous and is therefore subject to a principal house.

A filial house, properly so called, therefore, is not a moral person distinct from the principal house. Nor does it have its own chapter or council; but its members, if they possess the necessary qualifications, form part of the chapter or council of the principal house. A filial house can, however, have its own superior, but the superior possesses no authority except that which is delegated to her by the superior of the principal house, and the authority must be exercised within the limits of that delegation.

Nevertheless, a filial house is a true religious house. Consequently, the same conditions are required for its erection, functioning, and so on, as are necessary for the erection of every religious house.

18. ERECTION OF A RELIGIOUS HOUSE

For the erection of a **monastery of nuns,** that is, of religious with solemn vows, the approval of the Apostolic See and the consent of the local Ordinary are always required (c. 497, par. 1). This consent and the approval of the Holy See, given in writing, are required under penalty of invalidity, that is, without them the house or monastery is not recognized by the Church as a moral person and in consequence does not enjoy, unless by papal indult, any rights or privileges whatsoever (c. 497, par. 2; c. 100, par. 1).

Sometimes nuns who should profess solemn vows profess only simple vows in virtue of an Apostolic indult. When these nuns wish to erect a new monastery in a region where the causes for their indult do not exist, they need the permission of the Apostolic See and the vows they profess in the new region must be solemn vows (S.C. Rel., Oct. 11, 1922). For example, some nuns in countries with unsettled political conditions or laws against religion have been allowed by the Holy See to profess simple vows while retaining the legal status of nuns. If these nuns were to found a new monastery in a place where the above burdensome conditions did not apply, they would need permission from the Holy See, not only that of the local Ordinary; and they would have to pronounce solemn vows.

The approval of the Apostolic See and the written consent of the local Ordinary are also required **for the erection of any religious house for women in countries which are missionary territories** and hence subject to the Sacred Congregation for the Propagation of the Faith (c. 497, par. 1). The same permissions are required for the erection of any house which is exempt from the jurisdiction of the bishop.

If, on the other hand, the house or monastery to be established is only in an **institute of diocesan approval and is outside missionary territory,** the permission of the local Ordinary suffices for its erection. It must be remembered, however, that a religious congregation of diocesan approval cannot establish houses in another diocese without the consent of both Ordinaries: namely, the Ordinary of the place where the motherhouse of the congregation is located, and the Ordinary of the place where it is desired to establish the new foundation (c. 495, par. 1). The Ordinary of the place where the motherhouse is situated shall not in this case refuse his consent without grave reason (c. 495, par. 1).

Strictly speaking, it is not necessary to have the permission of the pastor in whose parish the new house will be established. However, it is wise to consult the pastor, especially in smaller localities, since the work of religious should be carried on in harmony with the pastor.

Before the erection of any religious house whatsoever, it must first be ascertained whether it will be able to provide suitably for the support of the community from its own resources, or by alms ordinarily received, or through other means of revenue.

The permission to establish a new religious house carries with it the authorization to carry on the works which are proper to the institute to which the house belongs; but the conditions under which the permission was granted must always be observed (c. 497, par. 2). For his own just reasons, the Ordinary can subject the permission which is requested to special conditions or restrictions, and these are obligatory as long as they are not contrary to any rights and privileges granted by the common law.

19. CONVERSION OF A RELIGIOUS HOUSE

In order to convert a religious house which has already been established to uses other than those for which it was originally founded, the same formalities are required as for the erection of a new house (c. 497, par. 4).

To other uses, that is, to uses which differ substantially from the original purpose of the house, as, for example, to change a cloistered monastery into a rest home, or a religious house which has been used for educational purposes into a hospital.

If, however, the change affects only the internal government and religious discipline of the house (for example, changing a house into a convent of strict observance, or converting a house used for the training of young religious into a rest home for old and infirm sisters), only the permission of the superiors of the institute, in accordance with the prescriptions of the constitutions, is required (c. 497, par. 4).

20. TRANSFER OF A HOUSE

When there is question, not of erecting a new house, but of transferring a house which is already in existence from one place to another, as long as it is within the same city or locality, the formalities for the establishment of a new foundation spoken of above are not required. The transfer must be made within the same city or locality, and never to a place which is at a notable distance from where the house was first situated (S.C. Bishops and Regulars, April 5, 1754). For example, a distance of one or two hundred yards would be allowed. But if the distance is two or three miles, then a *new* foundation rather than the transfer of a house which has already been established, would seem to be involved.

If a monastery in which the papal cloister is observed is transferred to another locality, it is necessary to secure permission from the Holy See to establish the cloister in the new place (S.C. Rel., Oct. 11, 1922).

21. SUPPRESSION OF A RELIGIOUS HOUSE

Whether a religious house is formal or non-formal, if it belongs to an **exempt religious institute,** it cannot be suppressed except by the authority of the Holy See (c. 498). And if it is a house of nuns, permission of the Holy See is necessary even if the nuns are not exempt.

If, however, it belongs to a **non-exempt congregation of pontifical approval,** it can be suppressed by the superior general, with the consent of the local Ordinary (c. 498). The house cannot be either validly or licitly suppressed if, in the judgment of the bishop, it should not be suppressed (c. 105, n. 1). The institute, however, has the right of appeal to the Holy See.

And, if the religious house belongs to a **congregation of diocesan approval,** it can be suppressed by the sole authority of the local Ordinary, after consultation with the superior general of the congregation (c. 498). However, when it is the last remaining house of the congregation, or the institute has only one house, then, since the closing of the house would mean the extinction of the institute, to suppress this one house, even when the institute is only diocesan, in virtue of canon 493, the permission of the Holy See is required (c. 498).

Whenever a religious house is closed, recourse *in suspensivo* (with suspensive effect) to the Holy See may always be made (c. 498). This means that, once an appeal has been made and until a response has been received from the Holy See, one is not bound to accept the decision of the Ordinary or of the superior general (c. 498).

If a religious house which has been closed belongs to a province or to a religious institute, the goods of the house, together with their accompanying obligations, become the property of the province or of the institute; always, however, without prejudice to the wishes of the donors. If the house is *sui iuris,* that is autonomous (cf. *supra,* n. 17, B), the goods may not be distributed among the dispersed members of the house but must be given to the Holy See (c. 493). The Holy See will consider the wishes of the donors and will give some of the goods to the members of the suppressed house should they need it for support in the world.

22. Repossession of a Religious House

Whenever there is question of reclaiming a religious house formerly possessed, the following norms are to be observed:

1) If the house was abandoned voluntarily, to reclaim it the same formalities as would be necessary for the founding of a new house must be observed (S.C. Bishops and Regulars, Nov. 17, 1617). The same is true with regard to a house which has been suppressed by legitimate ecclesiastical authority (cf. *supra,* n. 21), or one which was abandoned or destroyed with a period of more than one hundred years having elapsed since its destruction or abandonment (c. 102, par. 1).

2) On the other hand, if the religious have been violently expelled from their house, they and their institute retain full rights to reclaim it when this becomes possible; or, if the house has been destroyed, to rebuild it on or near its original site. This is true, at least, if after the violence has ceased, the time which has intervened has not invalidated the former right by legitimate prescription. Some maintain that the right to reclaim or rebuild is lost when more than a hundred years has elapsed since the dispersal of the community.

PART THREE

GOVERNMENT OF RELIGIOUS
WOMEN

I

LAWS FOR RELIGIOUS WOMEN

23. PAPAL LAWS

Religious men and women are subject to the laws and prescriptions which are contained in the Code of Canon Law or other documents of the Apostolic See. Not only those laws which pertain to them as religious, but also those which pertain to all the faithful bind them in conscience. The first and highest superior of all the faithful—religious, ecclesiastical or lay—is, and always will be, the Sovereign Pontiff. When one enters religion, one does not cease to be a Christian and a Catholic, and hence he or she is obliged to observe the universal laws of the Church as long as they are not contrary to the special laws of the religious state which the Church permits her children to embrace.

Hence the following must be noted:

1) Whatever is said in the Code of Canon Law concerning religious, even when expressed in the masculine gender, applies equally to religious women, unless it appears otherwise from the context or from the very nature of the case (c. 490).

2) With the exception of those laws which are contained in approved liturgical books or which are dictated by positive or natural divine law, the disciplinary laws of the Church which were in force at the time of the promulgation of the Code no longer bind unless they are contained either explicitly or implicitly in the Code (c. 6, n. 6). Liturgical laws or rubrics, even when they are not contained in the Code, remain in force unless they are expressly corrected by the Code (c. 2).

3) Legitimately acquired rights or indults and privileges granted by the Holy See to any religious institute, if they were still in use when the Code was promulgated and were not revoked, remain in force unless they are expressly repealed by the Code (c. 4).

4) Whenever there is a doubt as to whether any prescriptions of the Code differ from legislation which preceded the Code, the latter is to be followed (c. 6, n. 4).

24. Diocesan Laws

Diocesan laws and decrees oblige religious women who dwell within the diocese except when they are exempt from the jurisdiction of the bishop; and to the extent to which they enjoy this exemption. As we have pointed out, religious by their entrance into the religious life do not cease to be members of the faithful, and since the bishop has jurisdiction over all the faithful who live within the limits of his diocese, he has jurisdiction over religious living there unless the Sovereign Pontiff, the superior of all, including bishops, limits the episcopal jurisdiction.

Relative to the subjection of religious women to the authority of bishops, the following points should be kept in mind:

1) In virtue of canon 495, paragraph 2, if a religious institute of diocesan right is established in many dioceses, the constitutions may not be changed without the unanimous consent of each and every Ordinary of the dioceses in which the institute has houses. We say "unanimous" because if such consent were not given, the approval of each bishop which canon 495, paragraph 2 requires, would not be present.

2) If, by a special indult of the Ordinary, the faithful are dispensed from a common law (for example, from the ecclesiastical law of Fri-

day abstinence), religious dwelling in the diocese may use the dispensation if they are not prohibited from doing so by special vows or particular laws of their institute (c. 620). This is true even if the religious are exempt from the jurisdiction of the bishop (c. 620; cf. *infra*, n. 229).

When traveling in a diocese other than their own, women religious are not bound to the particular laws of that diocese unless such laws concern solemn legal acts or public order (c. 14).

25. RULE AND CONSTITUTIONS

Religious institutes are also governed by their own rule and constitutions (c. 489).

A rule, properly so called, **is the sum total of the fundamental statutes drawn up by the founder of an institute, or by others, to determine the particular end of the institute and the principal means by which it is to be attained.** There are four major rules recognized by the Church—those of St. Basil, St. Augustine, St. Benedict and St. Francis of Assisi.

The constitutions embrace all those particular laws, legitimately enacted and approved, which determine the practical application of the rule according to circumstances of time, place and persons. Ordinarily, however, especially in the recently founded religious congregations which seldom have a rule distinct from their constitutions, both terms are used to designate the laws proper to the institute. Nevertheless, the Sacred Congregation of Religious states that the special laws of religious congregations should be called *constitutions* and that the term *rule* should be applied only to the ancient rules of the religious orders *(Norms,* c. 4; cf. *supra* n. 8, B).

If, and to the extent that the formerly approved rules and constitutions of each religious institute are opposed to the canons of the Code of Canon Law, they are abrogated with the promulgation of the Code. On the other hand, insofar as they are not contrary to the Code, they retain their force (c. 489). Rules and constitutions should be brought into conformity with the Code, and two copies containing the necessary revisions should be sent to the Sacred Congregation of Religious for a second approval (S.C. Rel., Oct. 26, 1921).

If rules or constitutions which have been approved before the Code contain indults and apostolic privileges granted to an institute, these indults and privileges, even if they are contrary to the Code, are not necessarily abrogated. If they were granted by the Holy See, were not revoked, and were still in use in 1918, they may be retained (c. 4).

Moreover, if there are any dispositions of the Apostolic See which have been incorporated in the rule or constitutions, not as decrees of the Holy See, but as an integral part of the rule or constitutions, such dispositions, even if they are not confirmed by the Code, as long as they are not contrary to it, remain in force; not as Apostolic decrees, but as legislation which forms a part of the particular rule and constitutions.

When constitutions are submitted to the Holy See for approval for the first time, they must conform to certain norms drawn up by the Sacred Congregation of Religious (cf. *supra*, n. 9).

In approving new constitutions the Sacred Congregation of Religious usually proceeds in the following manner:

1) It suspends judgment for a time, and in the meanwhile draws up a list of critical observations in order that the text which has been submitted may be revised by the institute in accordance with these observations. This is done when the constitutions seem to be in need of extensive correction. Otherwise, the congregation makes the few corrections needed (*Norms,* n. 20; cf. *supra,* n. 8, B).

2) It then approves the corrected constitutions for a period of trial, for example, for five years or seven years (*ibid.*).

3) It gives final approval when it is finally judged that the text of the constitution is well formulated and is in conformity with the ends of the institute for which it was written (*ibid.*).

Once the constitutions of a religious institute have been approved by the Holy See they may not be changed by the local Ordinary, by the superior general, or by the general chapter of the institute. Changes may be proposed by the above mentioned superiors, but these changes cannot be validly made until they are approved by the Holy See. If an institute has not received papal approval, however, then the consent of the local Ordinary is sufficient for any addition or change in the constitution. However, if an institute of diocesan approval has spread to several dioceses, any change or addition in the constitutions would require the consent of the Ordinary of each diocese in which the institute is established (c. 495, par. 2).

26. CUSTOMS

Usages and customs, as long as they are laudable and lawfully introduced, may also have the force of law in religious institutes (c. 26).

Laudable: namely, customs which are introduced for a good purpose and which contribute to carrying on the work of the institute. Relative to this, it is to be noted that the following customs are not laudable: (1) customs which are opposed to the particular end of the institute or to regular observance; (2) customs which are opposed to the divine or natural law (c. 27, par. 1); and (3) customs which are expressly reprobated by a superior or by the law (c. 27, par. 2).

Lawfully introduced: that is, introduced with all of the guarantees and conditions which the law requires. Hence, the following customs are not lawfully introduced: (1) customs which are contrary to the common law of the Church, if they have not been in existence for at least forty continuous and complete years; that is, if they have not been in use without interruption for at least forty years (c. 27, par. 1); and (2) customs contrary to an ecclesiastical law which expressly prohibits future customs of whatsoever kind; these can never have the force of law unless they have been in existence from time immemorial, or at least for one hundred years (c. 27, par. 1).

27. ORDINANCES AND PRECEPTS OF SUPERIORS

Besides the rule and constitutions, every religious institute is governed by the orders and precepts of its superiors (c. 501, par. 1). What would be the use of giving power to superiors to govern the community if they could not give the members of the community commands which they are obliged to observe?

Ordinances or orders of superiors are prescriptions which the superior gives to the community in the form of norms or regulations. In other words, they are applications of the constitutions to particular cases. On the other hand, **precepts** are prescriptions made by the superior in the form of a true command, directing one or more subjects to do something, or to refrain from doing something. If the command tells the subject to do something, it is a positive, or *preceptive,* command; if it orders the subjects to refrain from some action it is a negative, or *prohibitive,* command.

Precepts may bind under pain of light or grave sin. If they bind under pain of grave sin, they are called **formal precepts** and should be given before two witnesses or in writing. Usually, the constitutions of each institute will state the form to be followed in giving a formal precept. Precepts given in institutes of religious women are known as **dominative precepts**. It is the more common opinion that dominative precepts cease to oblige when the superior who gave them goes out of office, even if they were given before witnesses or in writing (cf. c. 24).

Hence, a precept obliges under pain of sin in virtue of the obedience or subjection which every subject owes to her superior whenever a true command is given. Ordinances, on the other hand, oblige at most, only to the same extent as the constitutions, because it cannot be supposed that the prescriptions or norms given by a superior for the well-being of the community are more binding than the constitutions themselves. Therefore, if the constitutions, precisely as constitutions, merely oblige a religious to the penalty attached to the non-observance of these constitutions, a superior's ordinances, as such, cannot go beyond these limits.

Each religious institute is also governed by the ordinations or precepts of its chapters, held in accordance with its particular constitutions (c. 501, par. 1; cf. *infra*, n. 49).

II

SUBJECTION TO THE SOVEREIGN PONTIFF

28. Extent and Manner of this Subjection

All religious women are subject to the Roman Pontiff as to their highest superior (c. 499, par. 1).

All religious women; that is, all without exception, whether they are subjects or superiors and whether they are considered as individual members or as a community. This is evident because the Pope is the supreme head of all the faithful no matter to what category they may belong (n. 23).

Religious women are obliged to obey the Sovereign Pontiff not only by reason of the primacy of jurisdiction which he holds over each and every member of the faithful but also in virtue of the vow of obedience (c. 499, par. 1; cf. *infra*, n. 160). The vow of obedience pronounced by religious at the time of their profession is a public vow insofar as it is accepted in the name of the Church by a legitimate superior (c. 1308, par. 1). The Sovereign Pontiff is the supreme head of all who

45

are members of the Church, including religious, and hence, all religious, both men and women, are obliged to obey him not only as the other members of the faithful are, but also as religious in virtue of the vow of obedience. This does not mean, however, that religious commit a twofold sin if they fail to observe any command whatsoever of the Holy Father, for example, if they do not observe abstinence on Friday or if they do not hear Mass on days of precept. The vow of obedience has for its object, even relative to the Sovereign Pontiff, only that which is required by the nature of the religious state in conformity with the rule of the particular institute. Hence religious are obliged to obey the Pope "in virtue of the vow of obedience" only in those things which refer to the regular discipline of their particular religious institute, and which are in conformity with the rule and constitutions which they have professed (cf. *infra*, n. 160; cf. also *Summa*, II-II, q. 186, a. 5 ad 3).

There may also be monasteries of nuns immediately subject to the Holy See (c. 512, par. 1).

Immediately subject to the Holy See; that is, withdrawn from the jurisdiction both of the local Ordinary and of the superiors of the Order whose rule they profess.

29. THE SACRED CONGREGATION OF RELIGIOUS

Among the Roman Congregations, the Sacred Congregation of Religious, by the will of the Sovereign Pontiff, has charge of all the business pertaining to religious which is to be dealt with in the Roman Curia in a disciplinary form (c. 251).

In a disciplinary form; that is, in an administrative manner. Therefore, affairs which are to be treated in a judicial manner are to be referred to the competent sacred tribunal, even in the case of religious (c. 251, par. 2).

The following are subject to the Sacred Congregation of Religious: all religious of both sexes, whether in solemn or simple vows; those who, although they have no vows, lead a community life after the manner of religious; and members of the Third Orders Secular and secular institutes, without prejudice, however, to the rights of the Sacred Congregation for the Propagation of the Faith (c. 251, par. 1). The Sacred Congregation of Religious can bind religious and others subject to it in virtue of their vow or promise of obedience. Ordinarily however, unless the contrary is clear from the words or the matter treated, directives of this Sacred Congregation do not bind in conscience.

It is reserved exclusively to this Sacred Congregation to deal in an administrative manner with all the affairs which concern religious, whether they have to do with their government, discipline, studies, administration of goods, privileges of religious, or any other rights or duties of religious men and women (c. 251, par. 1). If a dispute arises between a member of a religious institute and one who is not a religious, the Sacred Congregation of Religious may refer the matter to another congregation or tribunal, especially if the non-religious party requests it and the request is judged opportune (c. 251, par. 2).

The Sacred Congregation of Religious has also the function of granting dispensations, which religious women, no matter for what motive, might have need.

30. Other Roman Congregations

Religious, as such, ordinarily are subject to the Sacred Congregation of Religious and not to other congregations. However:

1) If they have missions, everything pertaining to the missions, whether it concerns individual persons or the community, falls exclusively under the jurisdiction of the Sacred Congregation for the Propagation of the Faith (c. 252, par. 5).

2) Likewise, matters which, in virtue of canon 245, pertain to the Sacred Congregation of the Holy Office, remain within the competence of this congregation even when they concern religious (c. 247, par. 1 and 2).

3) Again, cases which pertain exclusively to the Sacred Congregation of the Council (c. 250), are to be treated by this congregation even when religious are involved (c. 251, par. 1 and 2). The cases which pertain to religious principally concern the making of a settlement with those who unlawfully hold goods belonging to religious (cf. c. 250).

31. Reports to be Sent to the Holy See

In order that the Holy See may be kept well informed as to the moral and material status of religious institutes, canon 510 of the Code of Canon Law prescribes that superiors of religious institutes are to send to the Holy See, at definite intervals, a report on the state of each religious institute.

In the case of religious women this report is obligatory: for all monasteries of nuns (S.C. Rel., July 9, 1947, n. IV); for all religious institutes of pontifical approval, with or without vows *(ibid.)*; for religious congregations or societies of diocesan approval in which community life is led; and also for secular institutes even if they are only of diocesan law *(ibid.)*.

This report must be submitted every five years, or more often if the constitutions so demand (c. 510).

For greater convenience and to render the examination of the reports by the Sacred Congregation of Religious more orderly, the Congregation in a decree of March 8, 1922, and in another decree of July 9, 1947, prescribed that, depending upon the place where the congregation or religious institute has its motherhouse, the quinquennial report on monasteries and women's institutes with vows is to be sent to Rome in the following order:

1) The first of the five years, the report is to be sent from Italy, Spain and Portugal.

2) The second year, from France, Belgium, Holland, England and Ireland.

3) The third year, from other nations of Europe.

4) The fourth year, from America.

5) The fifth year, from the other parts of the world. In this fifth year superiors general of sisters living a common life but without vows, the superiors general of secular institutes, and federations of monasteries throughout the world, are also obliged to submit a report.

The five year period began to be computed from the year 1923, and this is the fixed date for determining the year in which each group is to submit its report in the future.

Furthermore, this obligation is to be fulfilled by the superior general of the institute (c. 510), or by the major superior of a monastery of nuns which is independent (S. C. Rel., *op. cit.,* n. IV).

In **institutes for women which are of papal approval,** with the exception of monasteries of nuns, the report must be signed by the superior general and her council, and by the Ordinary of the place where the superior general and her council reside, and it must be presented to the Congregation of Religious by the superior general (*ibid.*, n. VII).

In **institutes of diocesan approval,** however, the report, signed by the superior general and members of the council, is to be sent to the Ordinary of the place where the motherhouse is located. This Ordinary must present it to the other Ordinaries of places where the institute has houses to obtain their observations, and then setting down his own opinion, he is to sign the document and forward it to the Sacred Congregation of Religious (*ibid.*, n. IV).

In the case of **nuns,** on the other hand, the major superior with her council must draw up a brief report; she and her council are to sign it and present it to the local Ordinary if they are under his jurisdiction, or to the regular superior if they are immediately subject to him. The local Ordinary, or the regular superior, after noting any observations which they may deem opportune, are to sign the report and send it to the Sacred Congregation of Religious (*loc. cit.*).

The manner of drawing up this report is described in instructions issued by the Sacred Congregation of Religious. The last instruction, listing the questions which are to be answered in the *Quinquennial Report,* was issued December 9, 1948. At this time, the Sacred Congregation of Religious also published an official version of the questionnaire in English (cf. C.L.D., Vol. III, p. 163).

III

CARDINAL PROTECTORS

32. Definition of a Cardinal Protector

The cardinal protector of a religious institute is that cardinal of the Church to whom the Sovereign Pontiff, at the request of the institute, confides the care and special guardianship of the institute of which he is named protector. One and the same cardinal may be the protector of several religious institutes.

33. Origin of the Custom

The custom of having a cardinal to protect the rights of monasteries or religious institutes and to exercise a special watchfulness over their well being is quite ancient in origin. It would seem that St. Francis of Assisi was the first to officially petition the Holy See to have a cardinal "as governor, protector, corrector of the brotherhood, in order that, prostrate at the feet of the Holy Roman Church and firm in the Catholic Faith, we may observe poverty, humility, and the Holy Gospel of our Lord Jesus Christ as we now firmly promise." The practice of requesting a cardinal protector from the Holy Father is observed today by almost all religious institutes of papal law, both of men and of women.

34. POWERS OF THE CARDINAL PROTECTOR

From the words of the Rule of St. Francis which we have just cited, it appears that in the past, at least in the Franciscan Order, the cardinal protector exercised true jurisdiction. But with the passage of time, both in the Franciscan Order and in other religious institutes, the cardinal protector's power of jurisdiction became more and more restricted until today it has ceased completely. Thus we read in the Code of Canon Law that:

1) The cardinal protector of any religious institute whatsoever possesses no jurisdiction (that is, he has no authority) over the institute or over any of its members (c. 499, par. 2). An exception is to be made only by an express provision (c. 499, par. 2). For example, if the cardinal protector should be assigned by the Holy Father as his delegate to carry out some business for the institute of which he is the protector, or, if he should be assigned as a visitator apostolic. In such cases, it is evident that he enjoys jurisdiction within the limits granted by the Holy Father.

2) The cardinal protector as such may not interfere in the internal discipline of the monastery or institute, or in the administration of the property of the same (c. 499, par. 2).

3) The proper office of the cardinal protector is to promote the good of the institute by his counsel and his patronage (c. 499, par. 2).

4) In accordance with a practice which has been introduced in the Roman Curia, the cardinal protector, instead of the local Ordinary, affixes the letter of recommendation to requests for dispensations, and to other matters sent by the religious to the Sacred Roman Congregations. Whenever the Congregations give a rescript in *forma commissoria*, they follow the custom of leaving the execution of the rescript to the cardinal protector of the institute.

The cardinal protector is frequently delegated to preside at elections of the supreme moderator of institutes committed to his care. Cardinals protector are usually included in the prayers, good works, and suffrages of the institutes in their care.

IV

SUBJECTION TO THE LOCAL ORDINARY

35. DEFINITION OF A LOCAL ORDINARY

The local Ordinary is the diocesan bishop, or whoever in the diocese fulfills the functions of a bishop, whether he be called an abbot or prelate nullius, administrator apostolic, vicar or perfect apostolic. A vicar general or vicar capitular is also classified as a local Ordinary (c. 198, par. 1). Hence the terms "local Ordinary" and "bishop of the place" have slightly different connotations, since one can be a local Ordinary without being a bishop. When, however, there is no particular need for making a distinction, the terms "bishop" and "local Ordinary" are sometimes used interchangeably to indicate the superior of a diocese.

As far as men and women religious are concerned, the local Ordinary is the Ordinary of the diocese in which a monastery or convent is situated, or in which the religious are assigned (c. 965).

The proper pastor of religious (relative to those things in which they are subject to him) is the pastor of the place in which the convent or monastery to which the religious belong is situated (c. 1221, par. 1; c. 1230, par. 5).

36. Extent of Dependence on the Local Ordinary

Nuns, if exempt, are subject to the local Ordinary only in those matters which are expressly provided for by law (c. 500, par. 2). Exempt nuns are those immediately under the jurisdiction of the superiors of their order instead of the local Ordinary. If they are **not exempt** they depend in all things upon the local Ordinary *(loc. cit.)*.

In order that this may be clearly understood, it should be noted that among monasteries of nuns affiliated with some particular religious Order (for example, with the Benedictine or Dominican Orders), some are united to the Order solely by reason of the habit they wear and by the rule they profess, without in any way being subject to the Order. On the other hand, others are united, either by reason of ancient custom or by a special indult from the Holy See, in such a way that they recognize the superiors of the Order with which they are affiliated as their lawful superiors. The superiors of the Orders, therefore, exercise true jurisdiction over the monastery.

The first type, even if they are affiliated with an exempt Order, are subject in all things to the Ordinary who acts either as the local Ordinary or as a delegate of the Sovereign Pontiff (c. 512, par. 1). The second type are subject in many things to the superiors of the Order with which they are affiliated, rather than to the Ordinary. The cases in which the monasteries of this second type depend upon the superiors of the Order and on the Ordinary will be pointed out when we treat specifically of these matters.

Sisters are subject in all things to the jurisdiction of the local Ordinary unless they enjoy an indult by which in whole or in part they are exempt from his authority (c. 500, par. 1; cf. *infra*, n. 40).

It should be noted here:

1) That the Ordinary may not in any way change the rule or constitutions of religious women of papal approval even if they are not exempt; but he may do so if a monastery or institute is only of diocesan approval. If an institute is located in a number of dioceses, be-

fore any changes may be made in the rules of the institute, the unanimous consent of each and every Ordinary in whose diocese the institute has houses is required, as we have pointed out above (n. 25).

2) Likewise, the local Ordinary may not interfere in the internal government and discipline of monasteries or institutes of papal law. However, he may and must be informed, especially at times of visitation, whether regular observance is maintained in conformity with their particular constitutions; whether sound doctrine and good morals have suffered in any way; whether the law of enclosure has been observed; and whether the sacraments are received with regularity. Whenever the Ordinary discovers any abuses he shall first make them known to the lawful superiors, and if they do not correct them he himself shall do so. If, however, a matter of grave importance arises, he shall take care of it immediately, and then shall inform the Holy See concerning what has been done (c. 618, par. 2, n. 2).

3) What the local Ordinary may or may not do relative to the administration of material goods of religious women will be pointed out in its proper place (*infra*, n. 97). Likewise, the powers of a bishop in a canonical visitation will be considered further on (*infra*, n. 53).

Without an apostolic indult, sisters in the strict sense of the word may not have any legal dependence on the Order to which they are affiliated (c. 500, par. 3). Thus, the supreme moderator of the Dominican or Franciscan Orders has no true jurisdiction over the various communities of Dominican and Franciscan sisters. However, this does not mean that spiritual direction and counsel may not be sought by sisters from the First Order to which they are affiliated. Such direction and counsel is useful and even necessary, if the sisters are to appreciate and live the spirit of the Order to which they are affiliated.

V

SUPERIORS

37. PROPER SUPERIORS

The proper superiors of a religious institute are those who are appointed or elected from among the members of the institute. They are called proper superiors to distinguish them from other superiors whom the institute may have, who are not members of the institute; for example, the local Ordinary.

Superiors of religious institutes are designated by various titles according to the different institutes and different offices they hold. Thus, for example, in some institutes of women, the local superior is called an Abbess, in others, a Prioress or President; in others, simply a Superior. The provincial superior is sometimes called a Provincial, at other times a Visitator, and so on. Likewise, the superior who is head of an entire institute does not always have the same title; ordinarily however, she is called a Superior General or Mother General.

Besides superiors properly so-called, there may also be vicar-superiors who do not act on their own authority but with the authority received from the superiors whom they represent and of whom they are the vicars.

38. MAJOR AND MINOR SUPERIORS

The Code divides the proper superiors of religious institutes into two groups—major and minor superiors (c. 488, n. 8).

Major superiors are the Abbot Primate, the Abbot Superior of a monastic congregation, the Abbot of an independent monastery (cf. *supra*, n. 17, B), every Superior General of a religious institute, the Provincial Superior, their vicars and all others who, under the title of Visitators, Assistants, and so on, have powers equivalent to those of provincials (c. 488, n. 8).

Minor superiors are all other superiors who hold a lower rank than those mentioned above.

In virtue of canon 490, it is evident that in religious institutes of women, those with the title of General, Provincial, President, Visitator or Assistant, and so on, are major superiors provided that they govern the office of presiding either over an entire religious institute or a particular province. The others are minor superiors.

It seems that the abbess of an independent monastery is also a major superior. In the Code (c. 488, n. 8) it is stated that the abbot of a monastery which is *sui iuris*, that is, a monastery that exists independently without forming a part either of a province or of a monastic or religious congregation, is a major superior; and in canon 490 it is prescribed that everything in the Code concerning religious, even when expressed in the masculine gender, applies equally to religious women unless it appears otherwise from the context or from the very nature of the case. No repugnance or difficulty arises in numbering among major superiors, abbesses, or prioresses or presidents of monasteries which are independent. Hence it seems that we must conclude that abbesses or superiors of monasteries which are *sui iuris*, that is, which have no other proper superiors except local superiors, should be named among the major superiors.

39. QUALITIES OF A SUPERIOR

A. Those not qualified to become major superiors.

1. Religious who have not completed their fortieth year when the

office of superior general of a congregation, or superior of a monastery of nuns, is in question; those who have not completed their thirtieth year when it is a question of providing a provincial or another major superior (c. 504).

Completed, that is, not merely begun. This is expressly stated in the Code (c. 504). The Holy See alone can dispense from this impediment.

2. Those who have not spent at least ten years from the time of their first profession in the institute to which they here and now belong (c. 504).

Ten years. These ten years of profession must be completed. This condition is not explicitly mentioned in the Code but it can be deduced clearly enough from the wording of the text. The words of the Code are to be understood in their literal sense unless from the context or from the matter of the law itself it is evident that they are to be interpreted in a broad or figurative sense. Now religious "professed for ten years" are those who have already completed ten years of profession and not only commenced them. Those who have only begun them have been professed, properly speaking, for only nine years. This is the interpretation which is also given in the Roman Curia to canon 504. The "ten years" should be computed in this case in conformity with canon 34, paragraph 3, number 3.

From the first profession. That is, from the first profession made immediately after the novitiate.

In the institute to which they here and now belong. This is prescribed in the Code to indicate that if a religious goes from one institute to another, she must spend ten full years in the new institute before she can be a major superior.

3. Those who have not been born of legitimate marriage (c. 504), unless they have been legitimated by the subsequent marriage of their parents. In general, those children are legitimate who are conceived in or born of a valid or putative marriage (c. 1114). Legitimation is an institute of the positive law, or a concession of a lawful superior, which attributes to a child born out of wedlock at least some of the juridicial effects of legitimacy. Legitimation may occur in different ways. That which occurs by a subsequent marriage renders one capable of being a major superior. Children legitimated in this manner are considered as the equivalent of legitimate children,

unless the contrary is expressly provided (c. 1117).

4. As well as excluding the above from the office of superior, the Code declares that the following may be removed from office, or declared incapable of holding office: superiors who, after a visitation has been announced, shall transfer religious to another house, without the consent of the visitator; likewise, all religious, whether superiors or subjects, who, personally or through others, directly or indirectly, shall induce any religious to remain silent or to conceal the truth in any manner whatsoever or not to answer with sincerity when she is interrogated by the visitator; and finally, those who, under whatever pretext, shall molest any religious on account of the replies she may have given to the visitator (c. 2413, par. 1).

B. Qualities required for the office of Local Superior

For **sisters,** the Code does not set down any special requirements relative to age or profession. Hence it is sufficient that the superior have the juridical qualities prescribed by the constitutions proper to her institute. For **nuns,** the Code requires that the local superior of a monastery, whether she be considered as a major superior or not, must have completed at least her fortieth year of age (c. 504).

Candidates, whether for the office of a major or a minor superior, must also possess all of the qualities which are required by the nature of the office to which they are elected or by the constitutions of each institute (c. 504).

40. POWERS OF A SUPERIOR

All superiors have dominative power over their own subjects in accordance with their constitutions and the common law (c. 501, par. 1).

Dominative power. In the present instance it consists in that power of commanding others which arises from a quasi-contract of obedience made in religious profession, in virtue of which the one who embraces the religious life makes herself subject to the government of the superiors of the institute. Even though it is founded on religious profession, dominative power does not necessarily presuppose religious profession. Novices and postulants, for example, even though they have not pronounced vows, are still bound in conscience to obey their rightful superiors by virtue of their free entrance into religious life.

The same is true of those who belong to institutes in which vows are not pronounced by the members.

In accordance with the constitutions and the common law. A superior, in virtue of her religious profession acquires the power to command other religious subject to her, but this power is not without restrictions. It cannot exceed the limits determined by the rule which the religious have professed, or by the laws which the Church has approved for religious (cf. n. 159).

A superior general has dominative power over all the provinces, houses and members of her institute in conformity with its constitutions (c. 502). Other superiors have only that authority which, in accordance with the constitutions or the common law, belongs to the office which they hold (c. 502).

No religious superior who is a woman can possess power of jurisdiction in the proper sense of the word. Ecclesiastical jurisdiction implies the power of spiritual rule over the faithful insofar as they are members of the Church. Hence it descends directly from the spiritual power which Christ granted to his disciples; and through his disciples, by means of the sacrament of holy orders, to their successors, the ministers of the Church. We know that women are excluded by divine decree from the ministry of the Church, and therefore they cannot hold any form of ecclesiastical jurisdiction in the strict sense of the word. Nevertheless, insofar as dominative power implies a certain jurisdiction or power to govern others, we may say, although in a broad sense, that women religious superiors have a certain jurisdiction over their sister-religious. This, however, is not true ecclesiastical jurisdiction.

By reason of their dominative power, women who are superiors have the following authority:

1) They can give commands, issue precepts and make regulations in accordance with the constitutions proper to their institute.

2) They can give penances to those who are guilty of faults. For example, they can impose fasting or certain pious practices. They can never, however, inflict true canonical penalties such as excommunication or interdict.

3) They can dispense from the observance of the constitutions, not indeed at will, but within the limits determined by the constitutions

themselves. They may not, however, dispense from the laws of the Church.

41. TERM OF LOCAL SUPERIORS

A. Houses of sisters

In **houses of sisters**, local superiors cannot hold office for more than three years. They can, however, on the expiration of this term, be immediately re-elected or reappointed a second time if the constitutions of the institute permit it, but not for a third time in the same house unless there is an interval between the second and third terms (c. 505).

Three years. This is to be understood as three years completed, and the years are to be computed as they are in the calendar (c. 34, par. 3); that is, the three year period comes to an end in the third year at the end of the same day of the month in which it was begun. For example, if the three year period were begun on March 1, 1960, it would terminate at the end of the day on March 1, 1963.

In the same house. A religious cannot be superior more than twice in succession in the same house, but if she goes from one house to another then she can be re-elected or appointed to the same office.

Unless there is an interval. The Code does not say how long this interval must be. Hence, if the constitutions say nothing regarding the matter, it is sufficient for the validity of re-election or reappointment that there intervene another person's election or appointment, even if this other person exercises the office for only a very brief time.

If the constitutions of the institute permit it. Thus, although the Code permits two successive terms, this would not be allowed if the constitutions should prohibit it.

B. Monasteries of nuns

In **monasteries of nuns** the superior is prohibited from remaining in office for more than three years. The constitutions are to be followed regarding re-election immediately after the first three year period. However, a *Circular Letter* of the Sacred Congregation of Religious (March 9, 1920), states that although in the Code there is no confirmation of the decision of Gregory VIII *(Exposcit Debitum,* January 1, 1583), in virtue of which the superiors of monasteries of nuns in

Italy were forbidden to remain in office for more than three years, nevertheless, by command of the Holy Father the Sacred Congregation will always require that such a prescription be kept in the constitutions of monasteries. Consequently, the abbess or superior of these monasteries of nuns is not immediately eligible for re-election after her first three year term unless a dispensation is obtained from the Holy See. In view of the fact that in monasteries of nuns the superior must necessarily be chosen from among the members of the community, the Holy See is lenient in granting this dispensation.

Does this prescription apply to monasteries in Italy alone as did the document of Gregory XIII, or does it apply to the whole world? It seems sufficiently clear that the prescription spoken of above applies to monasteries outside Italy as well as those in Italy. Otherwise, why should it be mentioned in a circular letter addressed to the Ordinaries of the entire world? Moreover, the phrase "although it is not incorporated in the Code," seems to indicate that this prescription is to be treated as though it were in the Code, and thus it pertains to monasteries in all parts of the world.

C. Schools and hospitals

The prescription preventing local superiors from remaining in office for a term exceeding three years does not apply to the principals of schools, directors of hospitals, or other officials, if they are not at the same time religious superiors (P.C.I., June 3, 1918). In other words, if in a religious house which has a school or a hospital attached, there is only one local superior who has charge of the school or hospital and at the same time has authority over the internal discipline and regular observance of the religious, this local superior may not be appointed for longer than a three year term. When this term expires she may be appointed to another, but not to a third unless an interval intervenes. If, on the contrary, there is one superior who directs the internal discipline and regular observance of the community and another superior, who is called director or president, and who merely has charge of the school or hospital as such, without any authority over the religious life of the sisters, this latter superior, director or president, may remain in office more than three years or even for life.

The prescription of canon 505 relative to the changing of local superiors is also to be applied to pious unions or congregations of women living a community life but without vows (P.C.I., July 25, 1926).

42. TERM OF MAJOR SUPERIORS

Major superiors also are to remain in office only temporarily unless the constitutions of an institute expressly state the contrary (c. 505).

Temporarily: that is, for a definite length of time, as for example, for three years, or for six years, according to the prescriptions of the constitutions.

Unless the constitutions of an institute expressly state otherwise. Hence if the lawfully approved constitutions prescribe that the continuance in office of the major superior is for an undetermined time, for example, until she is recalled from office, or even for life, the constitutions are to be followed. This is especially applicable to superiors general for whom this case is more apt to arise than for other major superiors.

Each religious institute may determine the length of time its major superiors may remain in office, for example, for three, four, five, six years, or more. The Code says nothing on the subject. It goes without saying, however, that once the constitutions are approved by the Ordinary of the place or by the Holy See, no changes relative to the tenure of office may be made without a new approval of the constitutions.

When her term of office has expired, a major superior may be re-elected, even without any interval, unless the particular constitutions expressly state the contrary. Just as the Code does not determine the length of office of major superiors, neither does it forbid their re-election. Relative to this question, however, it should be noted:

1) Regarding superiors general, the Sacred Congregation of Religious in the *Circular Letter* of March 9, 1920, informed diocesan Ordinaries that the repeated re-election of the same person to the office of superior general does not seem opportune in religious congregations in which the term of office is limited to a definite time. Not infrequently the institute suffers considerable harm from a too extended tenure of office by the same person. Even when the constitutions explicitly state that "the same person may be re-elected as superior general even for a third consecutive time provided that two-thirds of the votes be in her favor and the confirmation of the Holy See is obtained," it always must be understood that this is to be done only for serious and grave reasons, and not merely because of the simple will

of the voters or the fitness of the person. If these grave reasons do not exist or are not clearly set forth in the petition for confirmation, the Holy See will never confirm, the *Circular Letter* goes on to say, such a re-election; or rather, it will not grant a dispensation, because the person proposed is really ineligible for re-election. To avoid loss of time and useless recourse, the *Circular Letter* requests the diocesan Ordinaries who preside over such elections to inform the religious of the attitude of the Holy See on this point. Hence whenever the term of office of a superior general of a religious congregation is for a fixed time, to obtain a dispensation from the Holy See in the event of a re-election, the petition is to be based upon serious and grave reasons, explained and recognized as such by the diocesan Ordinary himself. The mere fitness of the person re-elected to fulfill the office is not of itself a sufficient reason for obtaining a dispensation.

2) The *Circular Letter* just cited makes no mention of the re-election of the same person as provincial superior. Hence the norms set down in the constitutions regarding the re-election of a provincial should be followed. Nevertheless the reasons which would lead the Holy See to look with disfavor upon the immediate re-election of a superior general also have value relative to the immediate re-election of a provincial. Thus one may reasonably conclude that the immediate re-election of the same person as provincial superior, even though permitted by the constitutions, is not advisable without grave and serious reasons.

3) If the Ordinary judges it opportune in some particular case to petition the Holy See for a dispensation, over and above the grave reasons which have induced him to do so, he should clearly report how many ballots were taken and how many votes the one postulated received. In addition, the Ordinary should state his own opinion on the matter (cf. *Circular Letter* cited).

Does the foundress of a religious congregation or of a pious society of persons living as religious have the right to retain the office of superior general until death, without a dispensation, even when the constitutions impose a time limit on the office of superior general? In conformity with a decision of the Sacred Congregation of Religious, March 6, 1922, a negative answer must be given to this question.

43. RESIDENCE

Superiors must live in their respective houses and must not absent themselves from them except in accordance with the norms of their particular constitutions (c. 508).

Superiors. This applies especially to local superiors because although provincial or general superiors should have a particular house for their residence, it is evident that by reason of their very office they cannot always remain in one and the same house. A local superior who negligently fails to fulfill this obligation of residence may be removed from office (c. 2381, nn. 1, 2).

44. DUTIES WITH REGARD TO PAPAL DECREES

All superiors are obliged to promote among their subjects a knowledge of existing laws and of new decrees of the Holy See regarding religious (c. 509, par. 1). The knowledge of existing laws and new decrees is sufficiently promoted if the laws and decrees are read in the refectory or in chapter. One of the questions of the *Quinquennial Report* concerns the manner in which this directive is put into practice.

Local superiors must also take care to have publicly read, on fixed days at least once a year, the constitutions of the institute, as well as the decrees which the Holy See shall order to be publicly read in religious communities (c. 509, par. 2, n. 1).

Which the Holy See shall order. The future tense is used here, and hence decrees issued for religious before the Code and which it was formerly the custom to read publicly, need no longer be read. Up to the present, there is no decree which must be publicly read in all religious institutes. In monasteries of nuns where there are extern sisters, the superior must see to it that the "statutes for extern sisters" are publicly read to them at least four times a year *(Statutes for Extern Sisters,* S.C.Rel., July 16, 1931, n. 127).

On fixed days: that is, on those days determined either in the decrees themselves or by each superior. It would be well to note these days in the calendar of the community or congregation, whenever they have their own calendar.

Every superior must also promote the observance of the decrees of the Holy See among her subjects (c. 509, par. 1).

45. RELIGIOUS INSTRUCTION FOR SISTERS

At least twice a month, the local superior shall see to it that a pious exhortation be given to all the religious of the house, and that catechetical and religious instruction be given to lay sisters and domestic servants (c. 509, par. 2).

Domestic servants are those lay people who live in the religious house and work for the community as servants or employees. The Code does not say whether the superior herself should impart the instruction and give the pious exhortations to her subjects. It is certain that she may do so, especially by holding the so-called chapters or spiritual assemblies of the community. Nevertheless, it is advisable for her to arrange, at least occasionally, to have the spiritual exhortations given by a priest who is duly authorized to give retreats and to preach to religious. It is also certain that in giving religious and catechetical instructions to lay sisters, or domestic servants, the superior may be assisted by a religious woman adapted to this work. The important thing is that the instructions are not omitted.

VI

CHAPTERS AND COUNCILS

46. CHAPTERS

A chapter in religious institutes is an assembly of several members lawfully convoked as delegates of the other members to treat authoritatively of the affairs of the institute.

Authoritatively: that is, a chapter has dominative power over its subjects; it can command them in accordance with the regulations of the constitutions and the common law (c. 501, par. 1; see also nn. 27, 40).

A chapter is general, provincial or conventual (local) according to whether it is made up of representatives or delegates of an entire religious institute, or of a province, or of a convent or monastery.

47. COUNCILS

A council in religious institutes is a group made up of certain members of a house or province or institute, who treat of the affairs of a house, province or institute together with the local or pro-

66

vincial or general superior. A council is conventual (local), provincial or general, according as it is convoked by a local, provincial or general superior. The members of a council are called counsellors or consultors.

The difference between a council and a chapter consists principally in this: a chapter, as we have just pointed out, possesses dominative power; that is, it can make decisions which oblige others even in virtue of the vow of obedience. The decisions of a council, on the other hand, have no binding force unless they are approved by the superior who presides over the council. This is true even if the constitutions grant to the counsellors not only a consultative, but also a definitive vote, as we shall see later on *(infra,* n. 50). Moreover, a council always presupposes a superior in charge who convokes the council—the members are counsellors of a superior; but a chapter may be held even though there is no superior with real jurisdiction in charge. The chapter itself, in conformity with the particular constitutions, can confer this jurisdiction upon itself, which is precisely what takes place when an elective chapter is also a legislative chapter.

48. NECESSITY OF COUNCILS

The Code (c. 516, par. 1) obliges the following superiors in religious institutes for women to have a council: (1) the superior general; (2) the provincial superior; and, (3) the local superior of formal religious houses; that is, houses to which at least six professed religious are assigned.

The constitutions of each institute are to determine who are to be members of the council, how long they stay in office, and how they may be removed (c. 516, par. 1).

The common law or the particular constitutions of each institute determine when these superiors are to seek the advice or consent of their council.

49. POWERS OF A CHAPTER

A chapter may be merely **elective,** or it may also be **legislative.** When a chapter is merely elective its powers are confined to what is involved in the election itself, in accordance with the common law and the constitutions (c. 507, par. 1). Once the election has been held and has been confirmed, the authority of the chapter ceases.

If, on the other hand, a chapter is also legislative, that is, if it also has the power to take part in the government of an institute or monastery, its authority may continue even after the election, in conformity with the particular constitutions of the institute.

A chapter, as we have pointed out above, has dominative power over its subjects (n. 46).

50. POWERS OF COUNCILS

The members of a council at times have a **deliberative**, or decisive, voice, and at other times merely a **consultative** voice, depending upon the prescriptions of the particular constitutions or the Sacred Canons (c. 516, par. 1).

The difference between the two kinds of votes in a council is that if the vote of the counsellors is merely *consultative*, the superior is not obliged to follow the decisions of the council but, notwithstanding the contrary opinion of the council, may validly do what seems most opportune to her. When the vote of the counsellors is *deliberative*, the superior, in those matters in which she is obliged to seek the advice of the council, must act, under penalty of invalidity, in conformity with the opinion expressed by the majority of the members of the council (c. 516, par. 1).

It is stated in the Code (c. 105, n. 1) that when the common law requires the *consent* of counsellors or of members of a chapter, the vote is understood to be deliberative; but when it mentions only *counsel* or *advice*, the vote is merely consultative. The Code requires the consent of the council in only four cases: for the appointment of a procurator (c. 516, par. 4); for the alienation of goods whose value is less than five thousand dollars (c. 534, par. 1); for admission to first temporary profession (c. 575, par. 2); and for dismissal of a religious in temporary vows (c. 647, par. 1). Particular constitutions, however, may require consent more often.

51. MANNER OF COUNTING VOTES

In chapters, that decision has the force of law which has been approved by the **absolute majority** of the voters, not counting invalid votes. However, after two inconclusive ballots, that decision will have the force of law which has received the approval of the **relative majority** of the voters. If a relative majority is not obtained after the third ballot, the one who presides should break the tie by her vote (c. 101, par. 1). Therefore, if the presiding officer is herself a qualified voter, she enjoys an additional vote when there is a tie on the third ballot. This procedure is to be followed in chapters and councils unless the common law or particular law expressly determines otherwise (c. 101, par. 1), or unless the chapter is holding an election. In this latter case, all other rules must be observed but the one who presides is not obliged to cast the deciding vote in the event of a tie. If she does not choose to do so, that candidate will be declared elected who is oldest in years of profession, or this failing to break the tie, the one who is oldest in age (c. 101, par. 1, n. 1).

An **absolute majority** exists when at least one more than half of all the valid votes are cast in favor of the same thing or person. A **relative majority** exists when, although the number of votes in favor of one side of a question does not constitute an absolute majority, they nevertheless exceed the number of votes cast for each of the other opinions taken individually. For example, if there are ten valid votes, at least six votes are required for an absolute majority; but a relative majority would be had if of the ten votes, four were cast for one person, three for another, and three for a third. The same is true of other similar combinations of votes.

There is nothing expressly stated in the Code regarding the manner of counting votes in councils. It seems to us however, that in accordance with the common law, the following is to be observed:

1) If the vote is deliberative, what we have said relative to counting votes in chapters is to be followed in councils. It seems to us that when the Code (c. 101, par. 1) speaks explicitly of chapters it intends to include councils as well.

2) If the vote is only consultative, however, then immediately after the first ballot, whatever may be the result of the vote, the superior may make the decision which seems best to her, since she is not obliged to act in accordance with the decision of the counsellors but is merely obliged to ask their opinion. The Code points out, nevertheless, that although the superior is not obliged to act according to the decision of the counsellors, it is not prudent to disregard their **unanimous judgment** unless the superior has grave and clearly preponderant reasons in favor of her decision (c. 105, n. 1).

VII

CANONICAL VISITATIONS

52. NATURE OF CANONICAL VISITATIONS

A canonical visitation is the examination or investigation, made by a legitimate superior either personally or through a delegate, regarding the government of the individual houses of a religious institute, the life of the members who dwell there, and the spiritual and financial condition of the institute itself. The legitimate superior empowered to make this investigation is determined for particular cases by the individual constitutions or the common law of the Church.

The purpose of a canonical visitation is to give to legitimate and responsible superiors the means of knowing the activities and persons confided to their care so that they may reprove subjects who are not faithful to discipline and regular observance, punish the culpable in order that they may mend their ways, encourage and reward their good subjects according to their merits, and suggest or even command means which are best suited to maintaining and developing the religious life and regular discipline ever more perfectly.

70

53. OBLIGATION OF CANONICAL VISITATIONS

The following are obliged to make a canonical visitation of religious women:

1) Major superiors, in conformity with their particular constitutions, at the time and in the manner prescribed by these constitutions. They are obliged to make the visitation in person, or, if they are impeded, through a delegate (c. 511).

2) The local Ordinary, at least every five years, must visit either personally or through a delegate:

(a) Every monastery of nuns subject to himself or immediately subject to the Holy See (c. 512, par. 1, n. 1). When the bishop makes a visitation of these monasteries he can examine everything which concerns both internal and external discipline and also everything which has to do with the administration of temporal goods (c. 535, par. 1, n. 1). Moreover, regarding the administration of temporal goods, it is stated in the canon just cited that a superior must give an account of her administration to the bishop once a year, or even more often if the constitutions so prescribe.

(b) Monasteries of nuns which are subject to regular superiors, but only regarding the observance of the law of enclosure (c. 512, par. 2, n. 1), or matters which have to do with the administration of temporal goods (c. 535, par. 1, n. 1). If, for a period of five years, the regular superior has not made a visitation of the monasteries immediately subject to him, the local Ordinary, in his visitation of these monasteries, can and must inquire not only about those things which concern the cloister and the administration of temporal goods, but everything which promotes the well being of the monastery (c. 512, par. 2, n. 1).

(c) All houses of sisters, if they are situated within the limits of his diocese. If the sisters are of diocesan right, the powers of the bishop are not limited in any way (c. 512, par. 1, n. 2). If they are of pontifical approval, whether exempt or not, the bishop in his visitation may investigate those things which concern the church, the sacristy, the public oratory and the confessionals (c. 512, par. 2, n. 2). He may also determine whether regular discipline is maintained in conformity with the constitutions, whether sound doctrine and good morals have suffered in any way, whether there have been any infractions of the law of enclosure, and whether the reception of the sacraments has been regular and frequent. If superiors, having been warned of the existence of grave abuses, have failed to remedy them, the Ordinary himself shall attend to the matter, and if it is a question of something of exceptional importance which will not suffer delay, the Ordinary shall decide immediately what is to be done, but he must afterward report his decision to the Holy See (c. 618, par. 2, n. 2).

If the sisters are of pontifical approval, the bishop may not interfere in the internal government of the house or institute. For example, he may not demand that one sister rather than another be assigned to a house, or that a house engage in one type of work rather than another. Likewise in the matter of temporal goods, the bishop can demand an account only of the dowries of the religious (c. 535, par. 2), and of funds which have been donated or bequeathed to the house for expenditure locally on divine worship or on works of charity (c. 535, par. 3, n. 2). He cannot interfere in the administration of any other temporal goods (cf. *infra,* n. 99).

3) In like manner, a regular superior must visitate, at least every five years, the monasteries of nuns subject to him, and he has the same powers which the bishop enjoys relative to monasteries immediately subject to the local Ordinary or to the Holy See (c. 512, par. 2, n. 1).

Since some monasteries are subject to a twofold authority, namely, to the bishop and to the regular superior, each of whom can make certain decisions independently of the other, prudence dictates that contradictions between what the bishop determines and what the regular superior commands are to be avoided. Hence before any commands are given or any decisions are made, there should be a mutual understanding between the two superiors. In any case, whenever divergent points of view arise, rather than give contradictory commands, it will always be better to refer the matter to the Holy See.

The following may make canonical visitations of women religious:

1) The Sovereign Pontiff, if he wishes to do so, since he is the Supreme Head of the entire Church (c. 218, par. 1).

2) Those delegated by the Sovereign Pontiff, especially the Sacred Congregation of Religious, to which the Pope confides the business of all religious throughout the entire world (c. 251; see also *supra,* n. 29). The delegates of the Sovereign Pontiff may be religious or secular priests. They may also be lay people, either men or women, when the exercise of ecclesiastical jurisdiction is not involved, and there is merely a question of officially entrusting to someone the task of determining the state of things in a monastery or religious institute.

Such a mission can be carried out very well even by a layman, or by a woman; as for example, by a religious of the same, or another institute. It is understood, however, that in such cases the visitator may only perform acts of purely dominative power, all acts of ecclesiastical jurisdiction being excluded (cf. *supra*, n. 40).

54. DUTIES OF VISITATORS

Visitators have the right and duty of interrogating any religious regarding all matters which they must know in order to carry on the visitation (c. 513, par. 1). The limits placed on visitators in these investigations can and ought to be defined by the common law, by the constitutions, and, in visitations made through a delegate, by the mandate in virtue of which the visitators act.

To obtain the truth, the visitator can give a precept or command to those being visitated obliging them to answer truthfully in virtue of holy obedience regarding everything about which they shall be lawfully interrogated. Moreover, if the visitator proceeds in a judiciary manner, he may demand that an oath be taken (c. 1944, par. 1). To proceed in a judiciary manner the judge must possess ecclesiastical jurisdiction, which can be given to clerics alone (c. 118); but to impose a precept in virtue of obedience, dominative power, which belongs to all superiors, even though they be only laypeople, whether men or women, suffices (cf. *supra*, n. 40).

If a visitator commands that all faults committed by other religious be revealed to him, this command should not be understood to extend to hidden faults. In regard to these faults the order of fraternal correction must still be followed. This is true for a twofold reason: first, because no superior may act contrary to the precept of Christ who commanded us that fraternal correction should be employed as long as there is hope of its being effective (see Matt. 18:15); and secondly, because a superior is not a judge of internal sins but only of those which are external, and he is the judge of these latter only insofar as they effect the good of the institute or its members. Hence as long as there is a well founded hope that fraternal correction can be employed effectively, and as long as a fault remains absolutely hidden, there is no obligation, notwithstanding the command of the visitator, to reveal secret sins, even though they are external, of one's sister religious.

The following are exceptions to the above rule:

1) Institutes in which religious expressly renounce the right to fraternal correction. In some institutes the members, in order to practice greater humility, agree to be publicly corrected anytime by any member of the community. Hence according to an old axiom of law, *Volenti et consentienti nulla fit iniuria,* when one wishes and consents to a renunciation of a right, no injury is done when others act contrary to that right.

2) Another exception is to be made in those cases which, although they cannot be said to be entirely public, have nevertheless certain external implications which give to a superior, as to any other judge, the right to demand, even under oath, that the truth be made known regarding the matter under investigation.

3) A third exception is to be made if the fault is such that there will be grave danger in not making it known immediately to the superior, or if there is no well founded hope that fraternal correction will be effective.

The visitator may not demand that the religious reveal intimate matters of conscience since they are not the object of any human law nor, consequently, of any precept. However, in this matter there should not be too much quibbling. Both superiors and subjects ought to seek in the visitation not only their own good but also that of the community. Therefore, all ought to act with the greatest mutual confidence and with the desire of making a worthwhile contribution to the common good, profiting by the maternal concern of the Church, which, in imposing canonical visitations, wishes to afford religious a most efficacious means of maintaining regular observance in convents and monasteries.

We shall consider later the question of the entrance of male visitators into the cloister of nuns (cf. *infra,* n. 201, B).

55. RIGHTS AND DUTIES OF THE VISITATED

All religious are under strict obligation to answer the visitator truthfully (c. 513, par. 1). Nor is it lawful for superiors to divert their subjects in any way from this obligation, or otherwise impede the scope of the visitation (c. 513, par. 1). As we shall see (n. 56), superiors who do so incur grave penalties. The obligation of answering questions relative to hidden matters, or relative to matters in which there is a well founded hope that fraternal correction will suffice, has been explained in the preceding number.

One may always have recourse to major superiors against the decision of visitators but not with suspensive effect, or *in devolutivo;* that is, one must carry out the commands of the visitator while the appeal is pending (c. 513, par. 2). Hence in this case the proverb *primus obediat deinde recurrat* — "One must first obey and then have recourse" — must be put into practice.

An exception is made to this rule only when a male visitator proceeds in a judiciary manner. A female visitator is excluded from proceeding in this manner because she cannot be given true ecclesiastical jurisdiction (cf. *supra,* n. 54). In this case, recourse may be had *in suspensivo,* that is, the obligation of obeying is suspended for the time (cf. *supra,* n. 21); therefore, one may have recourse and not carry out the sentence which the visitator has made as a judge (c. 513, par. 2). As a matter of fact, a male visitator may be invested with a twofold mandate: he may be assigned to investigate the regular life of a community or of a religious institute and to take steps which he believes necessary for good order and discipline; or he may be assigned to formally investigate and judge an individual fact or a particular person accused of some fault. In this latter case the law provides for recourse *in suspensivo,* as has been pointed out above, but in the former case recourse may be made only *in devolutivo.*

56. PENALTIES

Superiors who have transferred a religious to another house without the consent of the visitator after the visitation has been announced may be removed from office by the visitator (c. 2413, par. 1).

All religious, whether superiors or subjects, who, personally or through others, directly or indirectly, induce religious not to reply to the questions of the visitator, or to dissimulate or hide the truth, as well as those who under whatsoever pretext have molested any religious on account of replies which she may have given to the visitator, shall be declared by the visitator as incapable of obtaining any office which bears with it the government of other religious. Indeed, if they are already in possession of such authority they shall be deprived of office by their legitimate superiors (c. 2413, par. 1).

PART FOUR

SELECTION OF SUPERIORS

I

ELECTIONS

A religious may become the superior of an institute in several ways: by election, by postulation or by appointment. Hereditary succession in the office of superior, just as it is excluded in any ecclesiastical dignity, is not allowed in any religious institute whether of men or women. Thus if a superior appoints a religious to succeed her before she dies, this act is invalid. The most that a superior can do before her death, if the constitutions permit it, is to name a vicaress to take over the government of the house or institute until a new superior who succeeds the dead superior has been selected.

The Code contains nothing concerning the direct appointment of a superior by the lawful superiors. For validity, therefore, it is sufficient that the constitutions of each religious institute be followed. In an election or postulation, on the other hand, the norms contained in the Code, which we will explain in the next four chapters, are to be followed.

57. NATURE OF ELECTIONS

An election is correctly defined as the selection of a person capable

79

of filling a vacant office, made by those who have the right to make such a choice.

Vacant, because the Code absolutely prohibits under penalty of invalidity, a new election while a person lawfully invested with the dignity of office is still in charge (c. 150).

Made by those who have the right to make such a choice. Not all members of an ecclesiastical society enjoy the right of election, but only those who are endowed with certain qualities determined by the laws of the Church and the particular constitutions of each institute. Likewise, those who ordinarily enjoy such a right may lose it, because of some penalty; for example, those who are deprived of active voice in an election.

58. Laws Regulating Elections

In the election of religious superiors, the prescriptions of Canon Law must be closely observed (c. 507, par. 1). The Code treats of elections from canon 160 to canon 182; and although these canons deal with elections to ecclesiastical dignities and offices, without doubt they also apply to the election of religious superiors insofar as the nature of the case allows (c. 507, par. 1).

The constitutions of each religious institute which are not contrary to the aforementioned canons are also to be observed (c. 507, par. 1).

Which are not contrary to the aforementioned canons. Hence conditions or prescriptions contrary to the common law may not be inserted in the constitutions, and if such conditions or prescriptions are already contained in the constitutions they are to be corrected. In some cases, however, Canon Law allows contrary constitutions to continue in force; for example, canon 162, canon 171, canon 174.

59. Procedure in Elections

The election of religious superiors may be carried out either by ballot or by compromise. Quasi-inspiration, namely, an election carried out not by vote but by acclamation, even if all are inspired to agree unanimously on the same person for an office and by acclamation declare her elected, is not allowed (c. 160 ff.).

A. Election by ballot

Election by ballot is carried out in the following manner: each elector secretly designates, by a ballot, the person whom she chooses for the office; then those who are called scrutators or tellers collect the ballots, examine them and count them so as to know who has received a sufficient number of ballots to be elected. This manner of procedure is comprised of the following acts:

1) The writing of the ballot. One must clearly place the name of the candidate on the ballot, or at least identify her by a quality which is so characteristic that all ambiguity of the person designated is excluded. It is prescribed under penalty of nullity that the vote be "secret, certain, absolute [not bound by any conditions] and determinate" (c. 169, par. 1, n. 2). We refer to "the writing of the ballot," however, even if the ballots should be printed by hand. As long as secrecy is observed when the ballots are placed in the ballot box, the voting would not be irregular, much less invalid.

2) The collection of the ballots. In the Code it is stated that "the tellers shall see to it that the voting is done secretly, methodically, individually, and according to the order of precedence of each elector" (c. 171, par. 2).

3) The counting of the ballots. Having collected the votes, the tellers in the presence of the president of the election and in the manner prescribed by the particular constitutions or by legitimate custom shall first of all see whether the number of votes corresponds to the number of electors (c. 171, par. 2). If the number of votes exceeds the number of voters the ballot is null and void (c. 171, par. 3), and without proceeding further the ballots are to be burned and a new ballot is to be taken (c. 171, par. 4).

There is no mention made in the Code of the case in which the number of votes is less than the number of electors, perhaps because the diligence which the tellers must use precludes this hypothesis; or perhaps because it can be legitimately presumed that if the elector does not place her ballot in the ballot box she is understood to renounce her vote. However, to avoid all disputes it would be better to take another vote while the ballots are still folded.

4) The reading of the votes. From an examination of the ballots it can be determined how many valid votes each candidate has received (c. 171, par. 2).

Valid, namely, when all the requisite conditions are fulfilled (cf. *infra,* n. 66).

5) The announcement of the result of the balloting. This is accomplished by making known to the electors how many votes each candidate has received (c. 171, par. 2).

6) The burning of the ballots. The votes are to be burned immediately after each ballot (c. 171, par. 4).

Immediately, at least if another ballot is not taken in the same session; in this case the burning of the ballots may be postponed until the end of the session (c. 171, par. 4).

B. Election by compromise

Election *by compromise* occurs when the electors unanimously and in writing delegate one or many qualified persons chosen from among their own numbers or from those outside of the elective body to designate in their names for that one occasion the person to be elected (c. 172, par. 1). The persons chosen to make the selection are known as delegates.

In order that election by compromise be valid the following are required:

1) The convocation of the electors must be made in the same manner as for an election. Only after the electors are legitimately convoked and with their unanimous and written consent, is it permissible to proceed to the election by compromise (c. 172, par. 1). Unanimous consent is required only for the decision to make the selection by compromise; once this is decided all other factors that pertain to the selection (for example, the delegates, the conditions) may be decided by a simple majority.

2) The designation of qualified delegates (c. 172, par. 1). The Code neither states what nor how many conditions are required in order that the delegates be qualified. It merely notes that if the elections take place in a clerical religious institute the delegates must be priests (c. 172, par. 2). Hence in religious institutes for women, which are necessarily lay, the religious themselves, whether they are from that or another monastery, may be made delegates. Priests, male religious or the bishop may also be named as delegates. It is possible for only one delegate to make the selection.

3) Delegates whether men or women, under penalty of the nullity of the election, must:

a) Observe the conditions attached to the compromise, if these are not opposed to the common law. Conditions contrary to the common law are considered as not having been made (c. 172, par. 3).

b) If no conditions were attached they must observe the common law regulating elections, that is, the delegates in designating the person must proceed by way of election (c. 172, par. 3).

c) If the voters by compromise appoint only one person to designate a candidate for the office of superior, she may not elect herself (c. 172, par. 4). Likewise, if several were designated, no delegate can add her own vote to that of the other delegates who vote for her so as to effect her election (172, par. 4). A vote for oneself is always invalid, and it invalidates the election if it is the decisive vote (c. 170).

4) The compromise ceases and the right of election returns to the electors in the following cases:

a) If the college of electors, or at least the major part of it, revoke the mandate which permitted the compromise. This revocation, however, must take place before the delegates have begun to use the mandate (c. 173, n. 1).

b) If the conditions attached to the compromise were not fulfilled (c. 173, n. 2).

c) If the election or designation made by the delegates was invalid (c. 173, n. 3). When the election or designation made by the delegates is invalid for any lawful motive, the delegates may not proceed to a new election if their mandate has not been renewed.

60. TIME FOR ELECTIONS

Elections are invalid unless they are held within the space of time allowed by the common law or by the particular constitutions. This space of time is known as the *useful time* for elections (c. 161).

The Code designates as useful time for each election a period of three months to be computed from the day on which the notice of the vacancy was received (c. 161). There are, however, two exceptions:

1) When the particular or common law expressly determines otherwise (c. 161).

2) When it is a question of a new election which follows the renunciation of an office by one who, although validly elected, has not exercised the office. In this case, a new election must be held "within a month" from the day on which the renunciation became known (c. 176).

The terms month, three months, year, when used in connection with an election, are taken as they are in the calendar, without counting the first day the news of the vacant office is received, so that the useful time elapses at the end of the last day of the month of the same date. For example, if news of the vacancy of the office of prioress is received on the first of January, the month expires at the end of the first of February, three months at the end of the first of April (without taking into account that February may have 28 or 29 days and not 30 or 31), so that until midnight of April 1, there is still useful time for the election (cf. c. 34, par. 3).

If the election was not held within the useful time, the right of providing for the vacant office reverts to the superior who would have had the right to confirm the election, or to the one who has the next right of appointment (c. 178).

61. President of the Election

In every election there must be a president who authoritatively conducts the election (c. 171, par. 1). It would seem that the presence of a president is necessary for the validity of an election because it is something which is most important in conducting the election in a proper manner.

The president, as such, does not have a vote in elections; however, he or she could have a vote under some other title, for example, if the particular law of an institute grants it to him or her (c. 171, par. 1).

In the election of a superior of nuns:

1) If the nuns are subject to the Ordinary of the place he shall preside over the election either personally or through his delegate (c. 506, par. 2).

2) If, on the other hand, the nuns are immediately subject to the superior of an order with which they are affiliated, he fills the office of president. But even in this case the Ordinary should be duly in-

formed of the day and hour of the election so that he may assist at it, either in person or by a delegate, with the regular superior. If the Ordinary assists at the election, he is to preside (c. 506, par. 2).

The Pontifical Commission for the Interpretation of the Code was asked whether these words of canon 506 paragraph 2, "and if he assists, he presides," ought to be restricted to the case in which the bishop assists in person at the election or whether it is also to be applied to the case in which he sends a delegate. The Commission, on November 24, 1920, responded that the presidency always pertains to the Ordinary of the place, and not to the regular superior, whether the Ordinary assists at the election in person, or through a delegate.

When nuns are subject to a religious Order, must the regular superior or the superior of the nuns inform the local Ordinary in good time of the coming election? It seems to us that this is the duty of the nuns, and especially of the superior who is going out of office. Or, if she has already gone out of office, it is the obligation of the religious who takes over her duties, for example, the sub-prioress. Indirectly, however, it can be the obligation of the regular superior insofar as he would not be allowed to assist at an election of which the local Ordinary had not been informed. If the local Ordinary is not informed of the election and the regular superior presides, the bishop may annul the election.

In elections of sisters:

1) The local Ordinary either personally or by his delegate must preside over the election of a superior general (c. 506, par. 4). The Ordinary's office is not merely honorary; rather, it implys that he has true jurisdiction over the election (P.C.I., July 30, 1934).

When a religious congregation of diocesan approval has houses in many dioceses does it pertain to the Ordinary of the place in which the mother house is situated or to the Ordinary of the place where the election is held to preside over the election of a mother general? The Sacred Congregation of Religious, on July 2, 1921, answered negatively to the first part of the question and affirmatively to the second. Hence it pertains to the Ordinary of the place in which the election is held to preside over the election.

2) In other elections the particular constitutions or legitimate customs are to be followed in the choice of a president (c. 489).

In elections of nuns and also of cloistered sisters it is not necessary for the president to conduct the election within the cloister; rather, he must not enter the cloister, but together with the tellers he shall preside over the election at the grill of the parlor or chapter (c. 506, par. 2).

If a religious who has the right to participate in an election holds the office of president, she must take an oath before the election to fulfill faithfully the duties of her office and to observe secrecy concerning everything pertaining to the election, even when the election has come to an end. The same oath need not be taken when the president does not pertain to the electoral college (c. 171, par. 1).

62. TELLERS

Tellers in elections are those whose duty it is, together with the president, to see to it that the election is carried on in a lawful manner, to count the votes, and to make known the results of the ballots.

In every election besides the president there must be at least two tellers (c. 171, par. 1). It seems that tellers are required for a valid election.

At least two tellers. Hence there may be more if the particular constitutions prescribe it or also if the electors so desire.

In elections of nuns the tellers must always be two priests who are not ordinary confessors of the monastery (c. 506, pars. 2, 3).

It is not stated in the Code who is to select these priests. It is a reasonable presumption however, that whenever the particular constitutions are also silent, the choice is reserved to the president of the election. It does not seem practical that in the case of nuns, canon 171, paragraph 1, which in similar circumstances leaves the choice of tellers to the electoral body, may be applied. If the nuns are subject to a regular superior then he, rather than the local Ordinary, should appoint the priest tellers, since the preparation for the election pertains to him.

The tellers must not enter the cloister but they shall direct the election together with the president at the grill of the parlor or chapter (c. 506, par. 2).

In the election of sisters, the sisters themselves may hold the office of teller. Other people may also fulfill the office if the particular constitutions so provide or if such a practice is confirmed by custom.

When the particular constitutions or legitimate custom do not determine who the tellers ought to be, they are to be selected by and from the electoral college by secret ballot before the election (c. 171, par. 1).

By secret ballot. Here a difficulty presents itself: How can the election of tellers be held by a secret ballot when there are no tellers to count the ballots for the election of the tellers? It seems to us that one manner of procedure which is simple, certainly legitimate and effective, would be to propose to the electors certain names; then, by means of black and white beans the electors may express their assent or dissent through the secrecy of the ballot box. The proposal of names could fittingly be made by the president of the election. If this manner of voting is not acceptable then recourse must be had to the written ballot, the majority necessary to designate the tellers being determined from an examination of the ballots, and the number of ballots being regulated by the rules which we shall presently indicate *(infra,* n. 67). To proceed to this preliminary ballot it would not be necessary to designate tellers; otherwise the procedure could go on indefinitely. The president or others chosen by him will suffice to examine the ballots.

It is the duty of tellers to gather the votes, to see to it that the voting is done with care, according to the order of precedence among the electors, and that the votes remain secret (c. 171, par. 2).

If some of the electors in a monastery of nuns are ill, may the male tellers enter the cloister to collect their votes? This problem arises because of two seemingly contradictory canons. Canon 506, par. 2, prescribes that in the election of nuns the male tellers may not enter the cloister; whereas canon 168 states that "if any of the electors is present in the house in which the election takes place but cannot be present at the election by reason of ill health his vote shall be taken by the tellers (male) unless particular laws or legitimate customs provide otherwise." How are these two prescriptions to be reconciled?

It seems that when the particular constitutions or custom do not solve the question the following practice which is commonly in use is to be adopted: Two nuns who are electors are delegated by the tellers, or better by the one who presides over the election, to go to the infirm elector, receive her written and secret ballot and then carry it to the president of the election (cf. *infra,* n. 65).

The tellers must also count the votes which have been carefully gathered, and if the number of votes does not exceed the number of electors, open them in the presence of the president of the election and in the manner in which the particular constitutions prescribe; and finally, make known how many votes each candidate has received (c. 171, par. 2).

Before the election, the tellers, if they are members of the electoral college, must take an oath to fulfill their office faithfully and to observe secrecy concerning the proceedings of the election, even after the election has come to an end (c. 171, par. 1).

63. THE SECRETARY

In every election there must be a secretary to record accurately the proceedings of the election (c. 171, par. 5). She may be named, if this has not already been done in virtue of the particular constitutions, by the electors (c. 503). She may even be chosen from among the electors or from outside the electoral college. In the former case she has a vote in the election, in the latter case she has not.

The secretary together with the president and tellers must sign the acts of election (c. 171, par. 5).

64. CONVOCATION OF THE ELECTORS

The convocation of electors is the announcement made to them of the coming election and of the place and time in which it is to take place. All the religious who are members of the electoral college, that is, all the religious who have a right to vote in the election, must be convoked (c. 162, par. 1).

1) The convocation must be made by the president of the electoral college (c. 162, par. 1). Even when the president of the electoral college is not a woman religious but the local Ordinary or regular superior (cf. *supra*, n. 61), sometimes the convocation of the electors is made not by the Ordinary or regular superior but by the superioress who has charge of the house or institute, with the concurrence, of course, of the Ordinary or regular superior, relative to the place and time in which the election is to take place. We believe that this manner of acting is legitimate, because in doing so the superioress can consider herself a delegate of the Ordinary or of the regular superior.

In congregations of diocesan approval which have houses in a number of dioceses, the mother general of the community, and not the Ordinary of the place where the mother house is located, has the right to determine where the next election will be held. If the election is held outside the diocese where the motherhouse is located, then the Ordinary of the diocese where the election is held has the right to preside (S. C. Rel., July 2, 1921).

2) The convocation must be made in conformity with the particular constitutions or legitimate customs (c. 162, par. 1). If the constitutions or customs have nothing to say on the subject, the president of the electoral college is to determine the best manner of convoking the electors. It is absolutely necessary that one have moral certitude that all the electors receive notice of the election in sufficient time so that they may attend the chapter if they wish.

Those who are absent are to be convoked individually, that is, notice of the election is to be sent to them directly either by letter or in some other manner. Those who are present may be convoked collectively, either orally or by the sounding of a bell or by any other sign, as long as the electors have been previously informed that such a sign signifies the convocation of the election. When the electors are summoned individually, it suffices for validity of the convocation that the notice be sent either to the place of domicile or quasi-domicile of the electors, or to the place where they actually stay (c. 162, par. 1). It is sufficient, then, to send the notice or letter to the house where the religious is assigned or to the place where she is actually staying at the time.

Irregularities commited in the convocation of the electoral college sometimes render the election **invalid** and at other times they render it **rescissible.**

1) An election is invalid, if more than a third part of the electors were omitted from the convocation (c. 162, par. 3), unless the electors who were neglected were nevertheless present at the election (c. 162, par. 4).

2) An election is invalid, if the election is to an office which is to be held for life and the convocation of the electors was made before the person invested with the office was dead (c. 162, par. 5).

3) An election is rescissible, that is, one may petition for its annulment, if any member of the electoral college was neglected in the convocation and because of this omission was not present at the election. It is required, however, that the petition for annulment be sent

by the one not notified of the election to the lawful superior within three days after the election and that the case can be proven juridically (c. 162, par. 2).

Was neglected in the convocation; that is, if no notice of the election was sent her. Even if she was neglected she could still attend the election since convocation does not confer but supposes the right to vote (c. 162, par. 4).

Was not present at the election because of this omission. Hence if it can be proven that even if the elector had been informed in due time she would have found it impossible to attend the election, for example, because of illness, it does not seem that she may petition for annulment.

Legally speaking, electors may absent themselves from an election unless particular constitutions oblige them to attend. In practice, however, that is, in view of the common good, it may happen that even when particular constitutions grant one freedom in this matter, one may be obliged to attend an election when one's attendance can effectively contribute to the good of the community or can impede some evil. Active voice is granted not for one's own convenience but for the common good. Consequently, non-attendance at an election is never to be counseled even if one may be legally free to remain away.

May the electors hold a caucus before the election in order to discuss the various candidates? They may, if the purpose of the meeting is to make known the qualities of the candidates so that each elector with safe conscience can vote for one whom she believes most fitted to govern the community. On the other hand, if the purpose of the caucus is to induce the electors to procure votes for themselves or for others, then such a procedure is illegal, since c. 507, paragraph 2 states that all must abstain from seeking votes, either directly or indirectly, for themselves or for others. It is quite another matter if, instead of holding a true caucus, the electors freely and confidentially exchange counsels on the choice of a person to be elected. This assuredly may be done; it is even almost indispensable that it be done in order to direct the electors toward a probable majority which is necessary for the success of the election.

65. THOSE WHO CAN VOTE

The convocation of the electoral college having been lawfully made, only those electors have a right to vote who are present in person on the day appointed (c. 163).

Present in person. Canon 163 excludes the faculty of voting by letter or by proxy unless particular law rules otherwise.

However, if any of the electors is present in the house where the election is held but cannot go in person to the place where the chapter is held because of infirmity, the tellers must go to her to collect her written vote, unless particular laws or legitimate customs provide otherwise (c. 168). In the case of nuns, male tellers may not go in person to the infirm nun to take her vote but they shall delegate two electors of their choice to go and collect the vote from the infirm elector (cf. *supra,* n. 62).

One who does not belong to the electoral college may not be permitted to vote, under pain of rendering the election null and void. This, however, is not meant to be prejudicial to legitimately acquired privileges. In a particular instance, for example, the Sovereign Pontiff may grant a religious who has no right to vote, the permission to participate in an election (c. 165).

The following also are not qualified to vote: (1) those who have not the use of reason, for example, the insane (c. 167, par. 1, n. 1); (2) those who are under censure, or are infamous by law, but only after a declaratory or condemnatory sentence (c. 167, par. 1, n. 3); and (3) those who are deprived of active voice (c. 167, par. 1, n. 5).

If one of the religious just mentioned should be admitted to the election, in itself the election would be valid. It would be invalid, however, if the vote of such a religious were necessary to constitute the majority necessary for an election, or if one excommunicated by a declaratory or condemnatory sentence were knowingly admitted (c. 167, par. 2).

66. Qualities of a Valid Vote

In order that a vote cast by a legitimate elector be valid it must be:

1) *Free,* that is, freely cast (c. 169, par. 1, n. 1). Hence a vote is invalid if an elector either directly or indirectly was induced by grave fear or by deceit to vote for a particular person, or for several persons separately (c. 169, par. 1, n. 1).

2) *Secret,* so that the names of the candidates chosen become known

only when the ballots are opened and then without knowing who has cast the votes (c. 169, par. 1, n. 2). The common law does not set down any particular manner of secretly casting votes in an election except in the case of the election of the Roman Pontiff. Each institute, then, is left free to determine the most practical method of secretly casting votes. Ordinarily, this is done by balloting.

3) *Certain*, that is, there must not be any doubt as to the person designated (c. 169, par. 1, n. 2). For example, a vote expressed in the following manner would be null and void: I elect the one who will receive the greatest number of votes.

4) *Absolute*, that is, without attaching any conditions to it (c. 169, par. 1, n. 2). Moreover, if the conditions had been made before an election—for example, if one had promised to vote for a particular person under the condition that once elected she would act in such and such a manner or would do this or that thing—these conditions are to be considered as nonexistent (c. 169, par. 2).

5) *Determinate*, that is, it must designate individually the person to be elected; for example, by indicating her name and surname or the office for which she is a candidate in such a way that all ambiguity and uncertainty is excluded (c. 169, par. 1, n. 2). A blank ballot, therefore, is of its nature null and void and is not to be counted with the others.

6) *Made in person,* and not by letter or by proxy unless particular constitutions or particular law expressly permit it (c. 163). The manner of proceeding when an elector is infirm and cannot go to the place where the election is held has been already explained (cf. *supra,* n. 62 and n. 65). Even if an elector has the right to vote under several titles, she may cast only one vote (c. 164). Thus if one were a prioress and at the same time a counselor, she would still be able to cast only one vote, even though according to law both prioresses and counsellors have the right to vote. The only exception to the rule of one vote for one person occurs when particular law permits vote by proxy.

A vote cast for oneself is also null and void (c. 170). The observance of this canon is left to the conscience of each elector. In practice it is not easy to prove that one has voted for herself. Nevertheless, if in some particular case it is possible to prove that an elector cast a vote for herself, this vote must be considered null and void and not be counted in the number of votes which determine a majority (c. 101, par. 1, n. 1).

Furthermore, members of the electoral college must abstain from seeking votes either directly or indirectly for themselves or for others (c. 507, par. 2). This does not mean that the electors may not discuss among themselves the name of the person to be elected, as long as no pressure is brought to bear upon others.

In the examination of the ballots no account is to be taken of votes which for any reason whatsoever are invalid (c. 101, par. 1). A vote is not invalid if instead of writing, "I elect," one were to write, "I postulate." According to common law, a vote is valid as long as it certain and expressed without ambiguity. To have this certitude in an election to a definite office it is more than sufficient if the name is clearly written on the ballot, even if the elector, through ignorance or through error, has written "I postulate" instead of "I elect," or vice versa. To avoid any difficulty in this regard the ballot may read, "I elect or postulate."

67. THE NUMBER OF BALLOTS

Once a sufficient majority for a valid election is obtained, it is not permissible to continue balloting (c. 174).

Unless the particular constitutions which have been legitimately approved determine otherwise, it is never permitted to have more than three ballots. If the first two ballots are ineffectual because no one receives the necessary majority of votes required by common law or by the particular constitutions, on the third ballot she is to be considered elected who shall receive a relative majority of votes. If in this third ballot several candidates receive the same number of votes, the one who presides over the election may break the tie with her vote. If the superior is unwilling to do this, then she is to be considered elected, among those who receive an equal number of votes, who is oldest in years of religious profession; and if even this is not sufficient to break the tie, the oldest in age shall be considered elected (c. 101, par. 1, n. 1).

Unless the particular constitutions which have been legitimately approved determine otherwise. When the particular constitutions which have been legitimately approved determine otherwise in the matter of the number of ballots which may be taken, the constitutions, and not the Code, are to be followed. For example, if the constitutions state that only one ballot is permissible, or that more than three ballots are allowable, the prescriptions of the constitutions and not those of the Code are to be followed.

68. NUMBER OF VOTES REQUIRED

If the particular law (that is, the particular constitutions) does not determine otherwise, relative to the number of votes required for a valid election, the Code prescribes:

1) That person is to be considered elected who, after excluding any invalid votes, has received an absolute majority of the votes cast. And if this absolute majority was not obtained by any of the candidates on the first or second ballots, then on the third ballot that religious is to be considered elected who has received a relative majority of the votes (c. 101, par. 1, n. 1; c. 174; c. 507). (The meaning of absolute and relative majority was explained in n. 51, *supra*.)

2) When, on the third ballot, the candidates have received an equal number of votes, the one who presides over the electoral college may break the tie with her vote. If she does not wish to do so, then, as we have already pointed out, the candidate who is oldest in religious profession is to be considered elected. And if this does not settle the matter, then the one who is oldest in age is to be considered elected (c. 174; c. 101, par. 1, n. 1; cf. *supra*, n. 67). Hence in elections when an equal number of votes is received by the candidates, the president may, but is not bound to, break the tie by her vote; in the case of other decisions, on the other hand, she must do so (c. 101, par. 1; cf. *supra*, n. 51).

If the constitutions of a religious institute, which have been legitimately approved, legislate differently from the above relative to the number of votes and the number of ballots, then the constitutions are to be followed (c. 101, par. 1, n. 1; c. 507, par. 1).

The qualities required in the person to be elected have been explained above in number 39.

69. INTERSTICES

By *interstices* is understood that space of time which must transpire before the same person may be re-elected to the same office.

For **major superiors** the Code does not demand interstices of any kind; however, they may be imposed by the constitutions of each institute (n. 42).

A **local superior of nuns,** whether she be called prioress or abbess or by any other name, may not be re-elected without interstices when the three year period has elapsed (cf. *supra,* n. 41). A **local superior of sisters,** on the other hand, may be immediately re-elected a second time in the same house, that is, without interstices, if the particular constitutions permit this. She may not, however, be re-elected a third time without interstices (c. 505).

In the same house . . . without interstices, if the particular constitutions permit this. See the explanation above in number 41.

If grave reasons suggest or demand the re-election of a local superior for a third term, then she may be postulated, but not elected.

70. PROCLAMATION OF ELECTION

It pertains to the president of the electoral college to proclaim that religious elected who has received the required number of votes (c. 174). If the president of the electoral college is elected, it is better to assign the proclamation to the oldest teller.

The election is to be made known at once to the person elected, and within eight days at the most from the time that the notice is received she must declare whether she accepts the election or not. If she fails to do so within the allotted "useful time," that is, within the eight days, she loses every right acquired by the election (c. 175). "Useful time" means that time which is given for the exercise or prosecution of one's right; it is not computed if one is prevented from acting or is ignorant of one's rights.

If the person elected renounces her election, she thereby loses all rights acquired by the election even though she afterwards regrets the renunciation. She may, however, be re-elected (c. 176, par. 1).

If the election does not need confirmation, as soon as it has been accepted the person elected acquires full right to exercise her office immediately; but if confirmation is necessary, the one elected may not make use of her right until after the confirmation has been received (c. 176, par. 2).

Once the proclamation of election has been made the electoral college may not proceed to another ballot; it may do so only when the renunciation of the person elected becomes known with certitude or when the election has been annulled (c. 191, par. 2). Within a month after the renunciation has become known or the election has been annulled, the electoral college is bound to proceed to a new election; otherwise it loses all right to do so and the right of selection reverts to the superior who would have had the right to confirm the election, or to whom it pertains to appoint the superior in question (c. 176, par. 1; c. 178). This is the procedure set down in the Code. It should be noted nevertheless, that in the matter of elections, this particular point is usually modified by the constitutions of each religious institute. In this case, the legitimately approved constitutions, and not the common law, are to be followed.

71. RENUNCIATION OF ELECTION

Unless the constitutions expressly prohibit it, the one elected may always renounce the office to which she was elected (c. 184). She may do so immediately after the election or also after she has taken over the office. Superiors, however, shall not easily accept renunciation from office without a just and proportionate cause (c. 189, par. 1).

The following are the requirements for a valid renunciation:

1) The renunciation must be made directly to the person who, according to common or particular law, has the power to accept it or not accept it (c. 187, par. 1).

2) It must be made in writing by the person renouncing the election or else it must be made orally before two witnesses. It may also be made through a proxy, but in this case a special mandate is required. The written document of renunciation must be conserved in the archives (c. 186).

3) It must be made freely. Hence if it were caused by grave fear, unjustly inflicted, or by deceit or substantial error, or by simony, it would be, by this very fact, invalid (c. 185).

Once the renunciation has been validly made and accepted it may not be revoked (c. 191, par. 1). However, the person who has renounced the election may be elected again (c. 176, par. 1) or may acquire the office she has renounced by some other title (c. 191, par. 1).

Even after the renunciation has been made and accepted, the office becomes vacant only when notice of the acceptance of the renunciation is received by the person who has made the renunciation (c. 190, par. 1). Hence a superior who resigns an office remains in office until she receives notice of the acceptance of the renunciation by the legitimate superiors (c. 190, par. 2). A new election may not be held until the notification of acceptance is received.

Care is to be taken in informing the interested parties of the renunciation (c. 191, par. 2).

72. Confirmation of the Election

When confirmation by legitimate superiors is necessary for the validity of an election, the person elected either personally or through others must ask for such a confirmation within the space of eight days; otherwise she loses all right to the office unless she can prove the existence of a just impediment which rendered a petition for confirmation impossible (c. 177, par. 1). The Code does not state when confirmation of an election is required or by what superior it is to be made. Hence the particular constitutions are to be followed in this matter.

The superior to whom it pertains to confirm the election, not only may, but must confirm it, if the person elected possesses the qualities required by law (c. 177, par. 2). An exception is made to this in the election of a superioress general of a religious institute of diocesan approval. In this case it is reserved to the bishop of the place where the election is held to confirm or not confirm the election, according to his conscience (c. 506, par. 4). This is true even if the diocesan institute is located in many dioceses (S. C. Rel., July 2, 1921). Another exception is made when the constitutions legitimately confirmed by the Holy See give to the superioress, to whom the confirmation is reserved, the faculty of annulling the election. If the superior has this power, she may use it even in regard to elections in which all the requirements of law are fulfilled as long as she judges it opportune for the good of the monastery or of the religious institute.

Once confirmation has been given, the one elected acquires full right to the exercise of her office unless the particular law states otherwise (c. 177, par. 4). Before receiving this confirmation, however, the person elected may not interfere in any way whatsoever in the administration of things pertaining to her office. All acts executed in such circumstances would be invalid (c. 176, par. 3). If a person is elected to an office but turns it down, she may be re-elected to the same office. This is true also of a religious who does not receive confirmation after having been elected.

73. PROCEEDINGS OF ELECTIONS

All the proceedings of an election shall be recorded by the secretary; and, they are to be signed at least by the secretary, the president of the election, and the tellers (c. 171, par. 5).

The proceedings are to be accurately recorded in the archives of the monastery or of the province or of the motherhouse of the institute, depending on whether it is a local, provincial or general election (c. 171, par. 5). In certain religious institutes it is prescribed that when confirmation of an election is necessary the proceedings must be made in duplicate: one copy is to be placed in the archives and the other is to be sent to the superior to whom it pertains to confirm the election. This custom is praiseworthy and can be used to advantage in avoiding difficulties.

II

THE POSTULATION OF
SUPERIORS

74. MEANING OF POSTULATION

By the postulation of a superior is understood the request made by the college of electors to obtain as superior a religious who cannot be validly elected by reason of some impediment (c. 179, par. 1).

By reason of some impediment. The postulation of a religious who would be absolutely incapable of fulfilling the office in question by reason of natural impediments (such as lack of the use of reason) could neither validly nor licitly be made. Moreover, in order that the postulation be effective, the impediment in question must be not only canonical but also of such a nature that it can be and usually is dispensed. There are certain impediments, even of positive law, from which the authorities neither wish nor are accustomed to dispense, and in this case postulation is useless.

75. LAWFULNESS OF POSTULATION

Election by postulation is valid and lawful. It is not, however,

99

an ordinary process but is rather an extraordinary procedure, and may be employed only when it is not forbidden by the constitutions (c. 507, par. 3). An extraordinary and sufficient reason for the postulation of a superior would occur if a religious lacks some quality required by law—the requisite age, for example—but is more fitted for a certain office than another religious who has all the canonical requirements but does not possess the necessary natural qualities.

When an election is made by compromise the delegates do not have the right to postulate a superior unless special permission to do so has been granted to them (c. 179, par. 2). The meaning of election by compromise and of delegates appointed by compromise of the voters to make an election has been explained above (n. 59).

76. CONDITIONS FOR POSTULATION

Postulation is valid only when it is supported by a majority of votes. If it concurs with an election—that is, if some of the voters postulate as a candidate for an office a religious burdened by certain impediments, while other voters elect another religious who is truly eligible— then the postulation must be supported by two-thirds of the votes in order to be valid (c. 180, par. 1). For example, if there are nine electors and five postulate Sister N, three postulate Sister M, and one postulates Sister X, the postulation in favor of Sister N is valid since it is a question of postulation alone and Sister N has in her favor an absolute majority of the votes. If, on the other hand, five of the electors postulate Sister N, three *elect* Sister M, and one postulates Sister X, the postulation does not have enough support and therefore is invalid. When it concurs with an election, the postulation requires for validity that not merely a majority, but two-thirds of the votes be cast in favor of the postulated candidate. Hence at least six votes are necessary for the postulation of Sister N when her postulation accompanies a vote on eligible candidates.

The Pontifical Commission for the Interpretation of the Code was asked:

1) Whether, according to canon 180, par. 1, when a postulation concurs with an election, and on the first, second and third ballots the votes are divided between the eligible candidate and the postulate and neither the one postulated receives two-thirds of the votes,

nor the eligible candidate an absolute majority, is this eligible candidate validly elected by only a relative majority?

2) If, when there are several eligible candidates, whether the one validly elected is the one among them who receives a relative majority?

The Pontifical Commission, July 1, 1922, answered:

1) To the first question in the affirmative; that is, the eligible candidate is validly elected on the third ballot by a relative majority, the one postulated being excluded.

2) To the second question in the affirmative; that is, the one among the eligible candidates who receives a relative majority is elected always, the one postulated being excluded.

For example, if there are fifteen electors and on the third and last ballot candidate A was postulated with eight votes, candidate B was *elected* with seven, the postulation is not valid because it has not received two-thirds of the votes. Hence the one elected is to be preferred to the one postulated, even though the eligible candidate has one vote less than the postulate. Likewise, if there are fifteen electors and on the third and last ballot candidate A was postulated with eight votes, candidate B elected with four, and candidate C elected with three, candidate B is elected to the office notwithstanding the fact that postulate A had received an absolute majority of votes. Whenever a postulation occurs with an election, and the postulation does not receive two-thirds of the votes, it gives place to the election, whatever the number of votes in favor of postulation may be.

The results of the postulation must be sent under pain of nullity within eight days to the person who has the power of confirming the election, if he or she has the faculty to dispense from the existing impediment; otherwise it is to be sent to the Sovereign Pontiff or to another superior who has the requisite faculties (c. 181, par. 1). If the results of the postulation are not sent within eight days to the competent superior, not only is the postulation invalid, but if the electors cannot prove that the delay was due to a cause over which they had no control, they lose for this time the right of electing or postulating (c. 181, par. 2).

77. THE PROCEDURE OF POSTULATION

In postulating a candidate the vote is expressed with the word "I postulate" instead of "I elect," or another equivalent expression (c. 180, par. 2). If one uses the word "postulate" or the word "elect," or even if neither word is used, the vote is to be interpreted either as a postulation or as an election according to whether the candidate is eligible or merely capable of postulation (c. 180, par. 2).

For the rest, all the norms are to be observed which were set down above for the form and the manner of procedure for an election.

78. EFFECTS OF POSTULATION

Postulation does not confer any rights upon the candidate before confirmation is received (c. 181, par. 3). But once the postulation has been presented to the superior the electors may not revoke it without the consent of the superior (c. 181, par. 4).

The superior to whom it pertains may always reject the petition for a postulation (c. 181, par. 3). She has, however, the obligation of making known her rejection or approval within a month from the day on which the request was presented (c. 189, par. 2).

Unless the electors knowingly postulate a religious who is burdened with an impediment of such a nature that the dispensation could not be or usually is not granted, the electoral college re-acquires the right to proceed to another election or postulation if the request for postulation is rejected. If the electors did postulate one with such an impediment, then the appointment of the new superior devolves by law upon the superior who would have the duty to confirm the postulation (c. 182, par. 1).

If the postulation is admitted this must be made known to the person postulated and, under penalty of losing every right to the office, she must manifest within eight days her acceptance or rejection of the office (c. 182, par. 2; c. 175).

If the candidate accepts the office, she acquires, from that moment and without further confirmation, all rights pertaining to the office (c. 182, par. 3), unless the constitutions require other conditions for the exercise of the office, as was said above relative to elections (n. 72).

III

INVALIDITY OF ELECTIONS OR POSTULATIONS

Elections and postulations are absolutely invalid in the following cases:

1) If lay people in any way interfere in the election or postulation to the detriment of the necessary freedom of the electors (c. 166).

2) If a person not belonging to the electoral college is allowed to vote, without prejudice, however, to lawfully acquired privileges (c. 165). The mere presence of an outsider does not invalidate the election.

3) If a religious without active voice is allowed to vote and it is certain that without this vote the person elected or postulated would not have received the required number of votes (c. 167, par. 2).

4) If the number of votes exceeds the number of electors (c. 171, par. 3).

5) If in the convocation more than a third part of the electors are neglected (c. 162, par. 3), and the neglected were not present at the election (c. 163, par. 4).

IV

APPOINTMENTS BY SUPERIORS

The lawful superior acquires the right of appointing and instituting a religious superior directly for an office, to the exclusion of the electors, in the following cases:

1) If the election was not made within the prescribed time (c. 178; cf. *supra*, n. 60).

2) If the electoral college was punished with deprivation of the right to elect (c. 178).

3) If the postulation was not sent within the prescribed time to the superior who has the power to confirm it, unless the electors can prove that it was impossible for them to do so (c. 181, par. 2; cf. *supra*, n. 76).

4) If all the electors renounce their vote.

Except in these four cases mentioned in the common law, the Ordinary of the place may not disband the chapter of an institute of pontifical approval and personally choose the superior, unless the constitutions of a particular institute would permit it.

The power of selecting a superior reverts to the superior who would have had the duty to confirm an election or to the superior who, according to the particular law, must provide superiors for the vacant offices if the electors fail to do so (c. 178).

V

HONORARY TITLES

By honorary titles are understood those names by which offices or dignities are designated in religious institutes; for example, the title of Abbot, General, Provincial or Prior or Prioress are honorary. If no office or dignity corresponds to the title, it is exclusively honorary; for example, when a religious is called an Abbot, but is not in reality the superior of an abbey.

79. PERMISSION FOR HONORARY TITLES

It is only logical that one who is invested in her religious institute with a certain office or dignity may and ought to be given a title corresponding to that office or dignity. But, on the other hand, may religious who have no offices or who are not invested with any dignities be given titles merely as an expression of honor? To this question the Code wisely answers:

1) Among religious, exclusively honorary titles corresponding to major offices are tolerated as long as the religious to whom these

titles are given have really exercised such an office and the constitutions do not expressly prohibit it (c. 515). For example, the title of Ex-Mother-General, or Ex-Mother-Provincial, is tolerated when the constitutions permit it and when the person who uses such a title was in reality a mother general or a mother provincial.

2) In all other cases, exclusively honorary titles are prohibited in religious institutes of both men and of women (c. 515).

PART FIVE

CONFESSORS AND CHAPLAINS

I

CONFESSORS

80. KINDS OF CONFESSORS

In present day law five categories of confessors for religious women are usually distinguished: ordinary, extraordinary, supplementary, occasional and special.

Ordinary confessors are those who are lawfully designated to hear habitually the sacramental confessions of all of the members of a particular convent or monastery of religious women (c. 520, par. 1).

Extraordinary confessors are those who are designated to hear the confessions of all of the members of a convent or monastery at least four times a year (c. 521, par. 1).

Supplementary confessors are those who, besides the ordinary and extraordinary confessors, are habitually approved by the bishop to hear the confessions of the members of a convent or monastery, and who in particular cases may be called without the necessity of having recourse to the local Ordinary (c. 521, par. 2).

Occasional confessors are all those who are approved for hearing

111

the confessions of women and who in exceptional circumstances may validly and licitly hear the confessions of women religious (c. 522).

Special confessors are those who, for a special reason, are appointed to hear the confessions of certain religious for the tranquillity of their conscience or for greater progress in the spiritual life (c. 520, par. 2).

The difference, therefore, among these many kinds of confessors consists in this: the ordinary confessor is appointed to hear the confessions of women religious *habitually*, whenever the rule prescribes confession or the religious request it; nor may women religious, without reason, go to others. The extraordinary confessor, on the other hand, is appointed to hear the confessions of women religious only *at certain times* during the year.

Supplementary confessors resemble the ordinary and extraordinary confessors since they may hear the confessions of the whole community habitually, as we shall point out *(infra, n. 83)*. However, they differ from ordinary and extraordinary confessors since women religious are not obliged to go to them for confession. Occasional confessors may hear the confessions of *only certain* religious and only in special and exceptional circumstances. Finally, special confessors are appointed to hear the confessions not of an entire community but only of one or other religious of the community, even habitually, and not only occasionally.

81. ORDINARY CONFESSORS

Every religious community of women must have an ordinary confessor (c. 520, par. 1).

Every community, even if it is not a formal house, that is, even if at least six religious are not assigned there, and even if they belong to religious institutes without vows (S.C.Rel., January 10, 1920). This requirement does not affect members of secular institutes but it does affect those houses of these institutes in which the community life is led *(Provida mater, III, n. 4)*.

Must have an ordinary confessor. Hence the community has the obligation to request him and the local Ordinary has the obligation to appoint him. If a monastery of nuns is subject to a regular superior, then it is his duty to present the ordinary confessor, but the local Ordinary must confirm him.

Each community should have *one* ordinary confessor, unless, because of the great number of religious or for any other just reason, it is necessary to assign two or more confessors (c. 520, par. 1).

On account of the great number. The number of religious may be considered great when it exceeds fifty.

Or for any other just reason. The Code does not determine what this just reason may be or when it exists. The presence of persons in the same house who speak different languages, or the diversity of categories in the same house (for example, novices, postulants and professed) are sufficient reasons for naming several ordinary confessors. The local Ordinary must decide which motives will justify the appointment of two or more ordinary confessors for one religious community. He may also, if he wishes, divide the community into several groups and assign a particular ordinary confessor to each group.

The ordinary confessor may be approved for three years and no longer (c. 526); nor may he be appointed to the same community for a second term until after the lapse of one year from the expiration of his first term (c. 524, par. 2).

For the same community. He may, however, be appointed immediately as the ordinary confessor of another community even when this community belongs to the same religious institute.

If, however, because of a lack of priests qualified for such an office, the Ordinary of the place finds it difficult to provide a new ordinary confessor, he may appoint the same confessor without any interruption to a second, or even a third, three year term. The only other time that an ordinary confessor may be reappointed for a second or third time is when the majority of the religious in the community, including those who in other matters have no right to vote, petition by secret ballot for the reappointment of the same confessor after the expiration of the first or second three year period (c. 526). In the latter case, another ordinary confessor must be provided for those who disagree with the majority, if they so desire it (c. 526). The Ordinary may reappoint the ordinary confessor when the community petitions for this; however, he is not held to do so.

The same priest, without any dispensation, may serve simultaneously as ordinary confessor for several communities (S. C. Bishops and

Regulars, September 1, 1905). Ordinarily, in order to reappoint an ordinary confessor to a third three year term without any interruption, it is necessary to obtain a dispensation from the Holy See. However, the bishops of the United States have special delegation to permit them to confirm ordinary confessors for even a fourth or fifth term of three years, if the majority of the household vote by secret ballot for his retention and if special provisions are made for the minority, if they so desire.

82. EXTRAORDINARY CONFESSORS

Besides providing for the ordinary confessor, the Code prescribes that to every community of religious women shall be given an extraordinary confessor who, at least four times a year, shall go to the religious house, and to whom all the religious shall present themselves, at least to receive his blessing (c. 521, par. 1).

At least four times a year. Consequently, he may be summoned or sent even more often, but it is obligatory for him to go at least four times a year. The custom of fulfilling this obligation in the week of the Ember Days is an excellent one, and it is law in many dioceses in the United States. But if no regulations exist in a diocese concerning the time for the extraordinary confessor to hear confessions, he may carry out his duties whenever he deems it opportune or convenient. It is the custom that the same priest act as extraordinary confessor all four times during the year, but this is not absolutely necessary. Thus the priest who is giving the annual retreat might, with the permission of the bishop, take the place of the regular extraordinary during the retreat.

All the religious must present themselves to the extraordinary confessor: subjects and superiors, novices and professed. Strictly speaking, postulants could "perhaps" be exempted because the canon obliges "religious" and postulants are not religious. In practice, however, there does not seem to be any purpose or utility in exempting them. Even though the Code states that the religious should present themselves to the confessor, it seems that in the case of sick religious, the extraordinary confessor should present himself to them. Otherwise the purpose of the canon would not be fulfilled.

At least to receive his blessing. Consequently, a religious is not obliged to go to confession to an extraordinary confessor, but she must present herself to him in the confessional, at least to receive his blessing. The reason for this prudent prescription is obvious. If certain religious were to present themselves to the extraordinary confessor and others did not, it could easily give rise to suspicions about the necessity for certain religious to have recourse to the extraordinary confessor. This naturally would be to the detriment of liberty of conscience. To exclude such inconveniences, the Church prudently prescribes that each and every religious without exception must present herself to the extraordinary confessor "at least to receive his blessing."

Extraordinary confessors are not bound by the obligation of a three year term. This was declared by the Sacred Congregation of Religious, December 7, 1906, and the Code does not indicate anything to the contrary.

The ordinary confessor cannot be appointed extraordinary for the same community until after the lapse of one year from the expiration of his first term; but the extraordinary confessor may be appointed ordinary immediately after the expiration of his term (c. 524, par. 2).

83. SUPPLEMENTARY CONFESSORS

The Ordinaries of the places where religious communities of women exist shall designate for each house some priests, besides the ordinary and extraordinary confessors, to whom in particular cases the religious may easily have recourse for the sacrament of penance, without having to apply to the Ordinary on each occasion (c. 521, par. 2).

In particular cases. Hence this is not always to be done, nor without sufficient necessity, or at least some spiritual utility. If religious could lawfully have recourse, always and at will and even when there was no motive, to the supplementary confessors, the office of ordinary confessor would become useless. Nevertheless, whenever a religious asks for one of these confessors the superior must permit it, nor may she "either personally or through others, either directly or indirectly seek to know the reason for the petition, or show opposition to it by word or deed" (c. 521, par. 3). The judge of the lawfulness and need of the request of the religious is, in all cases, the confessor, who certainly neither may not, nor ought to, exercise his ministry without a sufficient and reasonable motive. The confessor should be lenient in forming his judgment, but if he decides there was not sufficient reason to call him in as supplementary confessor, he should prudently inform the sister of this so the same mistake will not be made in the future. Sufficient cause would be absence of the ordinary confessor, necessity, peace of conscience, spiritual progress, or things of like nature.

It seems that the phrase "in particular cases" can be understood in the sense that the superior, without any other permission than that of the Code, may summon the supplementary confessor to hear the confessions of the whole community when the ordinary confessor is impeded from doing so. This represents a particular, that is, an extraordinary case, relative to the confessions of all the religious of the community.

No definite age is determined for a supplementary confessor. However, it is fitting to follow the age requirement of the ordinary and extraordinary confessors (cf. *infra*, n. 88).

84. Special Confessors

If any particular religious, for the peace of her soul or for her greater progress in the spiritual life, requests a special confessor or spiritual director, the Ordinary shall readily grant the request. He shall be watchful, however, lest abuses arise from this concession. If they do arise, he shall carefully and prudently eliminate them, while safeguarding liberty of conscience (c. 520, par. 2).

A special confessor is not subject to the law of a three year term. An ordinary confessor, when his three year term has elapsed, may be appointed special confessor for some particular religious. Furthermore, a special confessor for one sister may at the same time be the extraordinary confessor for the whole community. No determined age is required for the special confessor, but it is fitting that the age requirements of the ordinary and the extraordinary confessor be observed (cf. *infra*, n. 88).

85. Occasional Confessors

Every religious woman, for the tranquillity of her conscience, may validly and lawfully go to confession to any confessor whatsoever who is approved for hearing the confessions of women, as long as the confession is made in a church or an oratory, even though only semi-public (c. 522); or at least in a place lawfully designated for the confessions of women (P.C.I., November 24, 1920; February 12, 1935).

For the tranquillity of her conscience. These words should not be interpreted too rigorously. Therefore, in order to use the privilege granted by this canon it is not required that there exist a spiritual need which cannot be satisfied in any other way. It is a question of a privilege in favor of the conscience of a religious, and thus we may interpret this phrase in a broad sense; not, however, to the extent of taking away all meaning. Therefore, we may not say that if she wishes, a religious may go to any confessor whatsoever for any reason. We believe, however, that merely the hope of drawing some special spiritual fruit from the confession or also the impossibility of going to the ordinary confessor for the usual and prescribed weekly confession is sufficient reason to approach the occasional. The confessor is to judge the existence or nonexistence of a sufficient reason. If a just reason is not present, the confession would still be valid since the condition is required only for licitness. In order to take advantage of the privilege of the occasional confessor, it is not necessary that the sister go to a confessor already hearing confessions in an approved place. Rather, the sister herself, or more fittingly, her superior, may summon him to hear her confession (P.C.I., December 28, 1927). When an occasional confessor is summoned to hear the confession of an individual religious, others, even every member of the community, may use this as an "occasion" to go to confession, but the superior may not call an occasional confessor and ask him to hear the confessions of the whole community.

In a church or in an oratory even though it is only semi-public. The meaning of church and public or semi-public oratory will be explained below (n. 234; and Part 10, Chap. I).

To any confessor approved for hearing confessions of women. In the United States it is not customary to approve confessors for men only. Therefore, any priest who has diocesan faculties to hear confessions would satisfy this requirement.

Or at least in a place lawfully designated for the confessions of women. At one time there was a doubt whether "a place lawfully designated for the confessions of women" could also be understood to include confessionals for religious women. The reason for the doubt was the word *"mulierum"* employed by the Pontifical Commission for the Interpretation of Canon Law (cf. P.C.I., November 24, 1920). This word, when used in a generic sense, would seem to include religious women; in a strictly juridical sense, however, it seems to exclude them. Today there is no longer any doubt since the Pontifical Commission itself has manifested, although merely incidentally, its mind. By the words "a place lawfully designated for the confessions of women" ought to be understood, besides the confessional lawfully designated for the confessions of secular women, the confessional of religious women as well, whether it is situated in a church or in a chapel or in some other place approved by the Ordinary (P.C.I., December 28, 1927).

Moreover, on the basis of another declaration of the Code Commission (February 12, 1935), places designated by way of act for hearing confessions, in accordance with canon 910, paragraph 1, can be validly used in hearing confessions of religious women. Hence when illness or "real necessity" makes it physically or morally impossible to hear the confession of a sister or nun in a confessional, it may be heard in any apt place. For example, if a religious who is sick, even though not gravely ill, should ask for an occasional confessor, he would be able to go to hear her confession in the room where she is confined to bed. Because of her illness, the room becomes, here and now, the place legitimately approved for confession (c. 910, par. 1). The same is to be said if there is no confessional present, and a sister has a true need of going to confession. A confession made in these truly grave cases, even though it is made outside of the confessional (for example, in a parlor), is valid and licit. Thus by reason of canon 522 and the responses of the Code Commission the following useful principle may be formulated: *A priest having diocesan faculties for hearing confessions of lay women may validly and licitly hear the confessions of women religious in any place where he could licitly hear the confessions of lay women.* These restrictions imposed upon the place where the occasional confessor can hear confessions pertain to the validity of the sacrament (P.C.I., December 28, 1927).

Religious who are on a sea voyage may go to confession during the voyage to any priest on the boat who is approved for the hearing of confessions by his own Ordinary, or by the Ordinary of the place of departure, or by the Ordinary of the ports at which the boat calls (P.C.I., May 20, 1923; July 30, 1934). The same privilege is granted those on an air journey (Pius XII, Motu Proprio, *Animarum Studio,* December 16, 1947).

A religious may not leave the convent without the permission of her superior for the purpose of going to confession, since this would be contrary to religious discipline. If a religious is outside the house with permission, however, no further permission would be needed to enable her to go to confession to an occasional confessor. The superior is not obliged to grant permission to leave the house in order to go to confession. Superiors, however, should exercise great care and kindness in this regard so that the peace of conscience of the individual religious will be protected.

86. CONFESSORS IN CASE OF SERIOUS ILLNESS

All religious women who are seriously ill, even if not in danger of death, may, as often as they wish during their serious illness, invite any priest whatsoever to hear their confessions, provided that he is approved to hear the confessions of women. The superior may not directly or indirectly prevent them from making this request (c. 523).

All religious women; that is, nuns or sisters. Thus, the confessor of sick religious may enter the papal cloister.

Even if not in danger of death. In order that the confession be licit and valid, it is sufficient that the religious is seriously ill. At times, it is difficult to determine whether or not a religious is seriously ill, but the judgment of an experienced nurse or doctor may be followed. It is according to the spirit of the law to interpret this privilege loosely, but it does not seem that every time a sister is confined to her room, or that every time a doctor is called, she is "seriously ill." On the other hand, if she is confined to her room due to sickness beyond a week's time, or if she undergoes major surgery, it seems that she can be considered "seriously ill."

A religious who is gravely ill may use this privilege as often as she wishes, but it ceases when she begins to get better.

87. APPROVAL OF CONFESSORS

Approval of ordinary, extraordinary and supplementary confessors is to be given by the Ordinary of the place where the religious house is situated (c. 876, pars. 1, 2). This is true even if the religious house is directly subject to the Holy See, or a regular superior. In this latter case, however, the major superior has the right to present the confessor to the local Ordinary for confirmation (c. 525).

If a sister or nun requests a special confessor, he too must be approved by the local Ordinary (c. 520, par. 2).

Occasional confessors have no need of special approval, beyond that already received from the local Ordinary, to hear the confessions of the faithful, including women.

88. QUALITIES OF CONFESSORS

Confessors of religious women, whether they be ordinary or extraordinary, must meet the following qualifications:

1) They must be forty years of age, unless in the judgment of the Ordinary a just cause determines otherwise (c. 524, par. 1). Ordinaries, then, may grant a dispensation from age to confessors of religious women. If the Ordinary does not grant a dispensation, the confessors must have completed forty years (cf. *supra*, n. 39).

2) They must be distinguished by the probity of their lives and by their prudence (c. 524, par. 1), that is, they must be endowed with such doctrine, prudence and holiness of life as will enable them to guide others successfully on the road to perfection.

3) They have no authority in the external forum over the religious in question (c. 524, par. 1). They may not, then, be either superiors or vicars of the monastery with the right to interfere in the government of the monastery. The Code also states that ordinary and extraordinary confessors are not "to interfere either in the internal or external government of the community" (c. 524, par. 3). On the other hand, there is no reason why a confessor may not also serve as chaplain of the monastery.

3) Finally, an ordinary confessor may not be made extraordinary confessor of the same community until after the lapse of one year from the expiration of his office as ordinary confessor (c. 524, par. 2). An extraordinary confessor, however, is not subject to the law of interstices and may be made ordinary confessor without any interruption in his office as confessor (c. 524, par. 2; cf. *supra*, n. 81 and n. 82).

The Code does not prescribe any age for supplementary confessors, just as it does not require any special qualifications besides those demanded by the office itself. The same is to be said of occasional confessors.

When nuns or sisters are affiliated with a certain Order, it is fitting and useful to assign a priest of the same order to them as ordinary confessor, insofar as this is possible. Ordinarily, this aids regular observance and instills in the religious the true spirit of the Order. A decree of the Sacred Congregation of Bishops and Regulars, December 10, 1858, directed to the Ordinaries of Spain, counsels this. However, it is nowhere prescribed as an obligation. When this is done, it is preferable that a religious of another Order or a secular priest be assigned as extraordinary confessor.

89. REMOVAL OF CONFESSORS

For a serious reason the local Ordinary can remove both the ordinary and extraordinary confessor of women religious, even when the monastery is subject to regulars, and the confessor himself is a regular (c. 527).

The Ordinary is not bound to make known the reason for the removal to anyone except the Holy See (c. 527). If, however, the removal concerns a monastery which is subject to regulars, the Ordinary must inform the regular superior of the removal (c. 527).

90. OBLIGATIONS OF SUPERIORS REGARDING CONFESSORS

When any religious asks for an extraordinary or supplementary confessor, no superior, either personally or through others, either directly or indirectly, may seek to know the reason for the petition or show opposition to it by word or deed or in any way manifest displeasure (c. 521, par. 3).

Neither may a superior prohibit religious from going to confession, for the peace of their consciences, to any confessor who is approved by the Ordinary for hearing confessions of women, whenever the opportunity presents itself and the religious go to confession in a church or other proper place, according to the norms set down above (n. 85). Moreover, superiors may not inquire whether religious have actually done this, nor may they seek to know why the religious have acted in this manner (c. 522). The Code does not force superiors to allow religious to leave the convent in order to go to confession; it merely declares that a confession is valid and licit if made outside the religious house without the permission of the superior. Hence, granted that the opportunity presents itself, religious may make use of it and go to confession. But, they have no right to withdraw themselves for this reason from regular discipline or from obedience to their superiors. Thus a sister who is outside of the convent for some legitimate reason may lawfully make use of this opportunity to go to the parish church and go to confession without requesting permission either from the bishop or from her superior. She may not, however, demand permission from her superior to leave the house for the sole reason of going to confession. In this latter case, the superior may refuse permission if she thinks it well to do so; always remembering, however, the gravity of the case and the responsibility that she assumes if she refuses.

Moreover, a superior may not prevent in any way a religious who is gravely ill, even though not in danger of death, from inviting any priest to hear her confession as often as she wants during her illness, provided he is approved for hearing confessions of women (c. 523; cf. *supra*, n. 86).

If a superior does not conform to what is said above, she should be admonished by the local Ordinary. If she is found delinquent a second time, she should be removed from office by the Ordinary, who will immediately notify the Sacred Congregation of Religious of the matter (c. 2424).

91. MANIFESTATION OF CONSCIENCE

Superiors are strictly forbidden to induce their subjects in any way whatever to make a manifestation of conscience to them (c. 530, par. 1). If, however, religious freely and spontaneously wish to open their minds to their superiors, they certainly may do so. Indeed, it is even desirable that they approach their superiors with filial confidence (c. 530, par. 2).

Hence, even if the rule prescribes the so-called weekly or monthly conference with the superior, this must always be understood relative to external things; for example, occupations, work, bodily health or observance of the rule. Relative to internal matters of conscience, neither the rule nor superiors may demand any manifestation or revelation which the religious subjects do not wish to make freely and spontaneously. It is well, nevertheless, to have great confidence, "a filial confidence," the Code says, in one's superior.

II

CHAPLAINS

A chaplain of women religious is the priest who has charge of religious services, excepting confessions, in a house of women religious. It is obvious that women religious, not being able to exercise any acts of the priestly ministry, need the services of some priest to conduct the liturgical functions in their church or oratory which are necessary for their spiritual life. The priest who is assigned to perform these functions for the sisters is called the chaplain of the religious.

In monasteries immediately subject to a regular superior, the regular superior appoints the chaplain (c. 529); if the regular superior is negligent in the matter then the local Ordinary should appoint him (c. 529). If the chaplain is to preach to the nuns, then the approbation of the local Ordinary is required (c. 1337); however, if it is merely a question of celebrating Mass and conducting other religious functions, the permission of the regular superior suffices.

In all other cases the local Ordinary appoints the chaplains of women religious (c. 529). Since it is not prohibited in the Code, the chaplain may also be appointed the ordinary confessor.

124

92. CHAPLAINS AND THE LAST SACRAMENTS

The last sacraments are Viaticum and Extreme Unction. Regarding their administration:

1) **In monasteries of nuns**, the chaplain, with the express or tacit delegation of the ordinary confessor, may administer the last sacraments to the religious, independently of the pastor. As we shall point out *(infra,* n. 249), in monasteries of nuns, in virtue of canon 514, paragraph 2, it pertains to the ordinary confessor, or to the priest who takes his place, to administer the last sacraments. Among those who can and ought to take the place of the ordinary confessor in this instance, is included not only extraordinary confessors, but also the chaplains of the monastery, since they frequently find it easier and more convenient to be present for the administration of the last sacraments.

2) **In houses of sisters**, the chaplain may not, in ordinary circumstances, administer the last sacraments without the permission of the pastor to whom this function, even in this case, is reserved (c. 514, par. 3). There are however two exceptions:

a) If the bishop, in virtue of canon 464, paragraph 2, withdraws the convent from the jurisdiction of the pastor and confides it to the chaplain. In this case it is obvious that the chaplain, who by the will of the bishop takes the place of the pastor, may and ought to administer the last sacraments (c. 514, par. 3).

b) In case of grave danger of death. Under these circumstances any priest may give the last sacraments; so the chaplain may do so relative to the religious that he serves (cf. c. 850; and c. 938, par. 2).

93. CHAPLAINS AND FUNERALS

We shall point out later what is to be understood by funerals. Here we shall speak only of the celebration of funerals.

In houses of nuns or of sisters who are exempt from the jurisdiction of the pastor by general or particular law, the chaplain of the monastery or convent shall conduct the body of a religious or novice who dies there to the church or oratory of the monastery, and there shall celebrate the obsequies (c. 1230, par. 5).

The chaplain shall conduct the body to the church. He may not, however, enter the cloister. When a monastery is cloistered the religious themselves "shall bear the body to the threshold of the enclosure" (c. 1230, par. 5).

In other monasteries and religious houses which are not exempt from the jurisdiction of the pastor, the chaplain has no rights concerning things which pertain to funerals, whether the religious die in the monastery or outside of it. The pastor has full rights over the funeral in conformity with what is said in the sacred canons relative to the funeral of the faithful (c. 1230, par. 5).

PART SIX

TEMPORAL GOODS

I

POSSESSION AND ADMINISTRATION

Temporal goods are defined as all those things which are ordained by nature to the needs of temporal life.

By their nature. This term is used since, indirectly, temporal goods may also be used for spiritual needs; for example, divine worship, liberality, suffrages or good works for the dead.

94. Kinds of Temporal Goods

A. Movable and immovable

Movable goods are those which may be transported from one place to another without changing their nature; for example, a table, clothing, grain or money.

Immovable goods are those which cannot without some alteration be transported from one place to another since they are rooted in the ground; for example, a house or a field.

B. Ecclesiastical and "profane" goods

Ecclesiastical goods, whether movable or immovable, are those which are the property of the Universal Church or of the Holy See or of other ecclesiastical institutions recognized by the Church as moral persons. Ecclesiastical goods are called "sacred" when, by reason of a special consecration or blessing, they have been dedicated to divine worship; for example, a chalice. They are called "precious" when for artistic or historical reasons, or because of the material of which they are composed, they have a notable value (c. 1497, par. 1 and par. 2). **"Profane" goods** are all others which are not ecclesiastical.

95. RIGHT OF POSSESSING TEMPORAL GOODS

Not only every religious institute but also all lawfully established provinces and religious houses are capable of acquiring and possessing temporal goods, together with fixed revenues and endowments. An exception to this rule is made only when the constitutions expressly prohibit or restrict this capacity (c. 531). For example, the Capuchins may not possess any temporal goods whatsoever; everything they have is possessed by the Holy See. The Franciscan Minors are limited in their capacity to possess, since they may not own immovable goods.

Even when the capacity to possess is full and unlimited, however, this is to be understood only in the sense of being able to own all kinds of goods and not in the sense of being able to exercise freely any and every act of administration; for example, the alienation of an object whose value exceeds five thousand dollars, which, under pain of invalidity, may never be made by religious, without the express permission of the Holy See (c. 534, par. 1).

What we have said regarding the capacity of possessing in religious institutes is to be understood from the viewpoint of ecclesiastical law. The civil law in many places no longer recognizes religious institutes as moral persons with a right to possess temporal goods. However, in the United States, the right of religious institutes and houses to possess and administer goods is recognized and protected.

96. ADMINISTRATORS OF TEMPORAL GOODS

The administration of temporal goods must be confided to a person especially chosen for that work, who shall be called the bursar, administrator or procurator (c. 516, par. 2). The administrator, bursar or procurator, shall be called general, provincial or local, depending upon whether she administers the goods of the entire institute, or of a province, or of a house (c. 516, par. 2).

If the constitutions are silent concerning the manner of selecting the bursars or administrators, they shall be selected by the major superior with the consent of her council (c. 516, par. 4).

A superior general may not herself discharge the office of general bursar, nor may the provincial superior be the provincial bursar. A local superior, however, may discharge the office of local bursar if necessity requires it, although it is better to keep this office distinct from that of superior (c. 516, par. 3).

97. MANNER OF ADMINISTRATION

The property of an institute, province or house is to be administered in conformity with the constitutions (c. 532, par. 1); but engaging in business in a true and proper sense is forbidden and it must always be avoided (c. 142; c. 592). Administration includes all acts intended to preserve and to improve material goods according to their purpose and nature.

In brief, the type of business which is forbidden to religious is that which involves the buying of something with the intention of selling it unchanged and at a profit; or if changed, changed by hired labor.

When investing money the consent of the local Ordinary must be obtained by superiors in the following cases:

1) When the money to be invested constitutes the dowry of a religious (c. 533, par. 1, n. 2). (In the administration of dowries, certain other rules, about which we will speak later, must also be followed. Cf. *infra*, n. 105.)

2) When any money belonging to a monastery of nuns or to sisters of merely diocesan approval is to be invested in any way whatsoever (c. 533, par. 1, n. 1). This does not include bank deposits, however, even if a small rate of interest is paid, because a bank deposit is considered as a conservation rather than an investment of money. Money in a bank account remains in the dominion of the one who invested it and may be withdrawn if the need arises.

3) When funds are to be invested which were left to a religious house of nuns or sisters for the purpose of divine worship, or for works of charity to be carried on in the same place (c. 533, par. 1, n. 3). Many authors restrict this obligation to superiors of houses which belong to a non-exempt congregation.

4) If the religious are also subject to a major superior, his consent must also be obtained in the three above cases before investments may be made.

In all other cases which are not considered under the above paragraphs, it is sufficient, for the lawful and valid investment of money, to observe the particular rules and constitutions of the institute. What we have said regarding the first investment of money is to be observed also in changing the title in which the money has already been invested (c. 533, par. 2).

98. PERSONS IN CHARGE OF ADMINISTRATION

Lawfully constituted superiors can make purchases and perform the juridical acts of ordinary administration within the limits of their office (c. 532, par. 2).

Lawfully constituted, that is, regularly elected or appointed. Since acts performed by those who are not confirmed are invalid, superiors must wait till they are confirmed before they may administer goods (c. 176, par. 3).

Within the limits of their office. If a superior or any other official contracts obligations outside of those which belong to her office, these obligations are juridically invalid, or at least the institute is not responsible for them.

May make ordinary purchases. This refers to those purchases which are necessary to provide food, shelter or clothing, or which are needed for the ordinary upkeep of property.

Juridical acts of ordinary administration. These are, besides the contracts of buying and selling, gifts, loans, rents and all other acts of a similar nature, for which, according to the law of the church and particular constitutions, no other authority is required than that of the superior who places them.

Besides superiors, **the officials of the house or of a province or of an institute, as for example, the bursar or procurator, within the**

limits of their office, may also validly and lawfully incur expenses and perform the juridical acts of ordinary administration (c. 532, par. 2).

As far as other religious are concerned: if they have solemn vows, whatsoever act of administration they may perform without the explicit or at least implicit permission of the lawful superior is not only unlawful but also invalid (c. 579). If they have simple vows, whenever they act in opposition to the obligations contracted by the vow of poverty, their actions are illicit but not invalid (c. 579).

Whether it be a question of buying and selling, of alienation of goods, or of contracting debts, in order for the house or institute to be responsible for the acts of their respective superiors or officials, the following conditions must be fulfilled:

1) The superiors or officials lawfully instituted must act formally as superiors or officials of the monastery or of the institute.

2) They must act within the limits of their office.

3) Their acts must be those of ordinary administration.

If any one of these conditions is lacking, the monastery or institute is not held responsible for the acts of administration of its superiors or officials. Thus, for example, if the bursar of a monastery contracts a debt with a tradesman for provisions for the monastery, it is clear that the monastery is obliged to pay him; but if the bursar contracts a large debt with a fashionable clothier to make a rich wardrobe for her niece, and the clothier is aware of this, it is clear that the monastery has no obligation to pay the debt. In this case, the bursar has clearly acted outside of the limits of her office and has performed acts which cannot be called acts of ordinary administration for a bursar of a monastery of nuns.

Furthermore, the monastery and institute are responsible for the acts of administration of a religious only when they are done with the explicit or at least the implicit permission of the lawful superior. If, on the other hand, a religious who is not the superior or official of a monastery or institute performs acts of administration (for example, buys books or household goods, without any permission, not even implicit), the house or institute is not responsible for such acts of administration. Hence if a religious has simple vows, the creditors can take action against her, obliging her to pay with the goods over which, notwithstanding her simple profession, she still has radical dominion. But if she has solemn vows, nothing remains but to make reparation by returning, insofar as is possible, the things in their original state; that is, by restoring what has been unlawfully acquired if the things still exist. The monastery or institute is not obliged, strictly speaking, to do any more.

From what has been said it is clear how necessary it is to be cautious in choosing diligent superiors or officials of a monastery or religious institute. In giving permissions to their subjects to perform acts of administration and in watching over the manner in which the religious use these permissions, religious superiors must be diligent, because negligence or silence on the part of the superior when the religious abuses the permissions given, may be taken as a sign of tacit or implicit consent.

99. REPORT OF ADMINISTRATION

Over and above what is prescribed in the rule and constitutions, in **every monastery of nuns,** even exempt, there is an obligation of giving a report every year, concerning the administration of goods, to the local Ordinary, as well as to the regular superior, if the monastery is subject to one (c. 535, par. 1, n. 1).

As well as to the regular superior; that is, to both the local Ordinary and the regular superior, as the Pontifical Commission for the Interpretation of the Code declared, November 24, 1920.

This report must be made gratuitously; that is, neither the local Ordinary nor the regular superior may demand any payment, tax or contribution for his co-operation (c. 535, par. 1, n. 1).

If the Ordinary does not approve of the account of the administration furnished him, he can apply the necessary remedies, even including the removal from office, if the circumstances demand it, of the bursar and the other administrators. If the monastery is subject to a regular superior, however, the Ordinary shall request him to correct the abuses; in this case it is only when the regular superior fails to do so that the local Ordinary himself may deal with the case (c. 535, par. 1, n. 2).

In institutes of sisters of merely diocesan approval, the local Ordinary has a right of inquiring into the administration of all of the goods of the province or the individual houses (c. 535, par. 3, n. 1).

In institutes of pontifical approval, the local Ordinary has only the power to examine on the occasion of his visitation, or more often if he judges it opportune, the administration of the dowries of the religious (c. 535, par. 2). The administration of other goods is subject to inspection only by the proper superiors, in conformity with the constitutions of each institute.

In any institute of nuns or sisters, the local Ordinary always has the right to inspect the administration of funds which have been given for the purpose of divine worship or for works of charity to be carried out in the place where the religious house is located (c. 533, par. 1).

100. ALIENATION OF GOODS

Alienation of goods means the sale, exchange or donation of goods, or any other means of transferring dominion of property to another person. It is not alienation, but rather an act of ordinary administration, to sell shares or bonds in order to purchase other things. Hence such transactions should be regulated by the laws for administration of property discussed above (cf. *supra,* n. 97).

In order that alienation of goods belonging to a religious institute is valid, the following regulations must be observed:

1. When there is question of alienating **precious goods,** or other things whose value exceeds five thousand dollars, the authorization of the Holy See is always required, otherwise the contract is null and void (c. 534, par. 1). (Note: A notification of the S.C. for Religious, January 29, 1953, states that in the United States and Canada, "the limit beyond which the permission of the Holy See is required according to canon 534, paragraph 1," is five thousand dollars: C.L.D., IV., p. 203. The Apostolic Delegate to the United States has the power to allow religious institutes to alienate goods up to three hundred thousand dollars; cf. C.L.D., Supplement, c. 534).

Precious goods are those goods which have a *notable value* for artistic or historical reasons, or because of the material of which they are composed (c. 1497, par. 2); for example, a painting, an ancient piece of embroidery, or a chalice ornamented with precious stones. Even though their value is not five thousand dollars, these precious objects may never be alienated without the permission of the Holy See.

Regarding precious goods, the Sacred Congregation of the Council was asked: "May votive gifts (for example, medals or rings) be alienated without the permission of the Apostolic See"? On July 12th, 1919, the Congregation replied in the negative. Hence votive gifts, whatever their value, may not be alienated without the authorization of the Holy See.

The Sacred Congregation of Religious was also asked: "When may precious objects be said to possess a notable value?" That is, what constitutes "a notable value?" The Sacred Congregation made no reply to this question. About a century ago, on the basis of a decision of the Sacred Congregation of Bishops and Regulars issued May 1, 1840, a precious object was considered to possess notable value if it was worth fifty dollars. Today, however, this value has certainly increased to at least two hundred dollars in gold.

Finally, the question was asked: "Is the permission of the Holy See required to alienate at one transaction several articles of ecclesiastical property, when the value of the articles taken together is in excess of five thousand dollars?" The Pontifical Commission for the Interpretation of the Code on July 20, 1929, answered in the affirmative.

Other things which may not be alienated without the permission of the Holy See are all those movable or immovable goods, whether they are sacred or not, which belong to religious institutes; for example, a field, a house or rents, whenever their value exceeds five thousand dollars.

Hence, canon 534, paragraph 1, and the responses cited above, prescribe the following:

1) No goods belonging to religious may be alienated without the permission of the Holy See when it is estimated that their value exceeds five thousand dollars.

2) Without the aforesaid permission, no precious goods or votive gifts may be alienated even if their value is less than five thousand dollars.

2. When there is a question of alienating **non-precious goods,** the value of which does not exceed five thousand dollars, the following conditions must be observed:

1) **In institutes of sisters of pontifical approval,** the written permission of the superior given according to the terms of the constitutions and with the consent of the chapter or council, manifested

by secret vote, is requisite and sufficient (c. 534, par. 1).

2) **In institutes of sisters of diocesan approval,** the written consent of the local Ordinary, as well as that of the superior and the council, is necessary (c. 534, par. 1).

3) For **nuns,** besides the consent of the proper superior and of the chapter or council, the written consent of the local Ordinary is required; and if the nuns are subject to a regular superior, his consent is also required (c. 534, par. 1). In the three above cases, it does not seem that the permission must be in writing to be valid.

For the licit alienation of goods, besides what has been said above regarding validity, the following rules must be observed (c. 574, par. 1):

1) There must be a written appraisal of the goods to be alienated, made by at least two conscientious experts (c. 1530, par. 1, n. 1). Moreover, the goods must not be disposed of for less than they were appraised (c. 1531, par. 1).

2) There must be a just cause for alienation, such as urgent necessity, evident utility to the Church or piety (c. 1530, par. 1, n. 2).

3) The sale is to be done by public auction, or, at least, it is to be announced publicly, unless circumstances make a different course of action advisable. The goods should be sold to the one who, all things considered, offers the best price (c. 1531, par. 2).

4) Moreover, all opportune precautions must be observed in order that no damage or ill repute may come to the Church (c. 1530, par. 2).

5) Finally, the money obtained from the sale of the goods shall be placed in safe and productive investments (c. 1531, par. 3).

Gifts made from the goods of a religious institute are generally not permitted. Exceptions, however, may be made for just causes, such as almsgiving, if the consent of the superior, in conformity with the constitutions, is obtained (c. 537).

101. LEASES

To lease goods belonging to the Church, the following must be observed:

1) If the value of the lease exceeds five thousand dollars and lasts

over nine years, the permission of the Holy See is required for the renting of the property (c. 1541, par. 2; c. 534).

2) If the value of the lease exceeds five thousand dollars and does not last over nine years: for **sisters of pontifical approval** the permission of their proper superiors, in conformity with their constitutions, is sufficient; for **nuns**, on the other hand, and for **sisters of diocesan approval**, there is also required the written consent of the local Ordinary and of the regular superior, if the monastery of nuns is immediately subject to one (c. 534; c. 1541, par. 1).

3) If the value of the lease is less than five thousand dollars, then even if the lease lasts more than nine years, the permission of the proper superiors is sufficient in all cases (c. 1541; c. 534).

102. LOANS

May religious communities of women borrow, or make loans with the goods of the institute? They may do so, as long as when making loans they follow the norms pointed out above regarding the administration and the investment of goods of a religious institute (cf. *supra,* n. 97). When receiving loans they must observe the rules regarding debts (cf. *infra,* Part VI, Chap. 5); to contract or receive a loan, under any form, is merely to contract a debt.

103. PENALTIES

A religious who alienates ecclesiastical goods without observing the preceding norms, or one who merely gives consent to an alienation which is not made in the proper manner, not only performs acts which are invalid or illicit but may also be punished as follows:

1) If there is question of goods valued at less than one hundred seventy-five dollars, the religious shall be punished with appropriate penalties by the legitimate ecclesiastical superior (c. 2347, n. 1). (Canon 2347 states that one who alienates goods valued at one thousand francs may be punished by the superior. One thousand francs is one-thirtieth of the amount mentioned in canon 534, which religious can alienate without permission of the Holy See. One-thirtieth of the current maximum sum which religious can alienate without permission ($5,000), is approximately one hundred seventy-five dollars.)

2) If the goods have a value of over one hundred seventy-five dollars and less than five thousand dollars, in addition to the appropriate penalties to be imposed by the superiors, the guilty religious shall be deprived of elegibility for any future office. If she is at present a superior, a bursar or an administrator, she shall be deprived of the office she now holds (c. 2347, n. 2).

3) If the authorization of the Holy See is knowingly omitted when it is necessary, all who have concurred in the alienation of goods, by giving or receiving the goods, or by giving consent to the alienation, besides the penalties mentioned above, automatically incur excommunication *latae sententiae,* reserved to no one (c. 2347, n. 3).

4) Moreover, there remains an obligation to return the goods unlawfully acquired and to repair any damage caused by the unlawful alienation. This obligation may be enforced by ecclesiastical penalties (c. 2347).

II

DOWRIES

When used in reference to religious, **the term dowry signifies that sum of money or portion of temporal goods which the postulant brings with her to religion, with which to support herself in a becoming manner.** Just as it is customary in some countries to give a dowry to young girls who are to be married, in order that the husband may not have to carry all of the burdens of the family, so too, in order to provide for their support and ease the burdens of the institute, it is ordinarily expected that a dowry be given to young ladies who wish to enter a religious community. The size of the dowry is determined by custom or particular law of the community.

104. NECESSITY OF DOWRIES

In monasteries of nuns a postulant must always provide the dowry fixed by the constitutions or determined by lawful custom (c. 547, par. 1). **Sisters** may or may not be obliged to provide a dowry depending upon the constitutions (c. 547, par. 3). A dowry is more strictly required, and it must be larger, in a cloistered community than in *active* institutes, since the works of the members of these latter institutes, such as nursing or teaching, will provide for their support.

When a dowry is prescribed either by common law, by the constitutions, or by custom and the institute is of **pontifical approval,** the dowry cannot be waived either entirely or partially without an indult from the Holy See. But if the institute is of **diocesan approval,** it may not be waived without the permission of the local Ordinary (c. 547, par. 4). Bishops in the United States can dispense from the dowry for nuns or sisters by reason of their Quinquennial Faculties (C.L.D. IV, p. 76).

Something which would guarantee the future support of a candidate would not be a substitute for a dowry. Thus a teaching certificate, a college diploma, or some special aptitude in art or science does not take the place of the dowry. However, any one of the above promises of future support would be a sufficient motive for asking for a dispensation from the law of dowry. Thus if a woman who is a college graduate and a trained teacher wishes to enter the institute but cannot afford the dowry, she could not be accepted without a dispensation from the law of dowry, but because of the potential earning power that her degree and experience represents, it would be easy to get such a dispensation.

If the prospective religious lacks the means to provide a dowry, then the community may, if it wishes, supply one out of its own funds. If this is done, however, the norms for alienation of property must be observed, because even though these goods will be administered by the religious community, the dominion over them will pass to the religious and she will have a right to them if she leaves the religious life.

105. ADMINISTRATION OF DOWRIES

The dowries must be carefully and honestly administered in the monastery, or in the house of habitual residence of the mother general or provincial (c. 550, par. 1).

In the monastery; that is, in the case of nuns. *In the house of habitual residence of the mother general or provincial,* refers to sisters.

After the first profession of the religious, her dowry must be placed in a safe, lawful and productive investment (c. 549). To perform this task is the duty of the superior of the monastery and her council in the case of nuns, or of the superior general or the provincial and her council in the case of sisters. In either case the consent of the local Ordinary and that of the regular superior, if the monastery is immediately subject to one, is also required (c. 549, cf. *supra,* n. 97).

After the first profession. Consequently, during the postulancy and novitiate, the dowry, if it has already been given, must be preserved just as it was received. It must not be invested in any way unless the knowledge and consent of the postulant or of her parents, if she is still subject to them, is obtained. At most, the dowry may be deposited in a bank if it is a notable sum, in order to obtain interest from it.

Besides that of the regular superior if the monastery is subject to one. When this canon is interpreted literally, the question arises: Does a monastery of nuns which is subject to a regular superior for the investment of dowries also require the permission of the local Ordinary for this investment? Because of the decision of the Pontifical Commission cited above (n. 99), we maintain that when there is a question of monasteries subject to a regular superior, the lawful investment of dowries demands the permission of both superiors.

106. Obligation of Keeping Dowries

It is strictly forbidden to spend the dowries of religious in any enterprise, even for the building of a monastery or the liquidation of debts already contracted, before the death of the religious to whom the dowry belongs. While the religious are living, the monastery may dispose only of the interest (c. 549).

Before the death of the religious to whom the dowry belongs; because at death "the dowry of the religious, even those with temporary vows, becomes the property of the monastery or of the institute" (c. 548). It is evident that after the religious' death the dowry belongs to the monastery or the institute, and it may be administered and disposed of as any other goods.

The Ordinaries of the place where the dowries are held must diligently see to it that the dowries of the religious who are still living are conserved; and especially on the occasion of their visitations, they must exact an account of how they are administered (c. 550, par. 2).

Where the dowries are held. The dowries should be conserved and administered at the mother house (c. 550, par. 1), but if in any institute this is not done, the vigilance of which the canon speaks must be exercised by the Ordinary of the place where these functions are carried out.

A superior, even though exempt, who, contrary to the above provisions, shall dare to employ the money of dowries for other uses, shall be punished by the local Ordinary according to the gravity of her fault, including, if he deems it opportune, deposition from office (c. 2412, n. 1).

107. RESTORING OF DOWRIES

If a professed religious, with either solemn or simple vows, leaves the institute for any cause, her dowry must be returned to her intact, She has no right, however, to the interest already derived therefrom (c. 551, par. 1).

For whatever cause. Consequently, the dowry must be given to her, whether she leaves the institute freely or whether she is expelled; whether she does so lawfully with a dispensation, or unlawfully by apostasy from religion.

If the dowry has been lost, the case must be resolved according to the ordinary rules of restitution and payments of debts. Consequently, if the dowry is lost without any fault on the part of the monastery, for example, if it were stolen, there is no obligation to make restitution. However, if the community is at fault, the full amount must be restored.

If a professed religious does not leave religion entirely, but by virtue of an apostolic indult, joins another institute—for example, a Benedictine becomes a Dominican—during the novitiate, the interest on the dowry must be given to the new institute. After profession in the new institute the dowry itself must also be given to the new institute (c. 551, par. 2).

During the novitiate the interest on the dowry must be given to the new insitute; that is, if in the constitutions of the new institute or by formal agreement it was declared that a certain payment should be made during the novitiate. Otherwise during the novitiate there is no obligation to pay anything and the interest shall then be combined with the capital (c. 570, par. 1).

When, on the other hand, a religious does not go from one institute to another, but merely goes from a monastery or a house to another monastery or house of the same institute—for example, from a monastery of Dominican nuns in New York to a monastery of Dominican nuns in Chicago—then the dowry must be given to the new monastery from the day the change takes place (c. 551, par. 2).

At times it is difficult to determine how much money should be returned to a religious. For example, the dowry of a religious consists of two hundred dollars in interest-bearing investments which have increased or diminished in value by the time she leaves religion. Has she a right to the increased or diminished value, or is it sufficient merely to return the two hundred dollars to her? This problem, and similar ones, may be solved by the following principles:

1) If the dowry is held in its original form, whether it has increased or decreased in value, the original investment must be restored.

2) If, on the other hand, the investments have been changed to some other investments by acts of lawful administration, it is sufficient to restore the investments by which the dowry is here and now represented, whatever may be their value.

3) Finally, if the investments originally given as a dowry were sold and the money was deposited in the bank, it is sufficient to restore the sum of money which still remains from the sale of the investments. The reason is the same for all three answers: according to the laws of restitution a thing must be restored to its owner not as it was when given, but as it exists at the time of restitution, provided the temporary possessor was not the knowing cause of its diminution in value. This conforms with the juridical principle: *"Res fructificat domino; res perit domino"*; that is, whenever a thing increases it increases for the owner; if it perishes it perishes for the owner. (Note: In some religious communities all dowries are administered as one fund, and the religious agree to take back only the original worth of their dowry if they leave religion. This seems to be the most convenient and equitable manner of administering dowries.)

III

PIOUS LEGACIES
OR
FOUNDATIONS

Pious legacies or pious foundations are defined as temporal goods given to some ecclesiastical moral person—for example, to a church or to a religious community—which entail the obligation of saying masses, holding sacred functions, or performing some other works of piety or charity, perpetually or for a protracted period, in return for the revenue of the goods (c. 1544, par. 1).

All pious foundations, even if made orally, must be put in writing and the document carefully kept in the archives of the monastery to which the foundation belongs (c. 1548, par. 1 and par. 3).

108. Acceptance and Administration

When religious women are exempt, it pertains to the regular superior to whom they are subject to take care of the following (c. 1550):

1) He is to determine the minimum standards for endowments and the manner of distributing the income of the foundation (c. 1545).

2) He must give written consent to the institute or monastery for the acceptance of such a foundation (c. 1546, par. 1), being careful in this regard not to give consent until he has ascertained that the new obligation will be satisfied and that the income from the foundation corresponds to the obligations imposed, taking into consideration the custom of the place (c. 1546, par. 1).

3) He is to designate a safe place in which money or movable goods received shall be immediately deposited, so that, as soon as possible, they may be invested in favor of the foundation. The investment must not be made until after the superior has consulted his council and any other interested parties. The individual obligations should be explicitly enumerated at this time (c. 1547).

The only women religious who are exempt by law are nuns who are subject to the regular superior of their Order (c. 615). Some communities of sisters are exempt by papal privilege (cf. *infra*, n. 230). All other nuns and sisters are to be directed by the local Ordinary in regard to pious foundations.

If the religious are not exempt, all the rights of which we have just spoken belong, not to the regular superior, but to the local Ordinary (c. 1550). When it is a case, however, of the investment of the capital of legacies or pious foundations, whether the religious women are exempt or not, the consent of the local Ordinary is required (c. 533, par. 1, n. 3; c. 535, par. 3, n. 2).

The local Ordinary also has the right to examine the accounts of the administration of pious legacies when they have been made with the intention of being used for divine worship or works of charity in the territory of the diocese in which the monastery is located (c. 533, par. 1, n. 3; c. 535, par. 3, n. 2).

109. FULFILLMENT AND REDUCTION OF OBLIGATION

If the religious are exempt and are immediately subject to a regular superior, the following pertain to him:

1) He is to see to it that the pious requests of the donors are fulfilled (c. 1515, par. 2; c. 1550).

2) He is to reduce the obligations, unless it is a question of Masses.

if the execution of the obligations becomes impossible because of a decrease of the revenue or for some other reason not traceable to the negligence of the executors. In this case, all interested parties must be heard and the intentions of the founder fulfilled insofar as is possible (c. 1517, par. 2; c. 1550).

Unless it is a question of Masses, because to reduce the obligations of Masses "is exclusively reserved to the Holy See" (c. 1517, par. 2; c. 1550).

If the religious are not exempt, or, rather, if they are not immediately subject to a regular superior, the power of reducing the obligations or overseeing their fulfillment pertains to the local Ordinary (c. 1550).

(Note: The Code in canons 1517 and 1550 does not mention the regular superior but only the local Ordinary and the major superiors. Consequently, it might appear at first glance that when women religious are exempt the above mentioned powers belong to their major superior and not to the regular superior or to the local Ordinary. However, this is not a true interpretation of the canons because there is involved here a question of true ecclesiastical jurisdiction which can never be exercised by women religious (cf. *supra*, n. 40). Hence the power which the Code attributes to major superiors when speaking of religious in general, must be attributed in the case of religious women to the regular superior or to the local Ordinary.)

IV

GOODS GIVEN IN TRUST

Goods given in trust are temporal goods which a donor, either privately before his death or by a last will, gives to some religious or religious institute, and which carry with them the obligation of faithfully fulfilling the intentions of the donor.

Faithfully. It is left solely to the conscience of the one who receives the goods to fulfill the obligations imposed by the gift; no explanation need be given before the law or to other persons who might be interested. It is this condition which distinguishes goods given in trust from those left as legacies or pious foundations. When it is a question of legacies or pious foundations, the ecclesiastical authority must always intervene in regard to the constitution and fulfillment (c. 1544; c. 1546).

110. OBLIGATION OF REVEALING TRUSTEESHIP

Any religious who has received in trust, either as a donation or last will, temporal goods given in favor of the Church, of their religious house, or of other pious causes in the diocese, must report it to the local Ordinary and describe all such goods, both movable and im-movable, with the obligations attached to them. If a donor has ex-plicitly and absolutely forbidden this report, the religious shall not accept the trust (c. 1516, par. 1 and par. 3).

Pious causes. This expression in the present case must be taken in a broad sense, that is, for any work of religion or charity (c. 1516, par. 3).

Of the diocese; that is, the diocese in which the convent where the religious resides is located.

If the goods are left in trust for any other purpose than those in-dicated above, it is sufficient that the religious make the matter known to her major superior, in conformity with the constitutions (c. 1516, par. 3).

If we adhere strictly to the letter of the Code, we would have to say that the religious should make the matter known not to her su-perior but "to her proper Ordinary." However, it is only in clerical institutes that the major superiors are called the proper Ordinaries of the religious (c. 198, par. 1); in lay institutes, whether of men or women, the only Ordinary is the local Ordinary. Consequently, since canon 1516, paragraph 3, makes a distinction between the legitimate superiors who will receive the report concerning goods left for pious causes and goods left for other reasons, we must limit the obligation of the religious in this latter case to making the matter known only to the proper major superiors.

111. FULFILLMENT OF DONERS' WISHES

It pertains to the local Ordinary, when goods are left in trust for some work of piety in the diocese, or to the lawful superiors of the religious when the goods are left or given for another purpose, to see to it that the goods are placed in safe investments and that the in-tentions of the donor are fulfilled (c. 1516, par. 2).

Both the local Ordinaries and the lawful superiors of the religious may and ought to be vigilant, even using their right to hold a visita-tion, in order to insure that the donor's wishes are fulfilled. And the religious, whosoever she may be, is obligated to give an accurate ac-count of everything received and the obligations attached (c. 1515, par. 2; c. 1516, par. 1).

V

DEBTS

In the present instance, **a debt may be defined as any onerous contract entered into with another person by which goods are purchased and not immediately paid for; or money or other temporal goods are borrowed, with the obligation of returning them or their equivalent.**

112. Conditions for Contracting Debts

Superiors must not grant permission for the contracting of debts unless it is certain that the interest on them may be met from current revenue and that within a reasonable time the capital sum will be amortized (c. 536, par. 5).

Moreover, if it is a question of contracting debts or obligations **exceeding five thousand dollars,** the contract, canonically speaking, is absolutely null and void if the authorization of the Holy See was not first obtained (c. 534). For a debt **less than five thousand dollars,** in the case of *sisters of pontifical approval,* it is sufficient to obtain the written permission of the proper superiors, in conformity with the constitutions and the consent of the chapter or council manifested

150

by secret vote. In the case of *sisters of diocesan approval,* the written consent of the local Ordinary must also be obtained. In the case of *nuns,* to the written consent of the local Ordinary there must be added the written consent of the regular superior if the nuns are subject to one (c. 534, par. 1). It is only when debts of less than five thousand dollars are contracted by an act of extraordinary administration that permission is needed. There is no need for the superior or procurator to obtain permission every time she contracts a debt through an ordinary act of administration; for example, when she buys food, clothing or other articles needed for the everyday use of the community. However, many communities limit the amount that can be spent even in these ordinary acts of administration.

In the petition made to the Holy See, to the bishop or to the regular superior to contract debts and obligations, all other debts or obligations with which the corporate entity, that is, the monastery, or province or institute, is already burdened, must be expressed; otherwise the permission obtained is invalid (c. 534, par. 2).

Is the authorization of the Holy See necessary when after having contracted a debt of four thousand dollars the need arises to contract another debt of four thousand dollars? According to a letter of the Apostolic Delegate addressed to religious superiors in the United States (November 13, 1936, cf; C.L.D., II, p. 161), authorization of the Holy See would be required, "since the total of financial obligations will exceed five thousand dollars after the second borrowing."

113. THOSE RESPONSIBLE FOR DEBTS

If a **moral person,** that is, a monastery, province or religious institute, contracts debts and obligations, even with the permission of superiors, it is personally responsible for them (c. 536, par. 1). In other words, when a monastery is burdened with debts which it cannot pay, it does not follow that the religious institute or the province to which the monastery belongs is obliged to pay the debt for the monastery. Even if the lawful superiors, that is, the mother general, the provincial or the local Ordinary have consented to the contracting of the debt, the corporate entity which contracted the debt is always responsible for it.

If, on the contrary, the person who has contracted the debt is an

individual religious, to determine the responsibility for the payment of the debt we must determine whether the debt was contracted with or without the permission of the superiors.

If the debt was contracted without the permission of the lawful superiors, the religious, and not the institute, the province or house, is responsible for the debt (c. 536, par. 3).

Without permission. Consequently, merely implicit or tacit permission is sufficient to make the superiors responsible for payment of the debt. For example, if a superior sees one of her subjects contract a debt by buying or selling without authorization, and says nothing about it, her silence is sufficient to render the superior, and through her the institute, responsible for the debts or other obligations contracted by the subject. It is a general rule of law that "he who remains silent when he can and should speak out is presumed to consent." Thus it is evident how necessary it is for superiors to be vigilant in this regard.

The religious and not the institute is responsible for the debt; that is, granted that the religious is able to pay the debt. For example, if a religious has simple vows and possesses property, she must pay the debt; otherwise it becomes a case of bankruptcy.

When, on the other hand, a religious contracts debts with the permission of the superior, there are two possibilities:

1) If the religious has **solemn vows,** then the corporate entity whose superior granted the permission must bear the responsibility (c. 536, par. 2). For example, if a local superior grants the permission, the house is responsible; if the provincial grants it, the province is responsible; if the mother general gives the permission, then the religious institute to which the religious who contracts the debt belongs is responsible. In such cases only the corporate entity, not the individual religious, has the power of possessing property.

2) If the religious has **simple vows,** and acts on behalf of the institute, it is evident that the institute is responsible for the debt. If she acts on her own behalf, however, she must satisfy the debt from her own property (c. 536, par. 2). If a religious possesses no property with which to pay the debt, then, although the Code says nothing on this matter, it seems that the religious community presided over by the superior who has given the permission is responsible for the debt (cf. *supra,* n. 98).

PART SEVEN

ADMISSION INTO RELIGION

I

REQUIRED CONDITIONS

114. CONDITIONS FOR VALID ADMISSION

For valid admission of a woman into religion, the Code requires the following:

1) She must belong to the Catholic religion (c. 538). Consequently, non-baptized persons and baptized non-Catholics may not be admitted.

Those persons are also excluded who, though baptized as Catholics, join a non-Catholic sect after baptism (c. 542, n. 1). A *non-Catholic sect* includes not only a religious sect properly so-called (for example, Calvinism), but also any sect which professes aetheism or agnosticism (for example, materialistic or dialectical communism, nihilism or materialistic socialism) (P.C.I., July 30, 1934). This disqualification is dependent on an external and public affiliation with the prohibited organization. A simple denial of the faith or an internal assent to the tenets of some non-Catholic sect would not suffice to incur this impediment. On the other hand, Protestants and heretics born in

155

heresy, and then converted to Catholicism, may be received into religion without any dispensation (P.C.I., October 16, 1919).

2) She must be free from all legal impediments (c. 538). Hence the following are excluded:

a) Those who enter religion under the influence of violence, grave fear or fraud, or those whom superiors receive for the same reasons or under the same circumstances (c. 542, n. 1). Fraud on the part of the candidate would occur if the candidate made an insincere statement with the precise purpose of deceiving the superior, if in its absence, admission to the novitiate very probably would have been refused. Fraud on the part of the superior would occur if the superior made promises assuring the candidate of exemptions and privileges incompatible with the religious life.

An unreserved excommunication is automatically incurred by all persons, of whatever dignity, who in any way force a man or woman to enter a religious institute, or to make religious profession, whether it be solemn or simple, perpetual or temporal (c. 2352).

b) Married persons as long as the marriage bond lasts (c. 542, n. 1). The Code no longer makes any mention of the possibility of spouses entering religion when both of them by mutual consent propose to embrace the religious life. Neither does it make any mention of the ancient right granted to one or other of the new spouses to enter religion if within the first two months the marriage has not been consummated. Hence, it must be concluded that these two prescriptions of the old legislation are abolished by the Code and that once the marriage has been validly celebrated the spouses contract a diriment impediment to entrance into religion. On the other hand, there is no impediment for widows or for those whose union has been legally recognized as invalid (c. 542, n. 1).

c) Those persons who have been, or are now, bound by the bond of religious profession (c. 542, n. 1).

Have been professed; for example, those who left religion when their temporary vows expired, or those who have been dispensed from their vows. Those whose temporary vows have expired and wish to re-enter the institute which they left are included in this prohibition. Novices and postulants would not be included, however, since they were never professed. Former members of secular institutes are also exempt from this law, but even though there is no ecclesiastical impediment to the reception of a one-time postulant, novice or member of a secular institute, it is always wise to ascertain the reason why they left their former institute before accepting them.

Or are now professed; for example, fugitives, apostates or anyone, whether within or without the monastery or convent, who is now bound by the vows of religious profession.

d) Those who are in danger of being punished for a grave crime of which they have been or may be accused (c. 542, n. 1).

A grave crime; for example, murder, theft, or adultery.

Of which they have been or may be accused; hence, not for a hidden crime but only for one which is so well known that it has been or may easily be brought before an ecclesiastical or civil tribunal.

115. Conditions for Licit Admission

In order that admission into religion be not only valid but also licit, besides the conditions enumerated above, the Code requires the following:

1) The candidate must be inspired by a right intention (c. 538). Hence she must have a true vocation and a supernatural motive, such as saving her soul or serving God. Entering religion for purely human motives is not licit.

2) The candidate must be capable of bearing the burdens of religious life (c. 538). Consequently, the following are to be excluded:

a) The infirm who are incapable of practicing with regularity the austerities and other observances of religious life. An exception within the limits determined by the constitutions may be made in those institutes which are specifically destined to cultivate vocations among sick persons.

b) Those who are mentally ill or who possess so little intelligence that they cannot understand, and consequently cannot seek, evangelical perfection.

c) Those who are so physically deformed that to clothe them with the religious habit would be to expose it to contempt and derision.

d) Those who manifest tendencies or passions or other vices which are so ingrained that their correction can be prudently doubted; for example, those who are excessively irascible or those who have shown themselves incapable of controlling sensual passions.

3) The candidate must not have any debts which she is unable to satisfy (c. 542, n. 2). Consequently, the impediment ceases when such persons either by themselves or through others pay their creditors.

4) The candidate must not be liable to render accounts, and must not be implicated in secular negotiations in such a way that the institute may have reason to fear law suits and annoyances (c. 542, n. 2). If candidates find themselves in such circumstances they must first free themselves from the above mentioned impediments and then seek admittance into religion.

5) The candidate must not have parents or grandparents who are in great necessity and need their assistance (c. 542, n. 2). St. Thomas tells us: "He who is still in the world, and whose parents are in such a condition that without his help they could not provide for themselves in a fitting manner, must not leave them to enter religion, for he would disobey the divine precept which obliges us to honor our father and our mother" (Summa, II-II, q. 101, a. 4 ad 4).

In the canon cited, there is no mention of brothers or sisters, nephews or cousins. Consequently, although particular cases may arise in which charity may oblige one to put off entrance in religion to take care of brothers or sisters, as a rule there is no obligation for a person to abandon his own vocation merely to look after them.

What about the person who has already joined the religious life and her parents fall into a state of grave need? If the need arises before profession and cannot be alleviated in any other way, the prospective religious ought to return to the world, at least for a while, and help her parents. If the need arises after profession, we must make a distinction:

If, while not leaving religion, the necessary help can be given to the parents in some manner (for example, from the goods of the community if the superiors should judge this opportune), it is evident that there is neither necessity nor obligation to leave religion.

If, on the other hand, the necessary help cannot be given to the parents except by leaving religion, she would be obliged to do so. In this case there would be a conflict between the natural duty of aiding parents and the ecclesiastical duty of remaining in religion, a conflict which must be resolved by giving preference to the natural law and to the duties which flow from it. It is required, however, that the need be truly great and there be no other way of caring for it.

6) The candidate, if she is a widow, must not be required to stay in the world in order to provide for the welfare and education of her children (c. 542, n. 2). "It is not lawful for a person having children,"

says St. Thomas, "to enter religion without providing for their care and education. For it is written (I Tim. 5:8) that if any man has not care of his home, he has denied the faith, and is worse than an infidel" (*Summa,* II-II, q. 189, a. 6).

7) Finally, it is required that the candidate does not belong to the Oriental Rite when there is question of entrance into a religious institute of the Latin Rite (c. 542, n. 2).

It is understood that to these requirements imposed by the Code, there must be added the requirements which, either for validity or for mere legality, may be required by the particular constitutions of each institute.

II

TESTIMONIAL LETTERS

Testimonial letters properly so-called are documents given by competent ecclesiastical authorities to testify to the general qualities required in a candidate who wishes to enter a religious institute; for example, they may testify concerning a person's character, baptism, or marital status.

Testimonial letters must be presented ordinarily before the postulant enters the religious institute (c. 544, par. 1); but for a just cause it is sufficient to present them before admission to the novitiate (cf. c. 2411).

116. THEIR NECESSITY

True testimonial letters are required for those entering institutes of religious women only when the aspirant has been in a college, or a novitiate or postulancy of another religious institute (c. 544, par. 7). These letters are to be issued by the major superior of the former religious institute. A college in this context means a school devoted

160

to the training of young girls or women for the religious life. Thus if one was not at least an aspirant for another religious institute, a true testimonial letter would not be needed.

Other documents, similar to true testimonial letters, are also required before one may enter a religious institute of women. The following documents are required:

1) A certificate of baptism and confirmation (c. 544, par. 1). These certificates are not required when a person merely passes from one religious institute to another by virtue of an apostolic indult. In this case the testimony of the major superior of the institute which the person left is sufficient (c. 544, par. 5). In virtue of the Code, it is not required that the candidate have a statement from her bishop that she is not married and is free to enter the religious state, but this letter is required by the particular constitutions of several institutes.

2) A written statement relative to the character and conduct of the aspirant (c. 544, par. 7). This information can be acquired either from documents or from special investigations made by the superiors who are to admit the postulant.

3) If the candidate was a postulant or a novice in another religious institute or monastery, a letter which indicates why the candidate was dismissed or spontaneously left the former institute must be sent by the major superior of the former institute (c. 545, par. 4).

117. OBLIGATION OF GIVING TESTIMONIAL LETTERS

Superiors are obliged to give testimonial letters when they have been lawfully asked for them. If for a grave reason they believe that they cannot issue the requested letters, they are obliged within three months from the date of request to make known to the Holy See the reason for their silence (c. 545, par. 1 and par. 2).

For a grave reason; for example, if the civil authorities forbid it, or if grave threats are made in case the letters are given.

If the superiors of a religious institute, when requested by the superiors of another institute, are unwilling to give the sworn testimony spoken of above (n. 116, par. 3), the Ordinary shall take measures against them in order to force them to fulfill their duties. To this purpose he may inflict penalties, even the privation of office. If, notwithstanding the actions of the bishop, they still refuse to give the

162ADMISSION INTO RELIGION

sworn testimony, the matter is to be referred to the Sacred Congregation of Religious (S.C.Rel., November 21, 1919).

118. Manner of Giving Testimonial Letters

Testimonial letters or other information officially requested must be: (1) sent directly to the superiors of the religious institute and not to the aspirants themselves; (2) sent free of charge and under seal (*loc. cit.*); (3) sent within three months from the date of request (c. 545, par. 1); and (4) given under oath by the superior who issues them, when the aspirant was a postulant or novice in another institute (c. 543, par. 1).

119. Obligation of Secrecy

Anyone who has knowledge of information received through testimonial letters is strictly obliged to keep secret both the information itself and the names of the persons who supplied it (c. 546).

Anyone. Hence not only the superiors who have received the letters, or the examiners who learn their contents, but all, even strangers, who by chance may come to a knowledge of such information.

120. Penalties

Superiors who admit a postulant to the novitiate without the requisite documents mentioned in canon 544, may be punished, even by privation of office (cf. c. 2411).

III

THE POSTULANCY

The postulancy can be defined as that period of time which intervenes between admission into religion and entrance into the novitiate, during which time the aspirants live in the monastery or religious house and follow the common life under the vigilance of the superiors of the religious institute.

121. NECESSITY AND DURATION

In institutes of religious women with perpetual vows, whether simple or solemn, candidates must make a postulancy of at least six months before they are admitted to the novitiate (c. 539). If those concerned are extern sisters of a monastery, they must make a postulancy of at least a year (S.C.Rel., July 16, 1931). If the postulancy were shortened or omitted altogether, it would not invalidate the novitiate.

For at least six whole months, because the lawful major superiors may prolong the time prescribed for the postulancy, but not beyond

163

another term of six months (c. 538, par. 2). The superiors competent in this case are those mentioned in number 38 and 39, above.

In order to be valid, however, the postulancy need not be continuous.

Hence absence from the monastery for a certain length of time (for example, for fifteen or twenty days), does not seem to interrupt the postulancy. At most it will be necessary to make up the days of absence, although the Code does not even demand this.

Moreover, if a postulant leaves the monastery with the intention of not returning, and then changes her mind and returns within a few days, it seems that the time already passed in the postulancy may be added to the future days she will spend there making one morally united whole.

In institutes with temporary vows, that is, institutes in which neither solemn nor perpetual vows are taken, "the prescriptions of the constitutions regarding the necessity and duration of the postulancy are to be followed" (c. 539). If the constitutions prescribe a postulancy, it must be made, and in the manner and for the time prescribed; if the constitutions do not mention the postulancy there is no obligation to make one.

When the postulancy is completed is it necessary to begin the novitiate immediately or may one wait for a time? When the postulancy is completed, it is customary to begin the novitiate immediately, but it does not seem that this is obligatory. The Code says that before beginning the novitiate those admitted into institutes with perpetual vows must make a postulancy; it does not say, however, that the novitiate must immediately follow the postulancy. If the postulant, therefore, after making six months or even a year of postulancy, must put off her novitiate for a reasonable motive, even for a notable length of time, although not as much as a year, she does not seem to be obliged to repeat the postulancy.

122. PLACE OF POSTULANCY AND MANNER OF MAKING IT

The postulancy must be made either in the novitiate house or at another house of the institute where the discipline prescribed by the constitutions is faithfully observed (c. 540, par. 1). It may also be made successively at several religious houses as long as the houses fulfill the conditions of canon 540.

A religious of exemplary life shall have charge of the postulancy and the postulants shall be placed under her vigilance and care (c. 540, par. 1).

Postulants are to wear a dress that is simple and modest, but different from that of the novices (c. 540, par. 2). It seems that postulants could use their own clothes since the Code merely requires modest and simple dress. But most communities, in order to avoid affectation and singularity, provide a dress for postulants which resembles a religious habit.

The postulancy may be begun even before the age required for the novitiate; hence it may be begun six months before the completion of the fifteenth year. The Code does not expressly state this but it does say that the novitiate may not be begun before the candidate has completed her fifteenth year (c. 555, par. 1, n. 1).

Nothing can be exacted for the expenses of the postulancy except what the constitutions may prescribe for food and clothing or what has been determined by agreement at the beginning of the postulancy. If the postulant leaves the institute before entering the novitiate, all that she brought with her that has not been used should be returned to her (c. 570, par. 1 and par. 2).

In monasteries of nuns, the aspirants are bound by the law of enclosure during their postulancy (c. 540, par. 3). Those who wish to become extern sisters are an exception to this rule since they make their postulancy in the house of the extern sisters which is outside the cloister. Even they, however, must wear a habit which is modest and different from the habit of the novices (S.C.Rel., July 16, 1931, *Statuta,* n. 22).

The Code says "in monasteries of nuns," that is, in monasteries where the cloister is obligatory. However, if the law of enclosure is enforced in other religious houses, even though they are not houses of nuns, it seems that here too the postulancy must be made in the cloister. In these monasteries the aspirants from the time that they are admitted to make their postulancy may enter the cloister without special permission; but they may not leave the cloister without special permission, unless they intend to leave the religious institute for good.

If a postulant in a monastery of nuns leaves the cloister without proper permission she does not incur excommunication because this excommunication applies only to nuns who leave the monastery unlawfully after their profession (c. 601).

123. PRIVILEGES AND POSTULANTS

It does not seem that postulants enjoy the same privileges as professed religious. This appears to be true from the fact that the Commission for the Interpretation of the Code declared that postulants do not enjoy the privilege of religious in regard to funerals (P.C.I., July 20, 1929). If they do not enjoy any privilege relative to funerals, it seems that the same applys to other privileges. Perhaps an exception should be made, however, for indulgences which are proper to the institute.

Unless the constitutions state otherwise, postulants do not have the right to the suffrages of the professed. Suffrages are a right to spiritual goods corresponding to the burdens of the religious life; the postulants have not contracted any burdens and hence they have no correlative rights. In the case of novices, however, the Code expressly determines that they have a right to suffrages (c. 567, par. 1).

IV

THE NOVITIATE

The novitiate is defined as that space of time during which the candidates for the religious life may learn and try the rule of a religious institute, and the religious institute may test the candidate's character, conduct, spirit and ability before admitting her as a member (c. 565; c. 571).

The purpose of a novitiate in a religious institute is threefold:

1) It gives the novices an opportunity to practice the austerities of the religious life, to gain a knowledge of the rule and the manner of life, and thus to determine whether they are capable of faithfully observing the obligations which will be theirs.

2) It gives the religious institute an opportunity to judge the qualities of the postulant so that unworthy members may not be admitted.

3) For the good of the postulant and of the institute itself, it gives the new member an opportunity to become habituated to the kind of life which she must lead.

It is customary to distinguish between the canonical and constitu-

167

tional novitiate. The **canonical novitiate** is that which is prescribed and determined by the Code of Canon Law (c. 572, par. 1, n. 3). A **constitutional novitiate** is that which particular constitutions sometimes add to the novitiate prescribed by the Code to prolong it for a time determined by the constitutions; for example, for a second year (cf. c. 555, par. 2).

124. The House of Novitiate

Each religious institute must have one or several novitiate houses (c. 555, par. 1, n. 3). If a novitiate is begun in one house, it may be validly completed in another as long as the transfer does not take more than 30 days.

In institutions of papal approval the novitiate house is to be erected only with the permission of the Apostolic See (c. 554, par. 1). If the **institute** is **of diocesan approval** it suffices to erect it in conformity with the particular constitutions (c. 554, par. 1).

If an institute is divided into provinces there may be only one novitiate house in each province; to have more it is necessary to obtain a special indult from the Holy See. In this matter the Holy See does not grant indults except for a grave reason (c. 554, par. 2).

The Code, in the canon cited, forbids the erection of several novitiates in each province without the special permission of the Holy See; but it does not oblige each province to have its own novitiate. There may even be only one novitiate for an entire congregation, which, as a matter of fact, is customary in certain congregations which are divided into provinces.

The novitiate must be separated from the other parts of the monastery in which the professed religious dwell, so that, without a special cause and the permission of the superior or of the novice mistress, the novices may not communicate with the professed religious nor these latter with the novices (c. 564, par. 1). During the novitiate lay sisters must also dwell in a separate place (c. 564, par. 2).

The superiors shall assign to the novitiate house only religious of exemplary life (c. 554, par. 3).

125. Conditions for Admission

The conditions for admission to the novitiate are the following:

1) All the conditions enumerated above for the valid and licit admission to religion must be fulfilled (cf. *supra,* n. 114 and n. 115).

2) A certificate of baptism and confirmation and the testimonial letters referred to above (Part VII, Chap. 2) are also required (c. 544, par. 2).

The Code in canon 2411 expressly states that religious superiors who receive a candidate to the novitiate without the required testimonial letters shall be punished in proportion to the gravity of their guilt, even with deprivation of office.

3) The aspirant must have completed her fifteenth year (c. 542, n. 1; c. 555, par. 1, n. 1), and this condition is required for a valid novitiate (c. 555, par. 1, n. 1). The years must be computed in conformity with canon 34, paragraph 3, number 3; that is, not the hour, but rather the day of birth, must be considered, and the year ends at the termination of this day. For example, even if one is born at one o'clock in the morning on December 25, 1945, the fifteen years are completed at the end of the day of December 25, 1960; hence the novitiate cannot be begun until December 26 of that year.

4) The consent of the major superior, who has heard her council or chapter, is necessary before the candidate can be admitted to the novitiate. Whether the vote of the chapter or council is consultative or deliberative is to be determined by the particular constitutions (c. 543).

5) A dowry is always required in institutes of nuns (c. 547, par. 1). A dowry is necessary for sisters if this is required by their constitutions; otherwise, postulants may be received without one (c. 547, par. 3) (cf. *supra,* Part VI, Chap. 2).

When a dowry is prescribed it must be given to the monastery or institute before the reception to the habit, or at least its payment must be guaranteed in a manner recognized by the civil law (c. 547, par. 2). Furthermore, if a dowry is prescribed it cannot be dispensed with in institutes of papal approval, either in whole or in part, without an indult of the Holy See; in institutes of diocesan approval the permission of the local Ordinary suffices (c. 547, par. 4).

6) A canonical examination of the vocation of the postulant, made by the Ordinary of the place where the novitiate is located, or by his delegate, must be held at least thirty days before admission to the novitiate. This examination must be made without charge (c. 552,

par. 2). It is not forbidden, however, to make a donation to the monastery, to cover the expenses which the examiner has incurred. Neither is it forbidden to express the gratitude of the monastery for the inconvenience which the examiner has undergone by presenting him with a gift. On the other hand, taxes of any kind whatsoever are forbidden, even if it was formerly the custom to pay them (S.C.Rel., March 18, 1922).

In the examination it must be clearly determined whether the postulant understands the step she is taking, or whether she has been constrained or coaxed by others. Only when her free will and right intention have been clearly ascertained may she be admitted to the novitiate (c. 552, par. 2).

The examiner has no right to enter the cloister.

The superior is strictly obliged to inform the local Ordinary at least two months in advance of the approaching admittance of a postulant to the novitiate (c. 552, par. 1). A superior who is found negligent in this matter shall be punished, even if she belongs to an exempt religious institute, by the local Ordinary, in proportion to the gravity of the guilt, even with deprivation of office (c. 2412, n. 2).

7) A postulancy must be made in the case of religious women with perpetual vows (cf. *supra*, n. 121).

8) A retreat of at least eight full days is required before the postulant begins the novitiate; and, if her confessor shall judge it opportune, she will be permitted to make a general confession of her past life (c. 541).

Eight full days. Hence if the retreat is made for only eight days the postulant must be on retreat for the entire first and last days.

It is to be noted that not all of the conditions enumerated above are required *ad validitatem,* that is, under pain of invalidity. As we have pointed out, requirements for the novitiate do not affect its validity unless this is expressly stated (cf. *supra*, n. 113 and n. 125, par. 3).

126. The Right to Admit Novices

The right of admitting to the novitiate belongs to the major superiors with the vote of the council or chapter, according to the requirements of the constitutions of each particular institute (c. 543). The council or chapter which must be consulted depends upon the constitutions; usually it is the chapter or council of the novitiate house.

Superiors who admit an unqualified postulant to the novitiate (that is, a postulant who does not fulfill the conditions referred to above), shall be punished in accordance with the gravity of their guilt, even with deprivation of office (c. 2411).

Anyone, of whatever dignity, who forces a person to enter a religious institute, automatically incurs a non-reserved excommunication (c. 2352).

127. MANNER OF BEGINNING THE NOVITIATE

The novitiate begins with the reception of the habit, or in any other manner prescribed by the constitutions (c. 553).

Or in any other manner prescribed by the constitutions. Since there are congregations or institutes which do not have a special religious habit, it is indispensable in these cases that the constitutions determine when and how the novitiate begins.

In religious institutes in which the postulants are solemnly admitted to the reception of the religious habit, it does not follow that the novitiate must necessarily begin at this time. The ceremony of reception to the habit can be distinct from the beginning of the novitiate (c. 553). To avoid all doubts, it is always well to declare when the novitiate begins, and to do so publicly, that is, in the presence of the religious community or at least before two witnesses.

In institutes whose members wear religious habits, the habit prescribed for the novices by the constitutions must be worn throughout the whole period of novitiate unless special local circumstances determine otherwise (c. 557). If a professed religious transfers from one religious institute to another, she must wear the habit of novices of the new institute, even though she still has vows professed in the institute from which she has departed (S.C.Rel., May 14, 1923).

In institutes whose members are divided into two or more classes—that is, choir sisters, lay sisters or similar classifications—the novitiate made in preparation for one class is not valid for another (c. 558; cf. *infra*, Part XII, Chap. 1).

To begin the novitiate, the following conditions are required by the Code:

1) The postulancy made according to the prescriptions of the Code for religious with perpetual vows, or, according to the particular constitutions of the institute for other women religious (c. 539, par. 1). As we have pointed out above, in institutes with temporary vows, the postulancy may or may not be made, according to the prescriptions of the constitutions (cf. *supra*, n. 121).

2) Residence in a novitiate house (c. 555, par. 1, n. 3). As we have pointed out, the novitiate may not be made in any house whatsoever of the institute, but it must be made under penalty of invalidity in a novitiate house (cf. *supra*, n. 124).

128. DURATION OF THE NOVITIATE

In every religious institute the novitiate must be made for at least "an entire and continuous year" under pain of rendering the subsequent profession invalid (c. 555, par. 1, n. 2).

The year of novitiate must be calculated according to the calendar, so that if the novitiate began on October 1, it would be finished at midnight of October 1-2 of the following year, even though the year in question is a leap year (c. 34, par. 3, nn. 1, 3). Since the year must be entire, the novitiate will not be completed until the end of the day corresponding to the day on which it was begun. Therefore, the hour at which it is begun is not taken into account. For example, if the novitiate was begun at eight o'clock in the morning on September 29, the year of novitiate will not end at eight o'clock in the morning on September 29 of the following year, but at midnight on September 29-30. Consequently, profession may not be made until the morning of September 30 (cf. can. 34, par. 3, n. 3).

The year of novitiate is *continuous* if the novitiate is not interrupted (c. 34). We shall consider in the next section the various ways the novitiate can be interrupted.

Under pain of rendering the profession invalid. This was expressly stated by the Pontifical Commission for the Interpretation of the Code, November 12, 1922.

If the constitutions prescribe more than one year for the novitiate, the extra time is not required for the validity of the profession unless the constitutions expressly state otherwise (c. 555, par. 2). Thus it is evident that it is not contrary to the Code if the constitutions of a religious institute prescribe more than one year of novitiate. However, this additional time does not affect the validity of the profession unless the constitutions expressly declare that it is prescribed under pain of the invalidity of the profession. The second year of novitiate may not precede the canonical year unless express permission is obtained from the Holy See (P.C.I., February 12, 1935). Moreover, if this additional time is required it must be spent in conformity with the rules drawn up by the Code for the novitiate; otherwise, it could not be rightly called a time of novitiate.

When the novitiate prescribed by the Code or by the constitutions is completed, if there remains any doubt regarding the suitability of the subject, the major superiors can prolong the time of probation, but not beyond six months (c. 571, par. 2).

Consequently, if one year of novitiate is prescribed, the major superiors can prolong it, in particular cases, to eighteen months; if according to the rule, the novitiate is to last for two years, the major superiors can prolong it to thirty months. (For those who are included under the term major superiors cf. *supra,* n. 38 and n. 39.) It is probable that major superiors can prolong the novitiate even without the consent of their council, but it would not be well for them to do so.

129. INTERRUPTION OF THE NOVITIATE

The novitiate can be interrupted in several ways; according to the manner in which it is interrupted it is necessary to remake it in its entirety, under pain of an invalid profession, or, it is sufficient to supply the time that was missed (c. 556).

A. Interruption and invalidity

The novitiate is interrupted and must be recommenced in the following cases:

1) If the novice is dismissed by her superiors and leaves the convent (c. 556, par. 1). It seems, therefore, that if the novice has been dismissed by the superiors but has not left the convent, and the decision to send her away has been revoked before the novice has left the house, the novitiate would not be interrupted.

2) If a novice, without the permission of the superior, leaves the

house of novitiate with the intention of not returning (c. 556, par. 1). In order to interrupt the novitiate in this manner, therefore, three conditions must be present simultaneously: departure from the house; lack of permission for same; and the intention of not returning.

3) If a novice remains outside of the novitiate house for more than thirty complete days, whether continuous or not. In this case the novitiate is interrupted even if the novice has the permission of her superior and a very grave reason for absenting herself from the novitiate house (c. 556, par. 1).

Complete days. The thirty days must consist of twenty-four hours computed from midnight to the following midnight (c. 32, par. 1). Therefore, parts of days are not counted. This seems to be at least the more probable opinion.

Whether continuous or not; that is, whether the days follow one after another without interruption or not. As long as the sum total exceeds thirty, the novitiate is broken.

Even for a very grave reason; that is, even though the cause of the interruption is more serious; for example, grave illness, the destruction of the monastery, or transfer from one novitiate house to another (P.C.I., July 13, 1930).

Even if she had the permission of her superiors; that is, of her own religious superiors or the bishop. If permission has been obtained from the Holy See, then the novitiate would not necessarily be interrupted, since the Holy Father may dispense if he wishes from any prescription of the Code which contains a purely ecclesiastical law.

Outside of the novitiate house. Hence, although novices must ordinarily dwell in a separate part of the convent, if for some reason they should live for a time outside of the place of novitiate but within the novitiate house itself (for example, in the infirmary), the novitiate would not be interrupted since the novice is not outside of the novitiate house.

B. *Interruption without invalidity*

If the novice with the permission of her superiors, or under compulsion, has spent more than fifteen days, even though not continuous days, but not more than thirty days, outside the novitiate house but under the obedience of the superiors, it is sufficient for the validity of the novitiate that she supply the number of days spent outside (c. 556, par. 2).

More than fifteen days. If the sum total of the interruptions *does not exceed* fifteen days, the missed time may be made up at the discretion of the superiors, but this is not required for the validity of the novitiate (c. 556, par. 2). When one has been out of novitiate for more than fifteen days, all the missed days should be supplied, not merely those in excess of fifteen days.

Not more than thirty days. As we have seen, if the interruption exceeds thirty days, it is necessary to begin the novitiate again unless a dispensation is obtained from the Holy See.

The manner of computing missed days can be best understood if we pose the following question. Would a novice interrupt her novitiate if she left the convent at ten o'clock in the morning on Monday and returned to the convent at noon on Tuesday? She would not, because when the Code speaks of interrupting the novitiate it mentions days and not hours. According to the Code, a day consists of twenty-four hours to be computed from midnight to midnight (c. 32, par. 1). In the present case, therefore, though there would be a total of twenty-six hours absence, there would not be one full day's absence since there would not be twenty-four hours of continuous absence from one midnight to another.

If a novice is sent by her superiors from one novitiate house to another novitiate house of the same religious institute, the novitiate is not interrupted, even if the trip lasts more than a day. If it exceeds thirty days, however, the novitiate would be invalid (c. 556).

130. TRAINING OF NOVICES

During the novitiate, the novices must be placed under the direction of a mistress of novices and of other superiors whom they are bound to obey (c. 561, par. 2).

During the novitiate, the novices must principally devote themselves to the following (c. 565, par. 1):

1) They must study the rule and the constitutions. The rule and constitutions should be known and studied in their entirety and not merely in summary nor only those parts which have to do with novices and professed religious. Profession is made according to the

whole rule and consequently it is only right that it should be known in its entirety.

2) They must engage in assiduous prayer and meditations.

3) They must study those matters which pertain to the vows and the virtues.

4) They must remove bad habits through suitable spiritual exercises.

5) They must try to regulate unruly passions.

6) They must try to acquire the virtues.

7) They must study Christian doctrine. An Instruction of the Sacred Congregation of Religious (November 25, 1929) requires that, in every lay institute of religious men or women, all postulants and novices must be given a course in Christian doctrine so that they may review it and learn it more thoroughly; and they may not be admitted to profession unless they show through examination a sufficient knowledge thereof.

During the novitiate the **lay sisters** must not be assigned to duties which divert them too much from the exercises prescribed for the novitiate (c. 565, par. 3). Moreover, novices must not be *ex professo* assigned to teaching or to the study of letters, sciences or arts (c. 565, par. 3).

Ex professo. Hence, study or teaching must not become a fixed and obligatory part of the novitiate. However, it is not forbidden to have classes in English, Latin, music or other apt subjects about one hour a day, so that the novices will not forget what has been learned. This also gives the superiors an opportunity to test the talents and diligence of the novices. But the novitiate must never become a regular school and divert the novices from the exercises proper to the novitiate.

In religious institutes in which two years' novitiate are prescribed, when the canonical year has been made in conformity with the prescriptions of the Code, in the second year of the so-called constitutional novitiate, the novices, whether lay sisters or choir sisters, may devote themselves to exterior works, for example, to helping out in the infirmary or teaching school, so that they may acquire practice and experience in the complete life lead by the institute, provided that the prescriptions contained in the *Instruction* given on this point by the Sacred Congregation of Religious, November 3, 1921, are observed, namely:

I. It must be remembered that the novitiate is instituted to train the souls of the novices in regard to the removal of bad habits, the restraint of the passions, the acquisition of virtues, and the practice of the regular life through the study of the constitutions; this is done so that the novices may learn to make progress towards Christian perfection by the profession of the evangelical counsels and the vows, which progress constitutes the end of every religious . . . . Therefore, this Sacred Congregation orders that even during the second year of novitiate the development of the spiritual life is of primary importance.

II. It is lawful, however, for the novice to be employed in works of the institute during the second year of novitiate if the constitutions allow it. This should be done with prudence and moderation, purely for the instruction of the novices. They should never be so employed in these works that they perform them alone, for example, taking the place of absent teachers or instructors in schools, or ministering to the sick in hospitals; rather, they should be engaged in the work under the direction and supervision of an older religious who should instruct them and show them the way.

III. If it is ever permitted by the constitutions that a novice during the second year be sent out of the house to do the work of the institute, this should be permitted only in exceptional cases and provided some grave reason requires it. The reason should have reference to the novice; for example, that they cannot be sufficiently trained in the house, or that for some other reason they cannot remain there; but never under any pretext will the necessity or advantage of the religious institute itself be a sufficient cause, as, for example, if the novices were to be substituted for the regular members in the work of the institute, because of scarcity of workers.

IV. But whether the novices remain in the house or out of it, they must be withdrawn from all exterior works at least two months before profession, and if they have been out of the novitiate they must return to it, so that for two months before their profession they may prepare for it by strengthening themselves in the spirit of their vocation.

No novice may be sponsor at baptism or confirmation unless it is a case of necessity and she has the permission of at least the local superior (c. 766, par. 4; c. 796, par. 3).

Unless it is a case of necessity; that is, a case of true necessity, for example, if there were no one else to serve as god-mother. Outside a case of true necessity the permission of the Holy See would be required.

131. CONFESSORS OF NOVICES

Regarding confessors, all that has been said above relative to professed religious is to be applied in exactly the same manner to novices (c. 566, par. 1; cf. *supra*, n. 80 ff.).

132. TEMPORAL GOODS OF NOVICES

In regard to temporal goods of novices, Canon Law states the following:

1) There is no obligation to reimburse the religious institute for food and clothing furnished during the novitiate unless this is expressly stated in the constitution (c. 570, par. 1). However, the institute may require the payment of extraordinary expenses, such as the cost of surgery, since this does not fall into the category of "food and clothing."

2) Temporal goods which were brought to religion by the aspirant, and which were not consumed by use, must be returned to her in their entirety if she leaves the institute before making profession (c. 570, par. 2). Hence it is a good idea to make a list or inventory of everything the postulant brings with her when she enters the institute so as to avoid disputes in the event that she leaves the institute. A novice may not demand recompense for any work she did while in the novitiate. For example, if she taught school during the second year of novitiate, she has no right to ask to be paid for this work. In order to avoid difficulty in this regard, it is wise to have prospective religious sign a statement to this effect, valid in civil law.

3) If a novice leaves the religious institute, may she, in virtue of canon 570, paragraph 2, take along her religious habit if she made it herself? We think not. In the first place it is not fitting. Secondly, the canon gives the right to retain those things brought by the aspirant to religion, and even if the aspirant paid for it out of her own funds, she still did not "bring it to religion with her." It seems more logical to regard the habit as a gift made to the religious institute or as an expense connected with the novitiate for which the aspirant has no right to be reimbursed.

4) If the novice renounces in any way her rights or goods, or if she assumes obligations affecting them, the renunciation and the other

contracts are, according to canon law, not only illicit, but also invalid (c. 568).

5) Before the profession of simple vows, whether temporary or perpetual, the novice must cede, for the whole period during which she will be bound by simple vows, the administration of her property to whomsoever she wishes, and dispose freely of its use and usufruct, unless the constitutions determine otherwise (c. 569, par. 1).

If this cession and disposition were omitted because the religious did not have any property and subsequent property comes into her possession, or if, after making the cession and disposition she becomes under any title the possessor of other property, even if she has already made simple profession, she must make provision for the newly acquired property in the manner just explained (c. 569, par. 2).

Cession is the action by which the novice surrenders, for the time she is in religion, the care of her goods to a physical or moral person of her choice. If the institute will receive the cession, the novice may cede administration to it.

Disposition is the action by which the novice provides for the use and revenue of her goods while she is in religion. If she wishes, the novice may decide that the revenue from her goods should be added to her capital, or applied to the upkeep of her property. The novice is free in choosing the person who will benefit by the disposition, unless the constitutions of her institute determine otherwise (P.C.I., October 16, 1919). The novice is always free, however, in choosing the beneficiary of the cession.

If the novice possesses goods but is deprived of their administration and free use by the civil law, then the cession and disposition can be delayed until the religious does have full control of her property.

6) In institutes of sisters, the novices, before the first profession of simple vows, shall make a will of all the property they actually or may subsequently possess (c. 569, par. 3).

In institutes of sisters. Hence nuns are excluded, perhaps because they take solemn vows and must make a renunciation of all property at that time (cf. *infra,* n. 176).

All the property they actually or may subsequently possess. Hence one who possesses no property could make a perfectly valid will disposing of any property that might come into her possession later on.

Before profession the novice may freely make the religious institute the beneficiary of her will. After profession, however, she could not do this without the permission of the Holy See. The only time that a will may be changed is in a case of urgent necessity; then the permission of the major superior or local superior would suffice (c. 583, n. 2).

The will may not be changed during simple vows without the permission of the Holy See. However, if the case is urgent, the permission of the major superior or at least of the local superior suffices (c. 583, n. 2).

133. PRIVILEGES AND SPIRITUAL FAVORS

Novices, from the moment of their canonical reception of the habit, are considered by the law as religious insofar as favorable things are concerned (cf. *supra*, n. 4). Hence they enjoy:

1) All the privileges granted to professed religious (c. 614); and consequently:

     a) All the faithful owe them reverence and respect (c. 119).

     b) Those who injure them become guilty of sacrilege (c. 119); and they incur excommunication if they do them personal injury (c. 2343, par. 4; cf. *infra*, n. 222).

     c) In all law cases which may arise, whether civil or criminal, they must be tried by an ecclesiastical tribunal and not by a civil court, unless in some countries other special provisions have been made (c. 120, par. 1; cf. *infra*, n. 223, ff.).

     d) They are also exempt from the jurisdiction of the bishop and pastor if and to the extent that the professed religious of their religious institute are exempt (c. 615; cf. *infra*, Part IX, Chap. 4).

2) Moreover, novices enjoy all the favors and indults granted to the religious institute (c. 567, par. 1). Consequently:

     a) They may gain all the indulgences which the professed religious of the institute may gain.

     b) If they die before profession they have a right to the same suffrages as are prescribed for the professed members (c. 567, par. 1).

This prescription of the Code regarding suffrages must be observed even if constitutions approved before the Code expressly state the contrary (c. 489; P.C.I., October 16, 1919). If, however, this seems to be too heavy a burden, the institute may, with the approval of the Sacred Congregation of Religious, determine other suffrages; however, the new suffrages must be the same for the novices and for the professed with simple or solemn, temporary or perpetual vows.

134. OBLIGATION OF THE CLOISTER

In monasteries of nuns, a novice is strictly obliged to the law of enclosure. The Code does not expressly state this, but it implys as much when it states in canon 565, paragraph 1, that novices must be trained in all the observances of the religious life. Moreover, it would not be reasonable for the Code to impose the law of enclosure on postulants in monasteries of nuns (cf. *supra*, n. 122) and dispense novices from the same obligation. If a novice leaves the cloister without due permission, however, she does not incur excommunication (cf. c. 2342).

In houses of sisters, if there is a law of enclosure, the novices are obliged to observe it.

135. DEPARTURE OR DISMISSAL

A novice may freely leave the institute during the novitiate (c. 571, par. 1).

Freely; that is, by leaving she does no injury to the institute, nor has the institute any right to constrain her to remain. But this does not apply to a person who feels she has a vocation; no one may flee from this obligation since prudence demands that we do all that is possible to follow the vocation to which we feel called.

A novice may also be dismissed by the superiors or the chapter, in accordance with the constitutions, for any just cause; and the superiors or the chapter are not obliged to make known to her the reasons for her dismissal (c. 571, par. 1).

A just cause is always required; otherwise the superiors would sin against charity by unjustly preventing the novice from fulfilling her vocation and also by depriving the institute of a useful member sent by God for the good of the institute.

Once the novice leaves the novitiate she immediately loses all the rights and privileges she enjoyed while in the institute (cf. c. 123).

All the temporal goods which the aspirant brought with her and which were not consumed by use must be returned to her in their entirety (c. 570, par. 2).

V

THE MISTRESS OF NOVICES AND HER ASSISTANTS

The mistress of novices is that religious to whom the care and religious formation of the novices is entrusted (c. 559, par. 1).

The assistant novice mistress is that religious who is assigned to help the mistress of novices in the care and religious training of the novices (c. 559, par. 2).

136. NECESSITY OF THESE TWO OFFICIALS

In every novitiate there must be a mistress of novices (c. 559, par. 1).

Moreover, an assistant novice mistress shall be appointed whenever it is deemed expedient because of the number of novices or for some other just cause (c. 559, par. 2). Both the mistress of novices and her companion shall be selected in conformity with the constitutions (c. 560).

182

137. QUALITIES OF THE MISTRESS OF NOVICES

1) The mistress of novices must be at least thirty-five years of age (c. 559, par. 1); hence it is sufficient if she has begun her thirty-fifth year.

2) She must be professed for at least ten complete years; this time is to be computed from the date of her first profession of temporary vows in conformity with canon 34, paragraph 3, number 3 (c. 559, par. 1).

3) She must be distinguished for piety, charity, prudence and regular observance (c. 559, par. 1).

4) She must also be free from all occupations and duties which would impede the direction and care of the novices (c. 559, par. 3). In practice, this means that the office of local superior and novice mistress must not be held by the same person, even though this is not explicitly forbidden by the common law.

138. QUALITIES OF THE ASSISTANT NOVICE MISTRESS

1) The assistant novice mistress must be at least thirty years of age (c. 559, par. 2); hence it is sufficient if she has begun her thirtieth year.

2) She must be professed for at least five years; this time is to be computed from her first profession of temporary vows and these years must be complete in conformity with canon 34, paragraph 3, number 3 (c. 559, par. 2).

3) She must be free from all occupations and duties which would impede the government and care of the novices (c. 559, par. 3).

4) She must have all the qualities, such as piety, charity and prudence, necessary for the effective fulfillment of her office (c. 559, par. 2).

139. AUTHORITY OF THE NOVICE MISTRESS

The novice mistress, and she alone, has the right and the obligation of providing for the religious formation of the novices and the direction of the novitiate (c. 561, par. 1).

May the novice mistress demand that the novices manifest matters of conscience to her? She may not demand this in the strict sense of the word, but she certainly may exhort the novices to be entirely candid in making known to her, not their sins, but their particular difficulties and their personal spiritual and temporal needs. Otherwise, how can she train the novices in the true religious and spiritual life, as the Code commands her to do? (c. 565.) Hence a novice who is stubborn in this matter, gives evidence by this very fact of a poor and very weak vocation (cf. *supra,* n. 91).

No one is allowed to interfere in the internal government of the novitiate, except the superiors who are permitted to do so by the constitutions and the visitators (c. 561, par. 1).

In all those things which pertain to the regular and general observance of the monastery however, the mistress together with the novices is subject to the superior of the house (c. 561, par. 1).

The internal government of the novitiate embraces everything which, in conformity with the constitutions, is done by the novices as novices and in the novitiate; in this the mistress of novices is independent. On the other hand, insofar as she and the novices form a part of the community and take part in the community life, they are subject to the general government of the superior of the community.

140. Authority of the Assistant Mistress of Novices

The assistant is immediately subject to the mistress of novices in those things which pertain to the novitiate (c. 559, par. 2). Consequently, she has only that authority which the novice mistress either expressly or implicitly gives to her.

141. Obligations of the Novice Mistress

It is a matter of grave obligation for the mistress of novices to see to it that the novices confided to her care apply themselves assiduously to regular observance in conformity with the particular constitutions and the spirit of the institute (c. 562).

Furthermore, during the year of novitiate, the mistress of novices must present a report on the conduct of each of the novices to the chapter or major superior in the manner prescribed by the constitutions (c. 563).

142. Removal of the Novice Mistress or Her Assistant

If the constitutions prescribe a fixed term of office for the novice mistress and her assistant, they must not be removed during this time without a just and grave cause. When their term of office has elapsed, both may be relieved of their office, or they may also be reappointed. The same is true if they were appointed for an indefinite period of time (c. 560).

VI

THE VOWS

A vow is a promise freely made to God to do something which is possible and which is better than its contrary (c. 1397, par. 1).

A promise. Hence it is not simply a proposal to do or not to do something, reserving full liberty to do the contrary if one pleases; rather it is a deliberate act of the will to do or not to do something with the intention of binding oneself in conscience.

Made to God; for although in pronouncing vows we may invoke the aid of the Blessed Virgin and the saints and pronounce vows in their honor, nevertheless, a true vow must be made directly and principally to God with whom we intend to contract an obligation which will bind us in conscience.

Freely, since it is a question of an obligation which one contracts because she is willing to do so. Consequently, the profession of a vow requires a knowledge of what is promised and full liberty to make or not to make the promise. Ignorance, physical force or fear could thus invalidate a vow.

Of something which is possible, not only physically but also morally; it is not possible to will to do something which, all things considered, appears humanly impossible.

Better than its contrary. We know from the gospels that it is God's will that we tend to perfection: "You therefore are to be perfect, even as your heavenly Father is perfect" (Matt. 5:48). We also know that a vow must be pleasing and acceptable to God if it is to have any value. Now, if God wishes that we tend to perfection, how would it be possible for him to accept a promise which would bind us to something less perfect than its contrary? For example, we know that the gospels tell us it is more perfect to give up, in a spirit of poverty, even those goods which we could lawfully possess; the gospels also tell us that it is more perfect to fast in a spirit of Christian mortification than it is to give oneself to feasting. Hence we may, without doubt, make a vow of poverty with the intention of giving up even goods lawfully possessed; we may also make a vow to fast on Friday, although in ecclesiastical law fasting is not prescribed on that day. On the other hand, it would be inconceivable that one would take a vow to become rich or to take a vow always to give oneself over to feasting, since these actions are not as acceptable to God as their opposites.

143. KINDS OF VOWS

By reason of their *duration,* vows are **temporary or perpetual** (c. 574). *Temporary vows* are those which are made for a definite time; for example, for one year, or for three years. *Perpetual vows* are those which are made with the intention of binding oneself for life.

By reason of the *manner* in which they are made, vows are **public or private.** *Public vows* are those which are accepted by a lawful superior in the name of the Church. *Private vows* or vows of devotion are those which are made without this official acceptance by the Church (c. 1308, par. 1).

Each member of the faithful may oblige himself before God to do more than what is strictly necessary for salvation by taking vows. However, if ecclesiastical authority does not intervene to confirm these vows officially, declaring not only that it permits them, but that it also accepts them after the manner of a contract between the person who pronounces the vows and the Church (represented in the present instance by the superiors of the order or of the religious congregation), the vows are considered private. Thus "public" here is not used in opposition to hidden or secret.

By reason of their *effects* vows are **solemn or simple** (cf. c. 1308, par. 2). *Solemn vows* are those which are recognized as such by the Church; otherwise the vows are *simple*.

Thus the type of acceptance or recognition by the Church is the juridically indispensable condition needed to constitute a solemn vow. At the same time, it is an element which distinguishes it from a simple vow.

Simple and solemn vows also differ from one another by reason of the different effects which they juridically produce, as we shall point out later (cf. *infra,* n. 173 and n. 176).

Whether or not simple vows are intrinsically distinguished from solemn vows is disputed by canonists and theologians. Those who maintain that an intrinsic distinction exists between the two types of vows explain their position in the following manner: By a simple vow one offers to God only the use of the thing which is the object of a vow, for example, the use of riches; by a solemn vow one gives up not only the use but also the thing itself; thus one renounces not only the use of riches but also the riches themselves by giving up the right to possess them. Since there is an intrinsic distinction between giving up the use of a thing and the thing itself, solemn and simple vows are intrinsically distinct. The followers of Saint Thomas defend this viewpoint. It seems to be the better position since it gives to the solemn vow a special note of solemnity and explains how the profession is a true sacrifice or holocaust offered to God.

Solemn vows are always public and perpetual; while simple vows may be public or private, perpetual or temporary.

From the viewpoint of *dispensation,* vows are either **reserved or not reserved.** *Reserved* vows are those from which a dispensation can ordinarily be obtained only from the Holy See. Vows which are *not reserved* are those from which dispensation can be obtained from certain ecclesiastical superiors, or from certain confessors, without recourse in each case to the Holy See.

Since only the Sovereign Pontiff, the Vicar of Christ on earth, has the power to interpret the will of God on earth, only he can dispense from a vow made to God. Sometimes the Pope declares that in certain cases he reserves dispensation from vows to himself (c. 1309); at other times he allows dispensations from certain vows to be granted in his name by bishops, other ecclesiastical superiors or confessors. In the former case the vows are called reserved; in the latter case they are said to be not reserved.

144. NATURE OF RELIGIOUS VOWS

Vows made in religious profession are always public (c. 488, par. 1; cf. *supra*, n. 2); that is, they are accepted in the name of the Church by a lawfully appointed superior.

Religious vows, whether simple or solemn, are always reserved if they are validly pronounced in the religious institute. If the institute is one of **diocesan approval,** the vows are reserved to the bishop; if the institute is one of **papal approval,** they are reserved to the Sovereign Pontiff (c. 638; c. 640).

Religious vows oblige in conformity with the rule and constitutions of the institute, and in conscience, that is, under pain of sin (c. 593). Consequently, it is not within the power of the one who makes profession to determine the object of the vow, its extension, nor the manner in which it is to be observed; rather, each religious who makes profession is necessarily obliged to the observance of the vows as they are determined by the rule and constitutions of the institute.

Nevertheless, out of devotion, one may intend to promise God in the profession of vows, more than what the constitutions demand. For example, one may intend to make a perpetual vow of chastity even if the constitutions speak only of temporary vows, or one may intend to bind oneself in conscience to extend the vow of obedience to all lawful commands of superiors, even if the constitutions limit the vow of obedience to formal precepts. In such cases, however, obligations added out of devotion affect only the conscience of the one who makes the vows; neither the religious institute nor the superiors have any right or duty to take these obligations into account.

The binding force of vows and the effects of simple and solemn profession, temporary and perpetual, will be discussed later when we treat of the various types of profession (*infra*, Part VII, Chaps. 8-11).

145. BINDING FORCE OF PRIVATE VOWS

Private or devotional vows taken **before religious profession** in any religious institute, are suspended as long as the person who takes the vows remains in religion (c. 1315).

Are suspended. Consequently, the vows are not annulled nor is a dispensation given; there is merely a cessation of the obligation to observe them during the time that the person who takes them remains in religion. On the day that a religious licitly leaves her religious institute, she is again bound to the observance of vows taken before her religious profession.

Private or devotional vows taken **after religious profession** are valid if they are *compatible* with the other obligations of the religious state, and thus religious are bound to keep them.

Religious profession does not rule out the profession of other vows, as long as they do not interfere with the practice of regular observance. Consequently, if a professed religious takes a private vow of humility, for example, there is no reason why this should prove an obstacle to the practice of the three original vows. The exercise of this beautiful virtue will help rather than hinder the religious in her quest for observance and perfection. The same is true of some other private vows. In particular cases however, it is always wise to seek the advice of the confessor before pronouncing such vows.

If the private vows that a religious has pronounced after profession are neither useful nor *opportune,* they are to be considered as invalid if the one who made them is in solemn vows (c. 579), and they are rescissible by the superior if the one who made them is in simple vows (c. 501, par. 1; 1312, par. 1).

As we have pointed out, every lawful religious superior has governing or dominative power over her own subjects, in virtue of which her subordinates are obliged to obey her (cf. *supra,* n. 40). Consequently, if religious, after their profession, that is to say after they have promised obedience to the superiors of the religious institute, contract special obligations without any authorization, it is evident that superiors are not obliged to recognize such obligations. Hence, superiors may annul private vows taken by their subjects after profession (cf. *infra,* n. 161; c. 1312, par. 1). It is understood, however, that superiors, if they are to proceed licitly, must always seek the good of their subjects or of the community over which they preside. Hence, a just cause is always required if an annulment of private vows is to be licit (c. 1312, par. 1).

146. Dispensations from Vows

The local Ordinary may directly dispense vows which have been professed in an **institute of diocesan approval,** or he may do so indirectly by granting an indult of secularization which implicitly carries with it a dispensation from vows (c. 638; c. 640, par. 1, n. 2).

The local Ordinary, namely, the Ordinary in whose diocese the religious seeking a dispensation dwells, not the Ordinary of the place where the mother house is located.

On the other hand, religious vows professed in an **institute of pontifical approval** may be dispensed only by the Holy See (c. 638; c. 640). When a dispensation from public vows is obtained from the Holy See, the religious in question can refuse to accept it, unless the Holy See determines otherwise (S.C.Rel., August 1, 1922; cf. *infra,* Part XIII, Chap. 3).

If the vows are temporary, they cease automatically when a religious is legitimately expelled from the institute in which the vows were professed. It makes no difference whether the institute is of pontifical or diocesan approval, as long as the vows are temporary (c. 648; cf. *infra,* n. 281).

147. The Vow of Poverty

The vow of poverty consists in the renunciation of the ownership, or at least of the free use, of temporal goods, because of the desire for supernatural perfection.

Because of the desire for supernatural perfection. Those who profess this vow seek to fulfill the invitation to perfection addressed by Christ to the young man: "If thou wilt be perfect, go, sell what thou hast, and give to the poor . . . and come, follow me" (Matt. 19-21).

There are four possible degrees of the vow of poverty:

1) The first consists in the renunciation of superfluous goods.

2) The second consists in the renunciation of the free and independent use of necessary things.

3) The third results in the renunciation of ownership of all goods presently possessed, and of the capacity to possess goods personally in the future.

4) The fourth consists in the renunciation of the capacity of possessing temporal goods personally or in common.

148. NECESSITY OF THE VOW

The vow of poverty is required by the very nature of the religious state (c. 487). Hence St. Thomas says (*Summa,* II-II, q. 186, a. 3):

> The religious state is an exercise and a school for attaining the perfection of charity. For this it is necessary that a man wholly withdraw his affections from worldly things; as Augustine says, speaking to God: "Too little does he love thee, who loves anything with thee, which he loveth not for thee" (Confessions, Bk. X, Chap. 29). Now the possession of worldly things draws a man's mind to the love of them; hence it is that in the attainment of the perfection of charity the first foundation is voluntary poverty, whereby a man lives without property of his own, according to the saying of our Lord in Saint Matthew (19:21): "If thou wilt be perfect, go, sell what thou hast, and give to the poor . . . and come, follow me."

The second degree of poverty, however, is sufficient for the essence of religious life.

Is sufficient. Objectively speaking, if a more perfect vow of poverty is professed, then a more perfect form of religious life is embraced; however, the essence of the vow of poverty is present if the religious binds herself merely to the obligation of renouncing the free use of necessary goods.

149. OBJECT OF THE VOW

Temporal goods which have monetary value, whether movable or immovable (for example, houses, land or money), are the object of the vow of poverty. Even if these things are made by the religious herself, such as statues or painting, they still are the object of the vow of poverty if they have a monetary value.

Spiritual goods, such as honor, reputation, and all the other internal goods of the soul, do not fall under the vow of poverty. Consequently, even professed religious retain a right to their honor and good name.

Relics are not matter for the vow of poverty because they are spiritual things without a monetary value. If a relic were included in an expensive reliquary, it would indirectly fall under the vow of poverty. The same thing may be said of statues, medals or rosaries, which because of the material of which they are composed, have a sizeable monetary value.

Do manuscripts, especially those written after the profession of vows, fall under the vow of poverty? This question was proposed to the Sacred Congregation of Religious, and on July 13, 1913, it answered that for all practical purposes, manuscripts are included under the vow of poverty. This is only right because although manuscripts are the result of spiritual work, they are nevertheless material things and have monetary value. This is especially true if the manuscripts are not personal, but are ancient books, or copies of valuable or ancient books. Nevertheless, the present custom in religious institutes, even of solemn vows, in virtue of which religious keep their own manuscripts and take them with them when they are transferred from one house to another, just as they take their clothing, books of piety or of study, is reasonable and may be retained.

150. Effects of the Vow

The simple and solemn vow of poverty have different effects. The **solemn vow of poverty** has the following effects:

1) It implies the renunciation of both useful and radical dominion or ownership of all material goods possessed by the religious at the time of profession (c. 581, par. 1).

Useful dominion or ownership means the power of owning, administrating and using temporal goods, as well as receiving any profit that might result from them.

Radical dominion or ownership means the basic right of ownership of temporal goods, exclusive of the right to administrate and use them.

2) It implies that the religious will not be able to acquire material goods in the future, no matter in what manner they come to her. Neither will she be able to use the material goods of others or the community freely; nor may she receive the revenue from them (c. 582).

3) It implies the inability to make wills, to incur obligations, or to make contracts regarding the use, the revenue or the ownership of temporal goods, without the permission of the superior. All of these acts are null and void if performed without the requisite permission (c. 579).

The **simple vow of poverty**, whether temporary or perpetual, implies the following:

1) The renunciation of the free use of all personal temporal goods, even though the radical ownership of these goods may be retained (c. 580, par. 1).

2) The renunciation of the administration of the goods which are possessed, so that a simply professed religious cannot make contracts nor administer her goods in any manner whatsoever without the permission of her superiors (c. 569, par. 1). Consequently, a religious about to take simple vows must cede the administration of her property to another moral or physical person so that she will never administer them again without special permission of her superior. She must also dispose of the use and revenue of her goods. The latter may be added to the capital sum, but it can never be used without the permission of the superior (c. 569, par. 1). Simple profession does not imply a renunciation of ownership. Therefore, the religious in simple vows may retain title to all property possessed before profession and may acquire more (c. 580, par. 1).

A religious in simple vows who performed actions contrary to the above regulations would act validly even though illicitly. Thus a sister who sold her property or gave it away would make a valid sale or gift, even though it would be illicit (c. 579).

The vow of poverty, whether simple or solemn, also implies the renunciation of all goods which the professed religious acquires through her own industry and all goods which she receives insofar as she is a religious (c. 580, par. 3; cf. *infra,* n. 173).

Through her own industry. Industry as such is not the object of the vow of poverty but the fruits of industry are. "Industry" includes any mental or mechanical work, even if it involves a skill acquired before entry into religious life. In case there is some doubt as to whether a religious received goods "insofar as she is a religious," or as a private individual, the presumption is that she received them because she is a religious (cf. c. 1536, par. 1).

A religious, after the profession of either simple or solemn vows, may licitly use temporal goods only when she does so with the permission of her superior and in conformity with the constitutions.

Permission to use temporal goods may be explicit or implicit, express or tacit, actual or presumed. One of these permissions must be present for licit use of temporal goods because of the renunciation of the free use of temporal goods made by profession.

Hence **a religious may transgress the simple or solemn vow of poverty in two ways:** either by breaking the vow alone, that is, by sinning against the virtue of religion alone, or by sinning against the virtue of justice at the same time. In either case, the sin may be mortal or venial depending upon the amount of matter involved.

A religious with the simple or solemn vow of poverty violates the vow alone if, without the permission of her superiors, she accepts temporal goods from those outside her institute, or if she administers, uses, or alienates goods over which she still retains radical ownership. In all these cases the religious fails in the promise of poverty she has made to God, but nevertheless she does not violate the rights of others, and though she acts illicitly, she does not violate the virtue of justice.

On the other hand, a religious would sin against the virtue of justice as well as the vow of poverty if she voluntarily destroyed or wasted goods of the institute, or if she appropriated the goods of others, or the goods of the monastery without the permission of the superior. In these cases, the religious would not only be unfaithful to a promise made to God but she would also injure the rights of others and consequently she would sin against the virtue of justice.

In matters of poverty, actual permission to use something or to administer something is not always required. *Tacit* and *presumed* permissions are sufficient under the following conditions:

1) In the case of a tacit permission it must be truly tacit, that is, the superior must know what is being done, must silently assent to it, and not command its opposite.

2) In order to use lawfully a presumed permission, it is necessary that there be no possibility of asking the superior for the permission, that it can be reasonably presumed that if the superior were present she would grant such a permission, and that the superior is later informed of the subject's action.

151. PENALTIES

Before the Code, several penalties were prescribed in the common law against those who violated the religious vow of poverty in grave matters. Among these penalties, the most noteworthy was the privation of active and passive voice for a period of two years (Council

of Trent, Sess. XXV, Cap. 2). The Code, however, makes no mention
of these penalties, and consequently, although they may be included
in the constitutions of individual institutes, they no longer exist in
virtue of common law (c. 6, n. 5).

152. THE VOW OF CHASTITY

**The vow of chastity is a promise made to God to abstain from
matrimony and all internal and external carnal pleasure.**

To abstain from matrimony; since a religious is bound by the vow
of chastity, her marriage would be invalid or at least illicit (cf. *infra,*
n. 154).

And from all carnal pleasure. We know that in virtue of the sixth
commandment some degree of chastity is obligatory for all. However,
the Gospels encourage us to practice a more complete and excellent
type of chastity which involves not only abstinence from unlawful
carnal pleasure (this is a matter of precept for all), but also abstinence
from those carnal pleasures which are permitted in the married state.

We may thus distinguish three kinds of chastity: *conjugal chastity,*
which consists in abstinence from all carnal pleasures except those
which are involved in acts imposed, or at least permitted, in the
married state; the *chastity of widows or widowers,* which consists in
abstinence from all sensual pleasure by a person who at one time was
married but whose spouse is now dead; and *perfect chastity* which
consists in renouncing all pleasures of the flesh, even those which
would be permitted in the married state. Perfect chastity is called
virginity when this total abstinence from carnal pleasure has never
been interrupted by any voluntary act of sensual pleasure, either inside or outside the married state.

Both internal and external. The offering of a virginal body to
God would mean little if the soul is guilty of impurity.

153. NECESSITY OF THE VOW

All religious must profess the vow of chastity since it is an essential
part of the religious state (c. 487). In the words of St. Thomas *(Summa,*
II-II, q. 186, a. 4):

> It is necessary for the religious state to be free from everything
> which can impede the total dedication of self to the service of

God. Now, even the lawful use of sensual pleasures is an obstacle
to the complete giving of the soul to the service of our Savior.
This is true for two reasons: first, because all carnal pleasure, by
reason of its very vehemence, increases concupiscence and consequently the soul is held back from a perfect and exclusive
searching for God; . . second, because of the care which the
government of a family (wife, children, the administration of
temporal goods) necessarily implies. Thus St. Paul writes in his
first Epistle to the Corinthians (7:32-33): "He who is unmarried
is concerned about the things of the Lord, how he may please
God. Whereas he who is married is concerned about the things
of the world, how he may please his wife." Consequently, perpetual, that is, perfect continence, no less than poverty, is required for the essence of the religious state.

Perfect chastity or even the chastity of widows is sufficient for the
religious state. Virginity is certainly most desirable in one who enters
the religious state but it is not absolutely required. This has always
been the mind of the Church and also the custom always observed
in practice.

The Church forbids widows to enter religion only when their help
is necessary for the maintenance and education of their children (c.
542, n. 2). The Church likewise forbids, under penalty of invalidity,
the entrance of spouses into religion, even though they are living
apart, or even if both of them promise to observe perfect chastity in
the future (c. 542, n. 1). Married men or women may not be admitted
into religion while their spouse is still living without the special permission of the Sovereign Pontiff—a permission which is not easily
obtained.

154. JURIDICAL EFFECTS

The **solemn vow of chastity,** validly pronounced in religion, has
the following effects:

1) It renders invalid any future attempt at marriage (c. 579; c.
1073). For this reason the solemn vow of chastity is numbered among
the diriment impediments of matrimony (c. 1073).

2) It severs the bond of a marriage if the marriage has been contracted but not consummated (c. 1119); hence it also breaks the bond
of a formal espousal (c. 1017, par. 3). The dissolution of a non-con-
summated marriage by religious profession is final; the bond does
not revivify if the religious obtains an indult of secularization.

The simple religious vow of chastity has the following effects:

1) It renders a marriage illicit but not invalid, unless a special privilege intervenes (c. 579; c. 1058).

Unless a special privilege intervenes. Just as the Holy See has attached to the solemn vow of chastity the effect of invalidating a marriage, so also may it attach the same effect to a simple religious vow of chastity. In order that a simple vow have this effect an express declaration is required (c. 1058; c. 1073).

2) The simple vow of chastity also severs the bond of espousals. Among the "just causes" for which one is allowed to break the bonds of espousals, simple or solemn religious profession is clearly included (c. 1017, par. 3).

155. Transgression of the Vow

If a religious who is bound by the vow of chastity were to violate the vow, either externally or internally, she would commit at least two sins. Or, as some moralists hold, she would be guilty of an act which has the malice of two specifically different sins, that is, an act which would be contrary at the same time to the virtue of chastity and the virtue of religion. Unlike the other vows, the matter of the vow of chastity is coextensive with the matter of the virtue of chastity. Consequently, a sin against the virtue is necessarily also a sin against the vow, and hence two sins are always involved, one against chastity and the other against religion. Due to this, a religious should make known to the confessor that she is bound by the vow of chastity everytime she must confess a sin against this vow.

A sin against the virtue of chastity is a true sacrilege. A sacrilege is the profanation of a sacred person, place or thing. A religious who has taken a vow of chastity in a religious institute approved by the Church, has offered to God, with the consent of the Church, her body and soul so that she becomes a consecrated being, set aside to honor God by the perfect observance of the virtue of chastity. Hence by failing to keep her vow she violates a sacred thing and thus commits a sacrilege.

156. Penalties

Religious who violate their vow of chastity may incur the following canonical penalties:

1) A religious bound by a **solemn vow of chastity** who attempts to contract matrimony, *ipso facto* incurs excommunication simply reserved to the Holy See. The same excommunication is incurred by anyone, no matter who he may be, who attempts to contract marriage with such a religious (c. 2388, par. 1).

Anyone who attempts marriage. We know, as was pointed out above (cf. *supra,* n. 154), that the marriage of a person with a solemn vow of chastity is always invalid. Hence the persons in question can only attempt to marry without actually contracting marriage, and the censure punishes this attempt to marry. It follows that the censure is not incurred by concubinage, even though it be public; a religious or civil celebration of matrimony is required.

A religious with **simple perpetual vows** who contracts marriage, *ipso facto* incurs excommunication reserved to the Ordinary, but in this case the marriage is valid (c. 2388, par. 2).

With simple perpetual vows. To incur the censure, it is not sufficient that the religious merely belong to an institute in which perpetual vows are professed, she must have actually pronounced perpetual vows.

A religious with a **simple temporary vow of chastity** who contracts marriage does not incur any of the above penalties or censures. However, when she contracts marriage she commits a very grave sin against the vow of chastity.

157. THE VOW OF OBEDIENCE

The religious vow of obedience is a promise made to God to obey the lawful superiors of a religious institute, in conformity with the rule and constitutions of the institute, in all those matters which, directly or indirectly pertain to regular observance.

A promise made to God. Although religious with a vow of obedience are subject to the lawful superiors of the institute, the promise to obey these superiors is not made to them but to God and this constitutes the very essence of the vow.

To obey the lawful superiors of a religious institute. We shall point out later who these superiors are (n. 160). Here it is sufficient to note that the vow of obedience does not oblige a religious to subject herself, in virtue of the vow, to all superiors, but only to those to whom she expressly or implicitly promised obedience. Even to these superiors she is not subject in all things, but only in those matters which pertain to regular observance.

In conformity with the rule and constitutions of the institute. There are many means which are capable of leading one to the practice of Christian perfection, but among these means there are some which are more adapted to the end of the institute in which profession is made. These are set down in the particular rule and constitutions of the institute. The religious intends to commit herself to the practice of these means, and not any others, when she professes obedience. Hence superiors cannot command, in virtue of obedience, that which is contrary to the rule and constitutions.

In all those matters which pertain to regular observance. When a religious makes profession, she promises God to strive for Christian and evangelical perfection, which, as we have seen (cf. *supra*, n. 1 and n. 2), consists principally in the observance of certain practices of virtue which are capable of leading one to spiritual perfection.

Directly or indirectly. It can happen that many things which are not expressly mentioned in the rule and constitutions may, because of special circumstances, prove useful or even necessary to attain personal perfection or the end of the institute. It is evident that these things also become means which the superior may and ought to use for the good government of the institute, and hence they may become the matter of the vow of obedience.

158. NECESSITY OF THE VOW

The vow of obedience belongs to the very essence of the religious state (c. 487). This is proven by St. Thomas *(Summa,* II-II, q. 186, a. 5) in the following manner:

> The religious state is a school or training ground for tending to perfection. Now those who are being instructed or trained to attain a certain end must follow the direction of someone under whose control they are instructed or trained, so as to attain that end as disciples under a master. Hence religious need to be placed under the instruction and command of someone in regard to things pertaining to the religious life . . . . Now one man is subjected to another's command and instruction by obedience. Consequently, obedience is requisite for religious perfection, that is, for the religious state.

St. Thomas confirms this conclusion by another argument:

Religious perfection consists chiefly in the imitation of Christ, according to Matt., 19:21: "If thou wilt be perfect, go sell what thou hast and give to the poor . . . and come, follow me." Now in Christ, obedience is commended above all, according to Phil., 2:8: "Becoming obedient to death." Hence it is evident that obedience belongs to the perfection of the religious life *(loc. cit.).*

The vow of obedience, considered in itself, is more excellent than the vows of poverty and chastity. By the vow of poverty temporal goods are renounced. These goods belong to their possessor, it is true, but they are extrinsic to her person. By the vow of chastity something closer to man, something which forms a part of his very person, is renounced, but it is merely pleasure of the sensory order. The vow of obedience, on the other hand, demands the giving up of the will by subjecting it in many things to the will of lawful superiors. Since freedom and the will are much more noble and precious than all other temporal or corporeal goods or pleasures, it follows that obedience is more excellent that poverty or chastity.

The object of the religious vow of obedience is more extensive than the objects of the other two vows, moreover, it includes the other vows, because a religious who promises to obey her lawful superiors in conformity with the rule and constitutions of an institute, necessarily promises to live in conformity with this rule which always includes as essential elements the vows of poverty and chastity (cf. *supra,* n. 1). Hence it is, that in the formula of profession of some religious institutes (for example, in the Dominican Order), only the vow of obedience is expressly mentioned, but it implicitly includes the intention of taking the three vows of poverty, chastity and obedience.

159. THE OBJECT OF THE VOW

The specific object of the religious vow of obedience is the precept or command of the lawful superior whenever it is directly or indirectly in conformity with the rule and constitutions. The vow of obedience consists in the subjection of the will of the religious to the will of the lawful superiors of the institute in which profession is made. But this subjection of the will is not without limits; it is in conformity with the end and the legitimately approved rule of the institute, as we have seen above (n. 25). It is evident, therefore, as St. Thomas points out *(Summa,* II-II, q. 104, a. 5) that:

1) Obedience to lawful superiors when they command what is in conformity with the rule is binding in conscience, that is, it is binding under pain of sin. Some maintain that a command must be a formal precept to bind one under pain of sin by reason of the vow of obedience. But all agree that a religious at least sins against the virtue of obedience if she acts contrary to any precept of her superior, whether it is a formal precept or not. The sin against the vow or virtue of obedience will be grave or light according to the nature of the command or at least according to the gravity of the thing commanded. Thus there certainly exists an obligation for religious who have made profession to obey their lawful superiors.

2) When, on the other hand, a superior commands what is good in itself but is outside of the rule, that is, neither directly nor indirectly contemplated by the rule, to obey in this case pertains to the perfection of obedience, but it is not obligatory. For example, when a religious who belongs to an institute which has as its exclusive end the education of children is commanded by her superior to care for an impoverished sick person, it would be a good thing to obey since it could lead one to the heights of perfection, but obedience in this case would not be obligatory because the religious did not promise in her profession to care for the sick.

3) If instead of commanding something which is good, though not contemplated by the rule, a superior should command something which is against the rule, or still worse, if she should command something which is sinful, it is evident that a religious is not only not obliged to obey, but she may not obey. As St. Thomas concludes, *(loc. cit.)* such obedience would be unlawful. For example, if a superior should command a religious to transgress a precept of God or the Church; if she should command a religious not to observe the law of enclosure when the observance of the cloister is obligatory; in these and similar cases it is evident that religious are not bound to obey and that they must not obey.

Hence relative to this question we can distinguish with St. Thomas three kinds of obedience: one, sufficient for salvation, by which a religious avoids sin and obeys in all those matters in which she is obliged to obey; the second, a more perfect obedience by which a religious obeys her superior in *all* lawful matters; and a third, which is called indiscreet obedience, by which a religious obeys even in unlawful matters *(loc. cit.)*.

In order that a precept or command be binding in conscience, it is sufficient that it be included either directly or indirectly in the rule. As we have said above, there are many things which are not explicitly prescribed by the rule but which are included insofar as they may be opportune means to attain the end of the rule. All of these things fall indirectly under the rule and are the object of the religious vow of obedience. In case of doubt as to whether a thing is included in the rule, the presumption is always in favor of the superior. Hence it must be presumed that, if a superior commands something, it is at least implicitly included within the limits of the rule. Consequently, a religious is obliged in conscience to obey, at least until the doubt is settled.

On the other hand, all the prescriptions of the rule are the object of the vow of obedience only when this is expressly stated in the rule itself. Religious in their profession do not promise obedience to the rule, but only to conform their religious life to the rule; that is, they intend to oblige themselves to obey the rule in the manner and to the extent prescribed by the rule itself. Consequently, if in the rule it is stated expressly that each and every prescription obliges under pain of sin and in virtue of the vow of obedience, as is true in the rule of some Orders, then it is evident that the object of the vow includes all the prescriptions of the rule. But if in the rule it is stated that no prescription of the rule obliges under pain of sin, but only to the penalty which the superior may impose for the transgression of the rule itself (which is true of the rule and constitutions of the Dominican Order), then the prescriptions of the rule do not fall under the matter of the vow.

The precepts of God and of the Church which affect all Christians do not fall under the matter of the vow of obedience. However, religious are held to obey in virtue of the vow of obedience all ecclesiastical laws which pertain exclusively to them. The reason for this is substantially the same as that given above: a religious in making her profession intends to oblige herself to obey only her lawful religious superiors in conformity with the rule of her own religious institute. She does not intend to obey everyone nor does she intend that everything will be the object of obedience. Therefore, if a religious should break one of the commandments (for example, if she should tell a lie), she would not commit two sins, one against truth and another against the vow of obedience, but only one sin against truth. Likewise, if a religious eats meat on Friday or does not attend Mass on Sunday, she would not commit a sin against the vow of obedience, but she would be guilty of a violation of a precept of the Church.

160. OBLIGATION OF OBEDIENCE

In virtue of the vow of obedience, a professed religious must obey the following:

1) The Sovereign Pontiff, not only as the supreme head of the Church, but as the lawful and proper superior of the religious institute of which she is a member (c. 499, par. 1; cf. *supra*, n. 28). The reason for this is clear: it is in the name of the Sovereign Pontiff and with his authorization that the Order or religious institute has been founded, and it is in his name and in virtue of his authority that the religious superiors may receive the profession of members of their institute (cf. *supra*, n. 2; and *infra*, Part VII, Chap. 7). The Pope, then, is the supreme prelate of each and every Order and religious insitute, and religious owe him obedience in all things pertaining to religious life, not only as the supreme head of the Church but also as the superior of the institute.

2) By reason of their vow, professed religious must also obey the particular superiors of the institute of which they are members—that is, local, provincial and general superiors, major and minor superiors. It is to these superiors that the religious in her profession promises obedience, and it is to these superiors that she confides herself for direction in the daily exercise of religious perfection (cf. *supra*, n. 159).

In order that the commands of superiors be obliging, however, it is required that the superiors be validly elected or appointed and that they lawfully take possession of their office (cf. *supra*, n. 72).

3) Women religious must obey the local Ordinary in some things, but the Code does not expressly state whether they are bound to obey him by reason of their vow of obedience. It seems that in this regard the following distinctions should be made:

a) If in the formula of profession, obedience is promised to the bishop in addition to the proper religious superiors, then it is clear that there is an obligation to obey the bishop even in virtue of the vow of obedience. The same is to be said if it is prescribed in the constitutions that the local Ordinary should be obeyed, even if the local Ordinary is not mentioned in the formula of profession.

b) In other cases, it is not easy to say whether the obligation to obey the local Ordinary arises from the jurisdiction he has in the Church or by virtue of the vow of obedience. Those who maintain it arises from the vow base their opinion on the parallel which exists between the Pope and the bishops: in virtue of canon 499, paragraph 1, they maintain that religious owe obedience to the Pope by virtue of their religious vow; hence, within the limits of his jurisdiction, the same must also be said relative to the local Ordinary, and this is especially true if the religious belong to an institute of diocesan approval. Those who maintain that obedience is not owed to the local Ordinary in virtue of the vow, give the following argument: the obedience which is to be given by religious in virtue of the vow extends only as far as is promised when profession is made. Now, it is understood that the will of the Church expressed in the Code demands that religious give obedience to the Sovereign Pontiff even in virtue of the vow, but there is no mention made of the local Ordinary; consequently, the local Ordinary is excluded from this prescription. This opinion seems to be preferable.

4) If professed women religious of exempt institutes are under the jurisdiction of the superior of the Order to which they are affiliated, then they owe obedience to these superiors. However, they need obey them only in those matters in which, according to the constitutions or the common law, they are dependent upon the regular superiors.

If women religious are not exempt, their vow of obedience in no way obliges them to obey regular superiors of the Order to which they are affiliated. Moreover, if it is a question of sisters, the Code expressly forbids the aforementioned regular superiors to govern, without a special apostolic indult, religious congregations of women, even when they belong to the same order (c. 500, par. 3).

161. Effects of the Vow

The **solemn vow of obedience** renders the person bound by the vow incapable of contracting any new personal obligations, burdensome or contrary to religious life, without the permission of the lawful superior (cf. c. 579).

Incapable. By solemn profession a religious gives up, not only the use of her will, but the will itself (cf. *supra,* n. 158), and consequently, she is unable to contract onerous obligations in regard to the religious life without the permission of the proper superior to whom she is subject. If she attempts to assume such obligations, they are *ipso facto* invalid (c. 579).

Without the permission of the lawful superior. The implicit consent of the superior is sufficient, at least for the validity of the contract by which new obligations are assumed.

Any new personal obligation, burdensome or contrary to the religious life; that is, any personal obligation which is assumed on the religious' own initiative and which imposes an obligation contrary to the vow of obedience or the religious life. If some obligation is assumed by the whole community or by the entire institute, it is clear that the obligation is binding and obliges all the individual members of the institute. Likewise, a vow is binding if it is not onerous relative to the religious life, for example, a vow to practice humility (cf. *supra,* n. 145).

The **simple religious vow of obedience** renders rescissible by the superiors any obligation assumed by individual religious which are onerous to the religious life (c. 1312, par. 1).

Renders rescissible. Therefore, such obligations are not invalidly but only illicitly assumed. One of the important differences between the simple and solemn vows of obedience is that the solemn vow renders the religious incapable of contracting any personal obligation which is onerous to the religious life, while the simple vow makes such actions only illicit. The religious with solemn vows has consecrated to God not only the use of her will, but her very will itself, just as by the vow of poverty she has given up not only the use of temporal goods but the very capacity to possess them. Hence, she cannot validly perform an action contrary to the will of her superior since she no longer has a will of her own. The religious with the simple vow of obedience dedicates to God the use of her will in accordance with the rule and constitutions. Hence, she "retains" her will and may perform actions looked upon as valid by the law, even if these actions are performed without the permission of the superior.

But because those in simple vows have at least subjected themselves to the dominative power of their superiors, the superiors may declare that an obligation which is contrary to the religious state is no longer obliging (c. 501; c. 1312).

162. Transgression of the Vow

The transgression of the vow of obedience always involves two specifically different sins—one against the virtue of religion, and another against the virtue of obedience—or as some theologians say, it involves one sin with two specifically different malices. The religious who violates her vow of obedience sins against the virtue of religion because she violates a promise made to God; she sins against the virtue of obedience because a religious, even independently of the vow, is obliged as a subject to show reverence and submission to the precepts and directives of her superior.

Nevertheless, since the object of the virtue of obedience is more extensive than the object of the vow of obedience, a sin against the virtue of obedience does not always involve a sin against the vow. For example, a religious is bound to obey lawful civil authority, not however, in virtue of the vow, but only because of her duty as a citizen. On the other hand, the vow obliges religious to obey, in virtue of the vow, only the proper superiors, in the sense explained above (n. 160).

In order for the vow of obedience to bind under penalty of grave sin, it is necessary that the thing commanded be of a grave nature. Obedience is a virtue which admits of lightness of matter; hence the vow of obedience also admits of degrees in the manner in which it obliges. The transgression will be grave or light according as the thing commanded is of a grave or light nature. The thing commanded can be grave either in itself (for example, the command to go from one convent to another), or it can be grave by reason of circumstances. For example, if a superior commands a sister not to go to some particular place in order to protect the religious from grave moral danger.

The obligation of obeying is always grave when the command is accompanied by a formal precept. Thus, for example, when a superior commands something *in virtute Spiritus Sancti et sanctae obedientiae,* that is, in virtue of the Holy Ghost and of holy obedience, or, *sub praecepto formali,* that is, under formal precept, the command is given *sub gravi,* that is, under pain of mortal sin, and the subject must accept it as such, even if the thing commanded may seem to be of small importance.

163. PENALTIES

The Code does not determine any fixed penalty for transgressions against the vow of obedience. Penalties for such transgressions are ordinarily determined by the constitutions of each religious institute. Moreover, since superiors have the right to command in virtue of the vow, they themselves may determine the penalty for each transgression against their commands and they may determine the penalty before or after the transgression. The penalty itself may be imposed, if it is considered opportune, under obedience, that is, in virtue of the vow of obedience.

VII

RELIGIOUS PROFESSION

Religious profession, in a broad sense, **is any public affirmation of the will to practice any form of a life of perfection in conformity with the rule of a religious institute.** In this sense, even tertiaries of a religious order are said to make profession in the Third Order. In the strict sense of the word, however, **religious profession is the public profession of vows in a religious institute approved by the Church.** Hence the essence of a true religious profession consists in the profession of vows. But in order that the profession be valid, the vows must be public and they must be pronounced in the manner prescribed by the constitutions of each religious institute (cf. *supra,* n. 2).

Religious profession, when it has been accepted by the superiors of the institute in which profession is made, takes the form of a bilateral contract which is binding upon both parties. It obliges the religious to the observance of the rule and the vows, and it obliges the religious institute to recognize all the rights and duties which belong to the professed in virtue of the rule of the institute (c. 572, par. 1).

164. KINDS OF PROFESSION

Religious profession may be:

1) *Simple* or *solemn*. It is simple when simple vows are professed; it is solemn when solemn vows are professed (cf. c. 574, par. 1; cf. *supra*, n. 143).

2) *Temporary* or *perpetual*. It is temporary, when the vows are taken for a definite time, for example, for one year, three years or five years; it is perpetual when the vows are taken until death (cf. c. 574; cf. *supra*, n. 143). Simple profession may be temporary or perpetual, but solemn profession is always, and of its nature, perpetual (cf. *supra*, n. 143).

165. ADMISSION TO FIRST PROFESSION

Admission to first profession is governed by the following discipline:

1) When the novitiate is completed, the novice shall be admitted to profession if she is judged suitable, otherwise she shall be sent away. If a doubt arises regarding her suitability, the major superior, with or without consulting her counsel, can prolong the time of probation but not beyond six months (c. 571, par. 2; cf. *supra*, n. 128).

But not beyond six months. This is true whether the novitiate lasts for only one year, or for two or more years; the Code, realizing that the duration of the novitiate may differ from one institute to another, speaks in general of the power of superiors to prolong the time of probation for another six months (cf. *supra*, n. 128). The rules governing the interruption of the novitiate are not applicable to the six months of prolonged novitiate in all their rigor, certainly not under the penalty of invalidity of profession (cf. *supra*, n. 129).

2) To admit a novice to profession pertains to the lawful superiors with the vote of the council or the chapter, in conformity with the constitutions of each religious institute (c. 572, par. 1, n. 2; cf. *infra*, n. 166, par. 3).

We are not speaking here of admission to profession insofar as it implies the reception of profession; rather, we are speaking of the decision of the superiors regarding the worthiness of the novices to be admitted to profession and of the corresponding consent of the chapter or council. "Admittance to profession" and "reception of profession" must be clearly distinguished since they are two different juridical acts and are often in the power of different superiors.

The vote of the council or of the chapter is deliberative for first profession; it is only consultative for simple perpetual or solemn profession (c. 575, par. 2). If the superior chooses to prolong temporary profession (c. 574, par. 2), or if the constitutions call for a frequent renewal of temporary vows, the council or chapter need not be consulted.

3) In institutes of religious women, before novices are admitted to profession, a canonical examination of their vocation is required (c. 552, par. 2). This examination must be made at least thirty days before profession by the local Ordinary or by a priest delegated by him. Regarding the manner of conducting the examination and the penalties imposed upon superiors who fail to inform the Ordinary of the approaching profession, see number 125, above.

4) A spiritual retreat of at least eight whole days must precede profession (c. 571, par. 3). Consequently, if a retreat of only eight days is made both the first and last day must be spent entirely on retreat. From a strict interpretation of the Code it would seem that a retreat is obligatory only before first profession; the canon cited mentions only novices who are to take vows and hence it is speaking only of first profession. Regarding succeeding professions, the Code merely says that the rite prescribed by the constitutions must be observed (c. 576, par. 1). However, whether or not the constitutions prescribe a retreat before all professions, it certainly is in accordance with the spirit of the Code and in conformity with the nature of religious profession that at least a short retreat should precede every religious profession.

5) Novices who are sisters must make a will before profession; those who are nuns, however, are not required to do so (cf. *supra,* n. 132).

Superiors who admit an unsuitable candidate to profession may be punished, even to the extent of being excluded from office (c. 2411).

6) First profession must be made in the novitiate house (c. 574, par. 1), but this prescription does not affect the validity of the profession.

166. REQUIREMENTS FOR A VALID PROFESSION

In conformity with canon 572, the following conditions are required for a valid religious profession:

1) Legitimate age, that is, sixteen years completed for temporary profession, and twenty-one years completed for perpetual profession, whether simple or solemn (c. 572, par. 1, n. 1). The years must be computed in conformity with canon 34, paragraph 3, number 3 (cf. *supra*, n. 125). Hence profession cannot be made until the day after the year, or years, of novitiate is completed.

2) A valid novitiate must have been made (c. 572, par. 1, n. 3).

A *valid novitiate*; that is, one made under all the conditions enumerated above for a valid novitiate. If the novitiate is invalid, all ensuing professions are invalid.

It is not absolutely necessary that profession be made immediately after the novitiate. However, we must remember that the novitiate is closely connected with profession inasmuch as the novitiate is a preparation for profession. Therefore, the profession should not be put off for a long time, or indefinitely, and it should not be delayed at all if there is not a just cause for doing so. It should never be put off for more than six months unless for a most grave cause.

3) The consent of the legitimate superiors, in accordance with the particular constitutions of the institute; is necessary (c. 572, par. 1, n. 2). The constitutions of each religious institute must determine which superiors will admit to profession and how they must express their consent. The Code merely states that the vote of the council or of the chapter is required, and that it is deliberative for the first temporary profession, but only consultative for subsequent professions (c. 575, par. 2). Consequently, a superior cannot validly admit a novice to first profession if she has been rejected by the council or the chapter. As far as validity is concerned, however, a superior can admit a professed religious to perpetual or solemn profession even if the council or the chapter has rejected her. It is evident, nevertheless, that outside of very exceptional cases it is not prudent to act against the will of the council and chapter in this matter.

4) The profession must be made freely, without violence, grave fear or fraud (c. 572, par. 1, n. 4). Anyone, of whatever dignity, who in any manner forces a person to make religious profession, whether simple or solemn, temporary or perpetual, incurs excommunication (c. 2352).

5) The profession must be expressed in formal terms, that is, the

person who wishes to make profession must state expressly, through words, signs or writing, that she intends to do so (c. 572, par. 1, n. 5). In virtue of the Code, a tacit or presumed profession is no longer valid.

6) The profession must be received by the legitimate superior, either personally or by a delegate (c. 572, par. 1, n. 6).

The Code does not say who this legitimate superior is and so the constitutions of each institute must be followed. Generally speaking, however, in the case of religious women, it is not the bishop or the regular superior or the priest who presides at the ceremonies who receives the profession, but rather the local, provincial or general superior of the institute, or a sister delegated by one of these superiors.

In some institutes of women (for example, the Daughters of Charity of St. Vincent de Paul), the three vows of religion are professed, but they are not received by the superior. Instead of professing them before the superior the sisters profess them before God. Institutes of this kind are not true religious institutes; rather, they are pious unions or societies of men or women living in common without vows.

In the formula of profession in certain congregations of religious women of pontifical approval, no mention is made of the superior, but only of the local Ordinary or his delegate. In such cases, is the Ordinary or his delegate to be considered as the legitimate superior for receiving profession? The Pontifical Commission for the Interpretation of the Code replied to this question in the affirmative (March 1, 1921).

7) The formula of profession is not determined by the Code. However, it can be, and generally is, determined by the constitutions, and the use of the proper formula obliges under pain of invalidity, if the constitutions so state.

8) It is not required by the Code that the written formula of the profession be signed by witnesses. However, if witnesses are prescribed by the constitutions, and they usually are, they must sign the formula and under pain of invalidity, if the constitutions declare this (c. 576, par. 2).

167. VALIDATION OF AN INVALID PROFESSION

Religious profession may be invalid for many reasons, as is evident from what has been said above (n. 166). Hence **if the religious profession is null because of some external impediment,** for example, if it was made before the candidate completed her sixteenth year, it may be validated by a *sanation* granted by the Holy See, or by a renewal of profession when the impediment has been discovered and removed (c. 586, par. 1).

An external impediment. An external impediment as contrasted with an internal impediment is one that can be proven in the external forum.

It may be validated by a sanation. A sanation is a legal fiction by which some action, such as religious profession or marriage, which was invalidly performed, but which could have been validly performed with a dispensation from the impediment that made it invalid, is considered to have been validly performed insofar as the legal effects of the action are concerned. For example, if a religious made an invalid solemn profession, then her renunciation of property would have also been invalid. By a sanation of the profession, however, the renunciation is considered valid from the time of the original invalid profession.

Since the publication of the Code, a tacit profession, which occurred when a religious lived as though she had been validly professed, is no longer allowed as a means of validating a profession (c. 586, par. 1).

If, on the other hand, **the profession is null because of a purely internal defect of consent,** it is validated by the giving of consent provided that the consent on the part of the institute has not been withdrawn (c. 586, par. 2). A novice, for example, who, in pronouncing the formula of profession maliciously withholds her internal consent, the profession is certainly null and void. To make it valid, however, it is not necessary that she seek a sanation or even that she make known her fault, except to her confessor. If the superiors have not revoked their consent, it is sufficient that she internally give true consent and the profession becomes by that very fact valid.

When doubt arises as to the validity of the profession, that is, if

there be serious arguments against the validly of the religious profession, and the religious refuses to renew the profession or to petition for its validation, the matter shall be referred to the Apostolic
See (c. 586, par. 3). It is not lawful, therefore, either on the part of
the religious or on the part of the institute to remain in doubt regarding the validity of the profession. When a well-founded doubt
arises, it is necessary either to renew the profession, or to ask the Holy
See for a precautionary validation *(validatio ad cautelam)*, or to present the case to the Holy See so that it may be examined and it can
be determined what action should be taken.

May a religious ever leave her institute because of an invalid profession without consulting the Holy See? If it is objectively certain
that the profession is invalid, she may leave without recourse because
if the profession is certainly invalid, there is no bond which obliges
her to remain in religion. However, it is necessary to avoid scandal,
and hence, although there is no need of a formal process, the invalidity of the profession should be made known to others. If the religious
is only subjectively certain that her profession is invalid, then the
case must be referred to the Holy See. Before a state of life which
was to all intents and purposes publicly and freely accepted can be
set aside, a statement by public authority must intervene in which
the action by which the state was embraced is declared invalid. Otherwise, anyone who deluded herself into thinking her profession was
invalid would be juridically free to leave religion.

168. CEREMONIAL OF PROFESSION

In making the religious profession, the rite prescribed by the constitutions must be observed (c. 576, par. 1). However, everything in
the ceremonies of institutes of solemn or perpetual vows which refers
to the perpetuity of the religious state (for example, the blessing of
the ring or veil), is to be reserved for solemn or perpetual profession
(S.C.Rel., July 10, 1919). There is no prohibition against giving a
certain solemnity to the first profession of temporary vows, although
those ceremonies which signify perpetuity must not be used.

If profession is made or renewed during Mass, it may be made
immediately after the first gospel. Otherwise, it should be made in
the following manner: "The celebrant who is to receive the profession, after having consumed the precious Blood, turns toward the

candidates, holding in his hands the Sacred Host. Each candidate reads aloud the formula of profession and thereupon receives the Blessed Sacrament" (S.C.Rel., August 14, 1894).

The first profession must always be made in the house of novitiate (c. 574, par. 1), but this is not required for validity.

A written document signed by the person professed and at least by the superior before whom the profession was made, attesting to the fact that the profession has been made, must be preserved in the archives of the institute (c. 576, par. 2).

At least before the superior. It is a praiseworthy custom observed in many institutes to confirm the written declaration of the profession by the testimony of two witnesses.

In the case of solemn profession, the superior who receives it must inform the pastor of the place where the professed was baptized (c. 576, par. 2). Solemn profession is an impediment which invalidates matrimony and hence it is necessary to make a note of it in the baptismal record so that if for any reason a certificate of baptism is requested there will be a record of the fact that the person has taken solemn vows in a religious institute (c. 470, par. 2).

169. RENEWAL OF PROFESSION

When the period for which temporary vows have been professed has expired, there must be no delay in either pronouncing perpetual or solemn profession, or in renewing simple vows (c. 577, par. 1).

The Code forbids professed religious to be without vows even for a brief period of time. It should be noted, however, that in virtue of canon 34, paragraph 3, number 5, the profession may be renewed at any hour on the anniversary day of the previous profession. For example, if profession is made at eight o'clock in the morning on March 1, the useful time for renewing the profession is the entire day of March 1 of the following year. Thus, the vows endure for the entire anniversary day of the profession, if the profession has been made for one or more years.

The years in this case are to be taken as they are in the calendar, that is, without taking into account whether it is a leap year or not. For example, if profession is made on March 1, the year ends at midnight on March 1 of the following year, even if it is a leap year, that is, even if there are 29 instead of 28 days in the month of February of that year.

If there is a delay between the expiration of vows and their renewal, the new profession would be illicit but not invalid. It would be merely illicit since the Code does not say that a new profession must be made on the day that the old one expires in order to be valid (c. 577, par. 1). However, if such a delay occurs in the profession of temporary vows which must precede solemn or perpetual vows, then the computation of years is reckoned from the day on which the vows are actually pronounced, not from the day on which they should have been pronounced, because three entire years must be spent as a professed religious before one may profess perpetual or solemn vows.

The lawful superiors, that is, the superiors who have the power according to the constitutions to admit to profession, can, for a just cause, permit the anticipation of the renewal of temporary profession, but not by more than a month (c. 577, par. 2).

Solemn or perpetual profession may never be anticipated, not even by a few days. When the Code speaks of anticipating profession it mentions only the renewal of temporary profession and it in no way indicates that the three year period required for solemn or perpetual profession may be shortened. Hence when the temporary vows have expired, and it is considered opportune to delay the making of solemn or perpetual profession for a few days, for example, to await a certain solemnity or the return of the superior general, it is necessary to renew the temporary profession for the entire time which remains until the solemnity or the return of the superior general.

Religious profession must always be renewed publicly, that is, in the presence of the community or at least before the lawful superiors in accordance with the particular constitutions. A record of the renewal of profession must also be kept in the archives of the monastery. No external solemnity, however, is required.

Hence the private renewal of vows after Holy Communion or on a certain special feast day may be commendable as an act of devotion and as a confirmation of good will before God, but juridically it in no way affects, either as to time or obligations, the public profession which is made in the form prescribed by the Church. When temporary profession is renewed there is no need to repeat the canonical examination. This is required only before the first temporary profession and perpetual profession (c. 552, par. 2).

170. EFFECTS OF PROFESSION

Every valid religious profession, whether simple or solemn, temporary or perpetual, for the time of its duration obliges the religious to the observance of the vows, the rule and the constitutions (c. 593).

Even if the profession is temporary, no professed religious may leave religion before the time of her profession expires, unless she first obtains a dispensation from her vows (c. 644). If she does leave without this permission she commits a grave sin; and if she has made perpetual profession, she would become an apostate from religion (c. 644; cf. *infra*, n. 274 ff.).

Once religious profession is made, all private vows which were made before profession are suspended during the time that the professed remains in religion (c. 1315). If private vows are made after profession and they are contrary to the religious state, they are either invalid, or at least they may be annulled (c. 501, par. 1; cf. *supra*, n. 145).

They are suspended; that is, there is no longer any obligation to observe them if they were made before profession. However, they do not completely cease to exist, so they would immediately become obligatory again if the religious were to leave religion (cf. *supra*, n. 145).

Those who have made perpetual or temporary profession in any religious institute cannot at the same time belong to any Third Order, even if they belonged to it before profession. However, if a religious for some reason returns to secular life, she becomes once again a member of the Third Order she belonged to before profession (c. 704, par. 1 and par. 2).

Cannot at the same time belong to any Third Order. Here it is a question of a secular Third Order, because, as we have seen above, the general of an Order with which a Third Order is affiliated can permit a religious institute to adopt the rule of the Regular Third Order when the institute has been affiliated with the First Order (cf. *supra*, n. 8, C).

No novice or professed religious, except in case of necessity and with the permission of at least the local superior, may act as sponsor at baptism or confirmation (c. 766, n. 4; c. 796, n. 3). To be sponsor at baptism or confirmation outside of a case of necessity, a novice or professed religious must obtain a dispensation from the Sacred Congregation of Religious.

Even if the religious professes only simple vows, the goods that she acquires after profession due to her own industry or insofar as she is a religious, belong not to her, but to the institute (c. 580, par. 2).

By her own industry; as, for example, needlework, painting, teaching or writing.

Insofar as she is a religious; that is, when an offering is made to a person, not because she is Mary or Dorothy, but precisely because she is a religious, or the superior of the convent. In case of doubt a presumption exists that the gifts are given because the person receiving them is a religious (cf. c. 1536).

171. Profession in Danger of Death

Before the publication of the Code, in virtue of a decree of the Sacred Congregation of Religious, September 10, 1912, novices of any religious institute who were at the point of death were permitted to make profession even before completing their novitiate. However, if they regained their health, they had to renew their profession as if it had never been made. The Code makes no mention of making profession at the point of death and hence a doubt arose as to whether it is still permitted. The question was authoritatively settled by the Sacred Congregation of Religious, December 30, 1922, when it declared that profession at the point of death is still lawful and prescribed the following conditions regarding it:

1) The novitiate must have been canonically begun.

2) The formula of profession should be the same as that used in the institute outside the case of illness; and the vows should be pronounced without any determination of time.

3) Not only the major superiors, but also the superior of the house of novitiate, or her delegate, may receive the profession. And, it is not necessary that it be received in the novitiate house.

4) The religious institute may not claim for itself the temporal goods of the novice if she dies after having made profession.

The aforesaid profession made at the point of death ceases to have any effect, either on the part of the novice or on the part of the religious institute, if the novice regains her health. Consequently:

1) The novice who has recovered her health may freely return to the world if she wishes.

2) The institute is free to dismiss her.

3) She must continue her novitiate for the entire time required by the constitutions.

4) At the expiration of this time she must renew her profession observing all the formalities and conditions as though she had never been professed (S.C. Rel., *loc. cit.*).

The novice who is professed at the point of death, besides sharing in all the indulgences, suffrages and privileges of her particular institute, also receives a special plenary indulgence in the jubilee form (cf. S.C. Rel., *loc. cit.*).

VIII

SIMPLE PROFESSION

Simple profession is that in which only simple vows are professed (cf. *supra*, n. 143). It is either temporary or perpetual, according as the vows are taken forever, or for a definite period of time; for example, for one year, three or five years.

Before the sixteenth century, simple religious vows were entirely unknown. In religious institutes, whether of men or of women, only solemn vows were pronounced (cf. *infra*, Part VII, Chap. 9).

172. NECESSITY AND CONDITIONS

Simple temporary profession must always precede the profession of simple perpetual or solemn vows (c. 574, par. 1).

Simple temporary profession may not be made before the completion of the candidate's sixteenth year of age (c. 573). The years are to be computed in accordance with canon 34, paragraph 3, number 3, that is, profession may not be made until the day after the completion of the sixteenth year. Moreover, all of the conditions listed above for the making of all types of profession must be observed (cf. *supra*, n. 165).

The question as to which superior has the right to admit candidates to profession has been discussed above (n. 165).

173. EFFECTS OF SIMPLE PROFESSION

Simple profession, whether temporary or perpetual, always produces the following effects:

1) It renders acts contrary to the vows illicit, but not invalid. However, if particular constitutions approved by the Church should state that certain acts contrary to the vows are invalid when performed by religious in simple vows, then these actions must be considered null and void (c. 579).

Hence, according to the common law, matrimony contracted by a religious with simple vows is illicit during the period of the vows. Nevertheless, once contracted, the marriage is valid. Furthermore, a gift made from her personal property is illicit, but valid. But these and other actions could be rendered invalid by particular constitutions which have been approved by the Church.

2) A religious with simple vows retains the ownership or radical dominion of her property and the capacity to acquire more property unless the constitutions determine otherwise (c. 580, par. 1). However, she may not administer the property herself; therefore, before profession she must cede, for the whole period during which she will be bound by simple vows, the administration of her property to whomsoever she wishes (c. 569, par. 1). Unless the constitutions determine otherwise, or unless special permission is obtained from the Holy See, before making profession, she must freely dispose of the use and revenue of her property (c. 569, par. 1).

She must cede the administration. Hence she is not free to retain or not retain the administration of her goods; rather, before profession she must cede the administration of her property to others—even to the monastery or religious institute to which she belongs, if it so pleases her and the institute will accept it.

Revenue and use of personal property must also be effectively removed from the control of the religious. She may decide that the revenue will be added to her capital sum unless the constitutions forbid this (P.C.I., October 16, 1919), or she may decide to give it to some-one else.

If the religious wishes to change the document by which she sur-rendered administration, use and revenue of property, she may do so with the permission of the superior general in the case of sisters, and the local Ordinary in the case of nuns. The only exception to this rule occurs when the change will be made in favor of the institute and a notable part of the religious' property is involved; then the per-mission of the Holy See is required. Canonists agree that one-half a religious property would constitute a notable part, and many say that one-third of the property would constitute a notable part.

3) A religious who has made profession of simple vows in a congre-gation of sisters may not gratuitously abdicate the dominion over her property (c. 583, n. 1).

Gratuitously. Hence, as long as she receives compensation, for ex-ample, by a contract of buying and selling, loan, or any other onerous contract, she may cede dominion of her property. The apostolic autho-rization, spoken of in canon 534, is not necessary in these cases since the personal property of individual religious with simple vows are not ecclesiastical goods properly so-called.

In congregations of sisters. Nuns are not included in this provision of canon 584 since they have a different discipline. Within sixty days before solemn profession, nuns must renounce all the property they possess, unless they have a special indult from the Holy See, ced-ing it to whomsoever they wish, on condition, however, that the re-nunciation is valid only if solemn profession actually takes place (c. 581, par. 1, cf. *infra*, n. 176).

4) Once she has made simple profession, goods that a religious ac-quiries either by her own industry or *intuitu religionis,* that is, inso-far as she is a religious, belong to her religious institute (c. 580, par. 2, cf. *supra*, n. 170). From this it follows that a professed religious, if her temporary vows expire, or if she is dispensed from her vows, or if she leaves religion as a fugitive or apostate, has no right to compen-sation for work done in religion, no matter how much profit the re-ligious institute has derived from her endeavors.

Notice that the religious institute has a right only to those goods which come to a simply professed religious insofar as she is a religious. All other goods remain in the dominion of the religious. Even if the religious were to die without having made a will, the institute would not be able to claim any of her personal property but her dowry. All the rest would go to her legal heirs.

174. PENALTIES

If a religious with simple vows contracts marriage, she and the person who marries her automatically incur excommunication reserved to the Ordinary, but the marriage is not invalid for this reason (c. 2388, par. 2; cf. *supra*, n. 156).

IX

SOLEMN PROFESSION

Solemn profession is that profession in which solemn vows are pronounced. Solemn vows are by their very nature perpetual (cf. *supra*, n. 143).

175. REQUIREMENTS FOR SOLEMN PROFESSION

Solemn profession must be preceded by simple temporary profession which has lasted for at least three years (c. 574, par. 1; cf. *infra*, n. 179).

Solemn profession may not be made before the candidate has completed her twenty-first year of age. Consequently, although canon 574, paragraph 1, requires only a three year period of simple profession, if the novice has not completed her twenty-first year when the three years have elapsed, she may not make solemn profession. For this reason the Code states that the first profession which must precede solemn or perpetual profession must be made for a three year period or for a longer time, if the subject requires more than three years to attain the twenty-one years prescribed for solemn profession. For ex-

225

ample, if a novice makes profession when she is sixteen years of age, this first profession should be made, not for three years, but until she has completed her twenty-first year. The manner of computing these twenty-one years has been discussed above (n. 166, par. 1).

A canonical examination must also be held before solemn profession, in the manner and at the time described above. Moreover, those who may admit candidates to solemn profession have been named above (n. 165).

176. EFFECTS OF SOLEMN PROFESSION

Solemn profession renders acts contrary to the vows not only illicit but also invalid, if they can be nullified (c. 579). Thus if a religious with solemn vows attempts to contract matrimony it is automatically null and void; if she makes a contract of buying and selling without the permission of her superiors, it is invalid; if she makes an onerous vow which is contrary to the obligations of the religious life, it is likewise null and void.

A religious with solemn vows loses not only the administration and the use and revenue of her goods, but also the very ownership over these goods; for these reasons:

1) Within the sixty days which immediately precede solemn profession, a religious, unless her community has a special papal indult to the contrary, must renounce, in favor of whomsoever she wishes, all the property which she actually possesses, on the condition that her profession subsequently takes place (c. 581, par. 1). If she does make profession, then the necessary measures must be immediately taken to ensure that the renunciation be effective also according to civil law (c. 581, par. 2).

Must renounce all of the property which she actually possesses. Relative to these words of the Code we may ask a further question: Before solemn vows, must, or may a religious renounce property which she could acquire in the future? For example, if a religious possesses no personal temporal goods when she makes her solemn profession, but will certainly inherit property at the death of her parents or other relatives, may she renounce these goods before profession? In answering this question, it seems that certain distinctions must be made:

a) If it is a question of goods which will come to a solemnly professed religious after her profession by reason of her own industry or insofar as she is religious, then certainly she may not renounce these goods. They do not belong to her but to her religius institute (c. 580, par. 2).

b) If it is a question of merely possible goods, that is, goods which she has not a well founded hope of acquiring, but which it is merely possible that she may obtain, then she has no right to renounce them since she has no right to such goods.

c) On the other hand, if it is a question of goods which the religious holds in well founded hope (*in certa spe*), then they may be renounced before solemn profession if the religious chooses to do so. The right in "certain hope" is sufficient to constitute these goods among those actually possessed. This opinion is verified by the practice of many religious communities who allow their members to renounce future wills and legacies.

After the profession takes place, necessary measures must immediately be taken to ensure that the renunciation will be effective according to civil law. Hence, insofar as the Church is concerned, the renunciation must be made within sixty days before solemn profession and with the condition that it will go into effect only when profession is actually made. But one must wait until after profession has actually been made before taking steps to insure the effectiveness of the renunciation before the civil law.

Unless her community has a papal indult to the contrary. To give to the vow its full perfection, the Church ordinarily demands that there be a total renunciation of property. If, however, special circumstances, such as existed in France and Belgium in the last century, indicate that such a renunciation should be dispensed with, at least before the civil law, then the Church may and as a matter of fact does grant special permission to do so.

2) After solemn profession all goods which come to a religious in whatever manner (for example, by inheritance, will or gift), and which have not been legitimately renounced before profession, are disposed of in the following manner:

a) If the order to which the religious belongs is capable of ownership, the goods are acquired by the order in the manner determined by the constitutions, without prejudice, however, to special indults of the Holy See (c. 582, n. 1).

b) If the order is incapable of exercising dominion over goods, then ownership of the property is acquired by the Holy See.

Ownership of the property. The use and administration of

these goods, however, is to be regulated by the rule and constitutions of each religious institute.

The Capuchins may be cited as an example of a religious Order of
men incapable of possessing temporal goods, especially goods of an
immovable nature. There are no nuns, and much less any sisters, who
to our knowledge are not able to possess temporal goods; on the contrary, at least in the case of nuns, it is formally prescribed that each
nun have her own dowry which is to be kept and administrated by the
monastery (cf. *supra*, n. 105).

3) Solemn profession also dissolves a marriage which has preceded
profession and which has not been consummated (c. 1119).

177. REGISTRATION OF SOLEMN PROFESSION

The superior who receives the solemn profession of a religious is
obliged to inform the pastor of the place where the professed was
baptized (c. 576, par. 2). Furthermore, a pastor who receives notice
that a solemn profession has been made must make a note of this
fact in the baptismal record (c. 470, par. 2; cf. *supra*, n. 168).

178. PENALTIES

Solemnly professed religious who attempt to contract marriage, even
though it be merely by a civil ceremony, and all persons who attempt
to contract marriage with them, are not validly married and they automatically incur excommunication which is simply reserved to the
Apostolic See (c. 2388, par. 1; cf. *supra*, n. 156).

X

TEMPORARY PROFESSION

Temporary profession is that profession which binds, not until death, but for a definite period of time, for example, for one year, for three years, or until the age of twenty-one (cf. *supra,* n. 143). It is necessarily simple, because as we have pointed out above, only solemn vows are by nature perpetual (cf. *loc. cit.*).

This profession may be made for any period of time, in accordance with the prescriptions of each religious institute. A religious could make temporary profession throughout her whole life if the constitutions of her community prescribed this.

The first temporary profession must be made in the house of novitiate (c. 574, par. 1), but this provision does not affect the validity of the profession.

179. NECESSITY OF TEMPORARY PROFESSION

Ordinarily, temporary profession must always precede simple perpetual vows or solemn vows (c. 574, par. 1; cf. *supra,* n. 175 and

229

infra, n. 183). However, if a religious who already has perpetual vows joins another religious institute (for example, if a Franciscan becomes a Dominican), then, after the novitiate, she may immediately make solemn or simple perpetual profession in the new institute without first professing temporary vows (c. 634).

Temporary profession which precedes simple perpetual or solemn profession must usually be made for three years (c. 574, par. 1). However, the constitutions are to be followed if they require annual professions (c. 574, par. 1); but in this case no perpetual profession may be made until annual profession has been renewed three consecutive years.

If three years after her first profession, a religious will not have attained the age required for perpetual profession, then instead of making the temporary profession for three years, she must make it for the time that must elapse before she is twenty-one years old (c. 574, par. 1). In this case her vows will expire on the day after her twenty-first birthday, in accordance with canon 34, paragraph 3, number 3.

The three years of temporary profession which must necessarily precede perpetual or solemn profession may be prolonged by the legitimate superior, not, however, beyond a second term or three years (c. 574, par. 2). This second three years period must begin by the renewal of profession as soon as the first period has elapsed (c. 577, par. 1). The legitimate superiors in this case are those who could admit to solemn or perpetual profession.

Once temporary profession has been prolonged, it may later be shortened. Thus if it is prolonged for three years but the competent superior decides after two years to admit the subject to perpetual profession, the profession would be valid and licit provided the subject is willing.

180. EFFECTS OF TEMPORARY PROFESSION

Professed religious, if they have temporary vows, are concerned with the following:

1) They enjoy the same indulgences, privileges, and spiritual favors as the solemnly or perpetually professed, and if they die during the time of their temporary profession, they have the right to the

same suffrages (c. 578, n. 1). This is true even if the constitutions approved before the publication of the Code provide otherwise (P.C.I, October 16, 1919). If this equality of suffrages for all the members of an institute becomes too burdensome, then, according to the same response, each institute may amend this point of the constitutions and submit the amendment to the Holy See for approval.

2) They are obliged to the observance of the rule and constitutions, just as those who are solemnly or perpetually professed. They are not obliged, however—even in institutes in which the choral recitation of the divine office is obligatory—to the private recitation of the divine office, unless the constitutions expressly prescribe it (c. 578, n. 2).

3) They do not have active and passive voice in elections unless the constitutions expressly grant this right. Nevertheless, the time required for acquiring active voice (voting capacity) and passive voice (eligibility for office) is to be reckoned from the first temporary profession, unless the constitutions determine otherwise (c. 578, n. 3). For example, when it is required that a religious be professed for ten years before she enjoys active voice in elections, the time is to be reckoned, not from solemn or perpetual profession, but from the date of the first temporary profession.

4) They contract only those obligations which pertain to the simply professed, even if they belong to institutes in which simple perpetual or solemn vows are professed by some of the members. For example, if a cloistered nun who has temporary vows should contract matrimony, the marriage would be valid and the excommunication she would incur would be reserved, not to the Sovereign Pontiff, as is the case for nuns with solemn vows, but to the local Ordinary.

181. RENEWAL OF TEMPORARY PROFESSION

When temporary vows expire they must be renewed without delay, unless the religious wishes to leave the religious life, (c. 577, par. 1). Relative to this, the Code states:

1) The years spent in vows are to be computed as they are in the calendar, in accordance with canon 34, paragraph 3, number 1. Thus if a religious makes profession for one year on March 1, the year will end on March 1 of the following year, even if it is a leap year.

2) The profession may be renewed at any hour on the same day on which the year ends, without waiting for the following day (c. 34, par. 3, n. 5). For example, if a religious made profession for one year on March 1, 1959, then on March 1, 1960, she may validly and licitly renew her profession at any hour of the day, even though in 1959 she did not make her profession until a late hour, for example, at eight or nine o'clock in the evening.

3) Superiors have the power to permit the renewal of temporary vows to be anticipated for a just cause, but not by more than a month (c. 577, par. 2). Consequently, with the permission of superiors, temporary profession may be anticipated by one month; but it may not be postponed for even one day. When temporary profession is renewed in anticipation, it becomes effective only when the previous temporary profession expires. The manner of renewing profession has been discussed above (n. 169).

182. FREEDOM TO LEAVE RELIGION UPON EXPIRATION OF TEMPORARY VOWS

When the period for which the vows were professed has expired, a religious is absolutely free to leave the institute (c. 637), and if she does not intend to renew her vows immediately, she *must* leave the institute (c. 575, par. 1). Hence it is not within the power of a religious to prolong the period of the profession she has made, or to remain in religion without vows; if she does not intend to renew her vows then she must leave the institute.

The religious institute, for just reasons, may dismiss a religious when her vows have expired by forbidding her to renew them (c. 637).

For just reasons. These reasons must be examined in each individual case but need not be revealed to the religious. A religious may never be dismissed because of ill health unless she has fraudulently hidden the illness before profession. The superiors who may reject a religious for renewal of profession are the major superiors who could have admitted her (c. 637; cf. *infra*, n. 279).

The question of the dismissal of a religious with simple temporary vows during the time she is bound by these vows will be discussed later *(infra, n. 279)*.

XI

PERPETUAL PROFESSION

Perpetual profession is that profession in which a person promises to observe the vows of religion throughout her entire life (cf. *supra*, n. 143). It is simple or solemn according as the vows professed are simple or solemn (cf. *supra*, Part VII, Chap. 8).

183. CONDITIONS FOR VALIDITY

Perpetual profession, whether solemn or simple, is not valid: (1) if the religious has not completed her twenty-first year of age (c. 573; cf. *supra*, n. 166, par. 1); or (2) if she has not been in simple temporary vows for at least three years (c. 572, par. 2). Regarding this second point it must be noted that, the three year period of simple temporary profession which must precede perpetual profession must be complete. This holds true even if one of the temporary professions of the previous three years has been anticipated in virtue of c. 577, par. 2 (cf. *supra*, n. 181). Furthermore, this three year period may be prolonged, either because the person professed has not completed her twenty-first year when the three year term has elapsed, or because

233

the superiors decide that it is wise to do so; this prolongation however, should not last longer than another three years (c. 574, par. 1). Hence if a religious will not have attained the age required for perpetual profession after her first three year period of profession has elapsed, the three year period should be prolonged at the time of the first profession. Thus if a religious will not be twenty-one by the time her vows expire, her temporary profession should endure till her twenty-first birthday. On the other hand, if she will be twenty-one by the time her three year period of temporary vows expires, then the prolongation cannot be validly made until after these vows expire (c. 574, par. 2; cf. *supra*, n. 179).

Perpetual profession is not licit unless it is preceded by a canonical examination which is to be conducted in the manner and at the time indicated above (n. 125; cf. c. 552, par. 1).

184. OBLIGATION OF MAKING PERPETUAL PROFESSION

In every religious institute in which perpetual vows are taken, when the period of temporary profession has expired the religious must either make perpetual profession, or return to secular life (c. 575, par. 1). Consequently, in institutes of perpetual vows, perpetual profession may no longer be put off indefinitely according to the good pleasure of the religious or the superiors. When the time of the temporary profession has expired, including the prolongation if this has taken place, perpetual vows must be taken; otherwise the religious must return to secular life.

Perpetual profession may be made in any house, unless the constitutions prescribe, as they often do, that it must be made in the motherhouse or house of novitiate.

Grave motives are required to exclude a religious lawfully from perpetual profession (c. 637); although not as grave as those required for the dismissal of a religious during the time she is bound by vows, even though the vows are merely temporary vows (c. 647, par. 2). A religious may never be excluded from pronouncing perpetual vows because of ill health, unless before profession she has fraudulently hidden the illness (cf. *infra*, n. 279).

185. EFFECTS OF PERPETUAL PROFESSION

When a religious makes profession of perpetual vows, she contracts all of the obligations attached to these vows, according as they are simple or solemn (cf. *supra,* n. 173 and n. 176).

A religious with perpetual vows, whether simple or solemn, automatically becomes an apostate if she unlawfully leaves the religious house with the intention of not returning, or if lawfully leaving the house, she does not return to it, intending by this act to withdraw herself from the religious obedience due to her superiors (c. 644, par. 1). The meaning of apostasy from religion and the penalties attached to it will be discussed in detail later on *(infra,* 274 ff.).

186. PENALTIES

If a religious is in simple perpetual vows, she and whoever presumes to contract marriage with her automatically incur excommunication reserved to the Ordinary (c. 2388, par. 2); if she is in solemn vows, both parties automatically incur excommunication reserved to the Holy See (c. 2388, par. 1).

PART EIGHT

OBLIGATIONS OF RELIGIOUS WOMEN

Besides the special obligations which each religious contracts by making profession according to a particular rule, there are other general obligations which the nature of the religious state or the Church impose upon all religious. In this section we will consider these obligations.

I

PERFECTION, THE RULE AND CONSTITUTIONS

187. TENDING TOWARD PERFECTION

The difference between a life dedicated to the pursuit of perfection and the ordinary Christian life has been discussed above (n. 2). When we speak about the life of perfection, we understand a life which consists in the observance of the commandments and the evangelical counsels, which are summed up in the three vows of religion (cf. *Summa*, II-II, q. 184, a. 3).

Religious, by reason of their profession, are obliged to tend to religious perfection (c. 593).

To tend to perfection; that is, they have no obligation to be perfect when they enter religious life, but they do have an obligation to strive for perfection while they are religious. As St. Thomas points out: "It is clear that to strive for an end does not necessarily imply the attainment of this end; it is sufficient that one tend towards the end by one means or another" (*Summa*, II-II, q. 184, a. 3). Hence religious, the end of whose state of life is perfection, are not obliged to be absolutely perfect, but they are obliged to strive for perfection.

Religious may not strive for perfection in any manner whatsoever, but only in conformity with the rule and constitutions of their institute (c. 593). "He who embraces the religious state is not obliged to the practice of everything that can lead to perfection, but only to those things which are determined and fixed by the rule he has professed" (*Summa*, II-II, q. 184, a. 2). This rule, approved by the Church, is a sure means of perfection if it is faithfully observed. But religious who act contrary to the rule and constitutions out of habitual carelessness or contempt can commit serious sins against the obligation to tend to perfection (*Summa*, II-II, q. 186, a. 9).

188. Observance of the Vows

Religious are obliged to observe faithfully and integrally the vows they have taken (c. 593). This command is found in Sacred Scripture and is directed to all men: *Si quid vovisti Deo, ne moreris reddere:* "If thou hast vowed anything to God, defer not to pay it" (Eccles. 5:3).

Faithfully, during the entire time they are bound by profession, whether temporary or perpetual.

Integrally, both as regards the number of vows which have been taken, and as regards the extent of their obligation. There is no true religious state without the three vows of poverty, chastity and obedience (cf. *supra*, n. 1). Consequently, these three vows are necessarily required in every religious institute. Other vows may be added to these, for example, a vow to go to the foreign missions, or a vow to attend the infirm. Likewise, the matter of the vows may be more or less extensive in this or that institute; for example, the vow of poverty in religious Orders deprives a religious of the right of ownership, whereas in religious Congregations in which only simple vows are taken, a religious gives up only the active and free control of her personal goods but retains ownership of them (cf. *supra*, n. 150).

In themselves, the vows of religion bind one sub gravi, that is, under pain of mortal sin.

In themselves, because indirectly, by reason of a lack of sufficient reflection, full consent or lightness of matter, the sin may be venial (cf. *supra,* n. 150 and n. 162).

Since a vow is a sacred thing, a sin against it constitutes a sacrilege. Therefore, religious women should always notify their confessor that they are religious, so that the confessor will be able to make a proper judgment of the penitent's spiritual condition.

189. Observance of the Rule

Religious are bound to order their lives according to the rule and constitutions of their institutes (c. 593). The difference between the rule and the constitutions of an institute has been explained above (n. 25). A religious who treats the rule and constitutions with contempt commits a grave sin, and she also fails in her obligation to strive for perfection. Nevertheless, the rule and constitutions do not always, at least directly, bind under pain of sin.

Do not always bind under pain of sin. The obligation involved depends upon the rule itself. In many rules it is expressly stated that the rule as such does not bind the religious under the pain of sin, but she must merely accept penalties imposed by superiors for transgressions against the rule (cf. *supra,* n. 159).

At least directly. Indirectly, however, either because the rule is transgressed through contempt, laziness or culpable negligence, or because what is commanded by the rule has already been commanded by God and the Church, transgressions against the rule and constitutions can involve sin. It is difficult to excuse from at least venial sin a religious who frequently, and as it were habitually, fails to observe the rule (cf. *Summa,* II-II, q. 186, a. 2; a. 9 ad 3).

190. Obligation to Persevere

A religious has a strict obligation to persevere in the religious institute in which she has made profession (cf. *supra,* n. 169). As we have pointed out, profession is a bilateral contract which involves a strict obligation on the part of the religious institute and on the part of the religious to observe it.

On the other hand, when her vows expire a religious may freely leave religion (c. 637; cf. *supra,* n. 182). Let us remember, however, that the freedom to depart acknowledged here is a juridical and not a moral freedom. It is true that when her vows have expired, a religious is juridically free to renew them or not, but this does not mean that in conscience, if she has received the grace of a vocation, she may freely renounce this grace and abandon the field of labor to which she has been called by God. She would at least be lacking in prudence!

II

THE RELIGIOUS HABIT

191. THE HABIT OF EACH INSTITUTE

The particular habit of a religious institute is made up of the special form, quality and color of the exterior clothing worn by the members of the institute and which distinguishes them from the simple faithful and from members of other institutes (cf. c. 639). Moreover, the proper habit of a religious institute which has already been founded may not be adopted by a new institute (c. 492, par. 3).

Proper habit, namely, one that has special characteristics. Hence if the habit adopted by a religious institute has no special characteristics to distinguish it from the clothing commonly used by the simple faithful or by other ecclesiastics, it cannot become the exclusive habit of the institute.

It is also forbidden to assume the religious habit of an institute unless one legitimately belongs to the institute (c. 492, par. 3).

Unless one legitimately belongs to the institute. Persons who have left religion for one cause or another, as well as those who never be-

243

longed to a religious institute, are forbidden to wear the proper habit of a religious institute (cf. *infra,* n. 193).

192. WEARING THE HABIT

Professed religious, unless they are excused for a grave reason, must wear the habit proper to their institute both inside and outside the house (c. 596).

Unless they are excused; for example, if the wearing of the habit is forbidden by civil law, if it is contrary to local custom, or in times of revolution or persecution. In these and similar circumstances it is allowable to put off or at least to hide the religious habit.

For a grave reason. The gravity of the reason is to be decided, not by individual religious, but by the major superior, or in urgent cases, by the local superior (c. 596).

Novices, unless special local circumstances determine otherwise, must wear the habit prescribed for novices by the constitutions during the whole period of novitiate (c. 557). The habit of the novices may be the same as that of the professed.

Postulants must wear plain clothing. It is not necessary that they have a special religious garb; they may continue to wear their secular clothing, as long as it is plain and modest. But if they are given a religious garb, it must be different from that of the novices (c. 540, par. 2). This seems to be a correct interpretation of canon 540, paragraph 2, which has just been cited. The canon clearly forbids postulants to wear the full religious habit of the institute; it also forbids them to wear the garb of the novices, whatever it may be. But it does not oblige them to have a special type of dress, and hence they may continue to wear secular clothing as long as it is conservative (cf. *supra,* n. 122).

The religious habit, besides being plain, must also always be in conformity with poverty. Hence everything that savors of excessive frills or of luxury must be excluded.

It is not becoming for religious persons to wear objects of gold or silver, except those in common use, such as a watch or a small cross. A golden or silver ring, however, is permitted in certain institutes as a sign of mystical espousal of the soul to Christ. Nevertheless, it must never be expensive or adorned with jewels.

193. PUTTING ASIDE THE HABIT

The following are not allowed to wear the religious habit, even though they have been lawfully clothed with it:

1) Religious who have obtained an indult of exclaustration from the Holy See (c. 639), unless the Ordinary for special reasons determines otherwise (P.I.C., November 12, 1922).

2) Religious who have obtained from the Holy See an indult of secularization (c. 640, par. 1, n. 1).

3) Religious who are dismissed (c. 648; c. 669, par. 2).

4) Religious who leave religion at the expiration of their temporary profession (c. 492, par. 3).

In order to fulfill the above law it is not sufficient merely to conceal the habit. Canons 639 and 640 expressly command that the habit be removed, at least in its external form, and to lay aside the habit is not the same as merely concealing it. It would not be contrary to the law to wear the "little habit," that is, the small scapular such as the tertiaries of certain religious orders wear. In this way, the religious habit is not truly worn—at least not in its "external form."

III

THE COMMON LIFE

The term common life signifies a form of community life in which all the temporal goods of the institute are owned and administered in common, and in which each religious receives from the common fund whatever is necessary in the line of food, clothing and furnishings. In this form of life, the needed article, and not the money for it, should be given to the religious whenever possible. Distinguished from the common life is the **private life,** which implies that a religious provides for her own needs and sustenance out of her own funds, or out of the funds of the community, which she retains in her possession and administers. This money which a religious retains and administers is known as *peculium. Peculium* is independent or dependent according as it is possessed without or with the permission of the superior.

194. OBLIGATION OF THE COMMON LIFE

In every religious institute all must carefully observe the common life (c. 594, par. 1). Strictly speaking, the private life is not incompati-

246

ble with the essence of the religious state or the vow of poverty if pos-
sesion, use and administration of goods are under the supervision of
the superior. Nevertheless, it is evident that the private life is not
the best manner of practicing the vow of poverty and the religious
community life. With good reason, therefore, the Code obliges all
religious to lead the common life in the future.

195. OBSERVING THE COMMON LIFE

The common life should be observed in matters of food, clothing
and furnishings, in all religious institutes (c. 594, par. 1). Relative
to this, the Code points out that the furnishings of the religious must
be in accord with the poverty which they profess (c. 594, par. 3).
Thus the demands of poverty will not be exactly the same in all
religious institutes. More severe laws will be in effect in those communities which embrace poverty as one of the chief means to perfection.

Moreover, money and deeds of property must be deposited in the
common fund and they must also be administered in common (c.
594, par. 2). It follows, therefore, that both independent and dependent *peculium* are contrary to this canon. **Independent peculium**
is never allowed since it is directly contrary to the essence of the religious life and the vow of poverty. In ordinary circumstances, **dependent peculium** cannot be permitted since it is contrary to the
spirit of poverty and the precept of the common life. In extraordinary circumstances, however, dependent *peculium* may be permitted.
For example, if the practice is a centenary or immemorial custom
and the Ordinary deems it prudent to tolerate it lest a greater evil
arise (c. 5); or if a religious is traveling or studying away from any
house of her institute. Canonists agree that the small amounts of
money which religious are given, especially those engaged in the
apostolate, to retain and use for carfare and other expenses are not
to be considered *peculium*.

Whatever is acquired by professed religious, including superiors,
either by their own industry or by virtue of the fact that they are
religious, must be incorporated into the goods of the house, province
or institute, according to the prescriptions of the constitutions (c.
594, par. 2).

196. PENALTIES

Religious who violate the prescriptions of their constitutions regarding the common life in a serious matter shall be seriously admonished, and if they do not amend, they shall be punished, even with deprivation of active and passive voice, and if they are superiors, also with the deprivation of office (c. 2389).

IV

THE CLOISTER OR ENCLOSURE

The cloister, or enclosure, in the material sense of the word, signifies the place in which the religious dwell, apart from others, in order to devote themselves more freely to the service and contemplation of God. In the formal or more strict meaning of the word, **cloister, or enclosure, signifies the obligation of neither entering nor leaving the monastery or convent without lawful permission.**

197. KINDS OF CLOISTER

An **episcopal cloister** or common cloister is that which is prescribed by the common law or by the bishop for men religious or sisters with simple vows. A **papal cloister** is that which must be observed by nuns or religious with solemn vows. It is called papal because the ordinary power to dispense from it belongs to the Roman Pontiff alone, and it is governed by sanctions imposed by papal laws.

The papal cloister for religious women has recently been distinguished into the *major* papal cloister and the *minor* papal cloister.

(Cf. Instruction of the Sacred Congregation of Religious, *Circa Monialium Clausuram*, November 23, 1950. In this section on papal enclosure of nuns, all references will be to this instruction unless otherwise indicated.) The major cloister requires that the religious never set foot outside the monastery and that outsiders never enter it without a dispensation from the Holy See. The minor papal cloister permits religious to leave the cloistered part of the monastery without a dispensation from the Holy See in order to perform works of the apostolate; for example, to teach school or to catechize. In this less strict type of papal cloister the religious may go to a part of the monastery that is not cloistered with only the permission of the superior, or she may even leave the monastery under certain conditions, provided she is engaged in works of the apostolate. Requirements for entrance of outsiders to the monastery are also relaxed in this type of cloister. (Apostolic Constitution of Pope Pius XII, *Sponsa Christi,* November 21, 1950).

198. OBSERVING THE CLOISTER

The parts of the house subject to the law of enclosure must be clearly indicated (c. 597, par. 3). As we shall see, even in convents or monasteries of papal cloister there are places not subject to the law of enclosure; for example, the parlor, the chaplain's quarters and the guest rooms. Hence in order that the law be more easily observed, it is necessary that the limits of the enclosure be indicated by signs and other fitting means. In monasteries of nuns, all places subject to the cloister must be perfectly separated and closed off by means of doors, turnstiles and grills. No place which is a part of the cloister may remain open to easy access by outsiders.

Insofar as is possible, the parlor should be situated near the entrance to the convent or monastery (c. 597, par. 2).

199. DUTIES OF SUPERIORS

Religious to whom the custody of the cloister is confided shall be careful lest during the visits of outsiders the discipline be relaxed and the religious spirit be weakened by useless conversations (c. 605, *Instr. cit,* n. 37). Superiors must observe the prescriptions of the constitutions regarding visitors and they must make sure that they are observed by others (c. 606, par. 1).

The bishop has the responsibility to see to it that the law of enclosure is faithfully observed by the religious women in his diocese (*Instr. cit.,* n. 35). Even in the case of nuns who are immediately subject to a regular superior, the bishop may hold a formal visitation and inquire concerning the observance of this law (cf. c. 603; P.C.I., November 24, 1920). If he finds that the law is not faithfully observed, he may impose suitable penalties (cf. *infra,* n. 204 and n. 208).

200. ENCLOSURE FOR NUNS

In monasteries of nuns which have been canonically established, even though they are not formal houses, the major papal enclosure must be observed if the nuns are not engaged in external apostolic works. If the nuns do perform apostolic works, then the minor papal cloister must be observed (c. 597, par. 1; Ap. Const., *Sponsa Christi,* November 21, 1950).

Canonically established; that is, founded with the necessary permission and in conformity with the laws which the Church prescribes for monasteries.

Even though not a formal house, namely, monasteries in which less than six professed religious are assigned (cf. *supra,* n. 17, A).

Before the Instruction *Circa Clausuram Monialium* (November 23, 1950), nuns who professed only simple vows by reason of a papal dispensation, were not bound to observe the papal cloister (P.C.I., March 1, 1921). Now, however, nuns who wish to retain their title and juridical status, even though by way of temporary exception they profess only simply vows, must observe at least the minor papal cloister (*Instr. cit.,* n. 4).

201. THOSE SUBJECT TO ENCLOSURE

A. Major papal cloister

In monasteries where the *major papal cloister* is in force, the nuns, under pain of excommunication, must remain perpetually within the confines of the cloister after their profession. They may not depart from it, not even for a short time, except in those cases provided by law or when permission to do so is granted *(Instr. cit.,* n. 18).

After profession. Those whose temporary vows expire are free to leave the cloister without special permission. However, they would need permission to re-enter. Novices and postulants may leave the cloister only when they intend to depart definitively from the monastery (c. 601; *Instr. cit.,* n. 10). Even if there are customs to the contrary, novices and postulants may not leave the cloister on the occasion of a clothing with the habit or a profession.

Except in cases provided for by law or when permission is granted. The Instruction gives the following as some of the lawful reasons for departure from the cloister: danger of death; danger of serious injury from fire, flood, air raid or invasion; or need to fulfill civil duties such as voting. When possible, these cases of danger or need should be confirmed in writing by the Ordinary of the place if time permits; otherwise, he should be notified afterwards *(Instr. cit.,* n. 21, d).

Nuns may pass from one monastery to another of the same federation without special permission if it is allowed by the rules of the federation. Otherwise the permission of the Holy See is required *(Instr. cit.,* n. 20).

In the Instruction the Ordinary or religious assistant is encouraged to ask for habitual faculties to dispense from the law of cloister in certain cases which create a just motive for the dispensation *(Instr. cit.,* n. 25). Such cases are: care of health; need to consult a doctor; visiting sick nuns outside; or supervising fields or property. It is clear that the Instruction has mitigated to some extent the rules in regard to leaving the papal cloister (cf. c. 601).

When it is necessary, local Ordinaries, of their own authority, may permit the cloister to be extended to the chapel or even to the parlors, but only during the time of necessity and provided all the safeguards of the cloister are observed *(Instr. cit.,* n. 12).

B. *Major cloister and externs*

The law of *major papal cloister* also binds externs of whatever class, condition, sex or age, unless they have special permission to enter. Those who violate the major papal cloister are automatically under excommunication simply reserved to the Holy See (c. 600; c. 2342, n. 1).

Exception to the law limiting the entrance of outsiders to the major cloister are made only for the following people:

1) The local Ordinary, the regular superior, and other visitators delegated by them or by the Holy See, may enter the cloister at the time of the canonical visitation but only for the purpose of inspection and on the condition that they are accompanied by at least one cleric or male religious of mature age (c. 600; *Instr. cit.,* n. 26).

For the purpose of inspection. Hence it would not be lawful to enter the cloister at the time of visitation to conduct the interviews with the nuns. These must be carried on at the screen, unless one of the nuns is sick and cannot come to the screen. Only then is it lawful for the visitator to enter the cloister for personal visitation *(Instr. cit.,* n. 26, b). When the prelate or his delegate visits the monastery to carry out some other act beside visitation, such as examining the will of a candidate, presiding at an election or receiving a profession, the same rules apply.

2) The confessor and his substitute may enter the cloister to administer the sacraments to the sick and to assist the dying, provided due precautions are observed (c. 600; *Instr. cit.,* n. 27).

The confessor. This includes the ordinary, extraordinary and supplementary confessors, and any confessor approved for the hearing of confessions of women who is requested by any seriously ill religious to hear her confession. It also includes a priest who hears the confession of a dying nun. Only the occasional confessor is refused the permission to enter the enclosure for the purpose of hearing confession.

Or his substitute; that is, the substitute in administering the sacraments of Holy Eucharist and Extreme Unction, for example, the chaplain (cf. *supra,* n. 92). Even when a nun wishes to receive Holy Communion merely out of devotion, any priest who celebrates Mass in the monastery, or who is invited by the nuns, may take the place of the chaplain or confessor and enter the cloister to give Holy Communion to the infirm.

Provided due precautions are observed; namely:

a) In the administration of Holy Communion, the priest should be accompanied from his entrance to his departure by at least two nuns. The whole community may accompany the Blessed Sacrament if this is the custom of the place *(Instr. cit.,* n. 27, b).

b) In the case of confession, the priest should be accompanied as far as the door of the sick nun's cell by two nuns; after the confession is finished they must conduct him immediately to the exit *(loc. cit.).*

c) In the administration of Extreme Unction, or when prayers are said for the dying, the same procedure should be followed, except that the nuns who accompany the priest, and other nuns as well, may enter the room of the sick nun with the priest. Whenever the confessor, or any other priest, enters the cloister, they must immediately leave it when their ministrations are finished *(loc. cit.).*

3) Rulers of States, their wives, and those who accompany them, may enter the enclosure (c. 600, n. 3).

Rulers of states; hence not only emperors, kings and princes, but also presidents of republics; in a word, all those who are the highest rulers of a people or nation, whatever title they may have. The Commission for the Authentic Interpretation of the Code of Canon Law has declared that in the United States, wives of state governors and their companions may be admitted into the cloisters of religious men (P.C.I., March 26, 1952). It seems logical to apply this response to communities of women as well; therefore, it seems that state governors in the United States, their wives and their retinue, may visit the cloister of any monastery of nuns within their jurisdiction (cf. Regatillo, S.J., *Interpretatio Codicis Iuris Canonici,* Santander, 1953; p. 234).

Those who accompany them; namely, those who form a part of the retinue when the ruler enters the monastery; not just those who happen to be present when he arrives.

4) Cardinals may also enter the enclosure, and they may be accompanied by one or two attendants, either clerics or lay people if they belong to the Cardinal's family *(Instr. cit.,* n. 29, b).

5) Doctors, surgeons, artisans, and all those whose work is necessary for the care of the needs of the monastery may be permitted to enter the enclosure by the superior if she has at least the previous habitual permission of the local Ordinary for their admittance and due precautions are taken *(Instr. cit.,* n. 29 c).

Due precautions are taken. This means that the persons who are admitted into the cloister must be known from certain information secured in advance to be of excellent reputation and character, and that they must be accompanied by two of the nuns as they pass through the quarters of the community, and that no one of the nuns may speak to them unless it concerns the business for which they were admitted *(Instr. cit.,* nn. 30, 31, 32).

The habitual permission of the local Ordinary. It suffices to seek this approval at the beginning of each year, listing those persons whose services will be required within the cloister during the course of the year, for example, the doctor, the gardener or the carpenter. In case of urgent necessity, however, permission may be presumed *(Instr. cit.,* n. 29, c).

6) Except as provided in the Apostolic Constitution, *Sponsa Christi,* girls or women may not be admitted to the cloister to study, to test their vocation, or for any other purpose without the special permission of the Holy See *(Instr. cit.,* n. 33 a). The exception mentioned in *Sponsa Christi* concerns nuns who are engaged in the apostolate.

7) Extern sisters may enter the cloister upon certain occasions. In their regard, the Sacred Congregation has passed the following legislation (cf. *Statutes for Extern Sisters,* July 16, 1931):

a) Extern sisters must strictly observe the law of enclosure during the year of canonical novitiate (art. 31).

b) They must re-enter the cloister two months before the end of the second year of novitiate (art. 32).

c) When their work makes it necessary for them to enter the cloister, they may do so, but for as brief a time as possible, and with at least the habitual consent of the Ordinary (art. 33).

d) If they become ill, or if they are infirm because of old age, they may be admitted into the enclosure with the consent of the bishop (art. 107).

C. *Minor papal cloister*

The law of minor papal cloister prescribes the following in regard to the departure of the nuns from the monastery and the entrance of outsiders:

1) The parts of the monastery reserved exclusively to the religious and that set aside for works of the apostolate must be clearly marked *(Instr. cit.,* n. 43, 48).

2) It is absolutely forbidden under pain of excommunication simply reserved to the Holy See to introduce into the part of the monastery reserved for the nuns any externs, no matter what their sex, age or rank, except those mentioned above in the section on major papal cloister.

3) It is also forbidden for the nuns to leave the monastery after profession without permission under pain of excommunication similar to the one spoken of in the section on major papal cloisters *(Instr. cit.,* n. 60). However, nuns may leave the cloistered section of the monastery and go to the section reserved for works of the apostolate in order to attend to the work of the monastery with the permission of the superior. If the place where the nuns perform their works is outside the monastery, then they may go to this place, but only in order to carry out the work of the monastery and with the permission of the superior and the local Ordinary. The superiors and the local Ordinary have a grave obligation to see to it that the nuns leave the monastery only for the reason enunciated above *(Instr. cit.,* n. 50).

4) Only those people for whom the work is being performed may be habitually admitted to the section of the monastery reserved for work. For example, boys and girls who are pupils in the monastery school. Women may be admitted to this section if their admittance has some necessary connection with the work of the monastery, but men may not be admitted without the permission of the bishop *(Instr. cit.,* n. 53, a).

202. LIMITS OF THE ENCLOSURE

In **monasteries of major papal enclosure,** the entire part of the house where the community dwells, the orchards and garden reserved for the religious, and any other place that they frequent, are subject to the law of enclosure *(Instr. cit.,* n. 11, a). The public church, the priest's sacristy, the place where the priest hears the nuns' confessions, the guest house, the quarters of the extern sisters, and the parlor are not affected by the law of enclosure *(loc. cit.);* neither are the gardens and orchards which are not reserved for the nuns and into which they may not enter (c. 597, par. 2). As we have pointed out above (n. 201), the local Ordinary may extend the cloister to the above places when there is good reason for it.

Even if the monastery is exempt, it pertains to the local Ordinary to determine exactly the limits of the enclosure, or for lawful reasons, to change them (c. 597, par. 3).

Sections of the monastery reserved to the nuns should be closed off in such a way that, insofar as is possible, those within are prevented from seeing out, and outsiders are prevented from seeing in *(Instr. cit.,* n. 13, a). Hence:

1) Yards, gardens and sun decks must be enclosed with thick shrubbery or a suitable wall *(loc. cit.).*

2) Windows which face the street must be made of non-transparent glass, and they should be equipped with shutters and lattices in order to impede the view from either side. If there are sun decks or roof gardens, they too must be hidden from the public *(Instr. cit.,* n. 14 b).

3) Unless there is some stricter provision of particular law, the nuns should be allowed to see the altar, but they should not be visible to the faithful *(Instr. cit.,* n. 15).

4) The confessional should be so situated that the confessor is outside the cloister and the penitent is within *(Instr. cit.,* n. 11 b; n. 9).

5) The part of the parlor reserved to the nuns must be separated from the part destined for visitors by two securely fixed and separated screens or grills *(Instr. cit.,* n. 16).

6) At the door of the monastery, in the sacristy, in parlors, or wherever else they are needed, there should be a turnstile or wheel through which necessary objects may be passed. A small opening in this wheel is permitted so that one may see what is being put into it *(Instr. cit.,* n. 17).

In **monasteries of minor papal enclosure:**

1) The parts of the monastery exclusively reserved to the community should be marked off and separated from the parts used for apostolic work *(Instr. cit.,* n. 43). The parts reserved to the nuns are the cells, the choir, the chapter room, the refectory, the kitchen, the recreation room, and other places which are needed for community life *(Instr. cit.,* n. 44). In these places the same regulations that apply to the major papal cloister must be observed. Although the Instruction does not mention it, we believe that the local Ordinary has the right to determine definitively what part of the monastery should be strictly cloistered and what part should be reserved for works.

2) The same sections must be outside the cloister as in a monastery of major papal cloister.

3) There should be no possibility of seeing in or out of the place reserved for works. If the same privacy that is preserved in the sec-

tion reserved for the nuns cannot be observed in this section, the Ordinary of the place should see to it that the best possible arrangements are made *(Instr. cit.,* n. 47).

203. CUSTODY OF THE CLOISTER

The cloister in monasteries of nuns, even those subject to a regular superior, is under the vigilance of the local Ordinary who can correct and coerce delinquents, including exempt male regulars, even with penalties and censures (c. 603, par. 1; *Instr. cit.,* n. 35). If nuns are subject to a regular superior, the custody of the cloister is confided to him as well as to the bishop; therefore, he may inflict punishment on the nuns and others subject to him if they are found guilty in this matter (c. 603, par. 2; *Instr. cit.,* n. 35).

Within the monastery the custody of the cloister pertains to the superior *(Instr. cit.,* n. 36).

204. PENALTIES

In the case of **major papal cloister:**

1) Whoever, no matter of what class, condition or sex, violates the law of enclosure of nuns by entering their cloister without due permission, and likewise those who shall introduce or admit persons into the cloister, automatically incur excommunication simply reserved to the Holy See (c. 2342, par. 1).

By entering without due permission. According to St. Alphonsus, a person who violates the law of enclosure even by taking one small step into the cloister is considered to have incurred the excommunication if his whole body is inside the enclosure.

One who introduces an outsider is likewise excommunicated, whether it is one of the nuns or an extern who does this; for example, if a confessor would take a woman with him when he went to hear the confession of a sick nun, he would fall under this censure.

One who admits an outsider refers to those who are bound by reason of their office to exclude externs. Hence this refers to superiors and those who have custody of the entrance to the monastery.

2) Nuns who unlawfully leave the cloister after profession are also automatically excommunicated. This excommunication is simply reserved to the Holy See (c. 2342, par. 3).

Nuns. This term is to be taken in its proper sense; hence it signifies religious women belonging to a monastery where solemn vows are taken, whether they have already taken these vows, or have only temporarily taken simple vows, because these latter are also professed nuns. Novices and postulants are bound by the law of enclosure (*Instr. cit.,* n. 10); thus if they leave it unlawfully they commit a sin; however, they would not incur this excommunication if they left unlawfully since it affects only professed nuns (c. 2342, n. 3; c. 601, par. 1).

If a nun leaves the cloister with permission, but does not return to it on time, she does not incur the excommunication, even though she would sin gravely. The penalty of excommunication is incurred by those who unlawfully leave the cloister, not by those who stay away unlawfully. This may seem to be a fine distinction, but in judging penalties, such distinctions must be taken into account. They may seem like subtleties, but since penalties are strictly interpreted, such distinctions are very important.

Unlawfully; that is, without permission or case of urgent necessity as explained above (n. 201).

3) If the transgressors of the law of enclosure are clerics, besides being excommunicated, they shall be suspended for a time which in the judgment of the local Ordinary is proportionate to the gravity of their fault (c. 2342, n. 1).

4) The bishop and also the regular superior who has nuns subject to him, can correct and punish transgressors of the law of enclosure of nuns with other censures. However, a bishop can punish all transgressors, even exempt regulars, whereas the regular superior can punish only those subject to him (cf. c. 603, par. 1).

In the case of a **minor papal cloister:**

1) Those nuns who unlawfully leave the confines of the monastery incur excommunication simply reserved to the Holy See. Regarding this point the discipline for major and minor cloister is the same (*Instr. cit.,* n. 60).

Unlawfully; that is, without observing the norms outlined above in regard to leaving the cloister when there is some external work to perform (cf. *supra,* n. 201).

2) Those nuns who unlawfully go from the part of the monastery reserved to the community to that set aside for apostolic work should

be punished by the superior or the Ordinary of the place (*Instr. cit.*, n. 61).

3) Any outsiders, no matter what rank, sex or age, who unlawfully enter the part of the monastery reserved to the community, and anyone who introduces or admits them, automatically incur excommunication simply reserved to the Holy See (*Instr. cit.*, n. 62).

4) Anyone who unlawfully enters the section of the monastery reserved for apostolic work, and those who introduce or admit them, should be punished by the Ordinary of the place or the superior (*Instr. cit.*, n. 63).

205. ENCLOSURE FOR SISTERS

The law of enclosure must also be observed in the houses of sisters, whether the house is of papal or diocesan approval (c. 604, par. 1). The cloister in such houses, however, is not papal, but only episcopal, and though general norms for observing it are contained in the Code, the particular manner of observance varies according to the constitutions of each institute.

206. THE EPISCOPAL CLOISTER

In houses of sisters, the law of enclosure consists in not permitting persons of the opposite sex to enter the place included in the cloister (c. 604, par. 1). However, the following may be admitted into the houses of sisters for adequate reasons:

1) All those who are exempt from the law of enclosure of nuns (cf. *supra*, n. 201).

2) All those whom the superiors for just and reasonable motives, deem it opportune to admit into the cloister (c. 604, par. 1).

This form of cloister, therefore, as far as the common law of the Church is concerned, is much less extensive than the law of enclosure for nuns. It places no limitation on the sisters in regard to leaving the convent, and it forbids the entrance only of persons of the opposite sex, and even they may be admitted if the superior deems it opportune.

207. LIMITS OF THE CLOISTER

If the entire house is exclusively set aside as a dwelling for religious, then the entire house is subject to the law of enclosure, with the exception of those places designated above when we spoke of the cloister of nuns (cf. c. 604; c. 599; cf. *supra*, n. 202).

If the house has annexed to it a boarding house for resident students, or a house for religious or educational purposes, then, although it is not necessary to observe the cloister in the places set aside for such purposes, at least one part of the house is to be reserved for the exclusive use of the religious and is to be subject to the law of enclosure, if this is possible (c. 604, par. 2; c. 599, par. 1).

Even in those places which are not subject to the law of enclosure because they are set aside as a boarding house or for religious or educational purposes, persons of the opposite sex are not to be admitted except for a just reason and with the permission of the superiors (c. 604, par. 2; c. 599, par. 2).

208. PENALTIES

The bishop can, in particular circumstances and for grave reasons, safeguard the enclosure, even in monasteries of sisters, with censures. At all times, however, he must be vigilant in having it duly observed and in correcting any abuses in this respect (c. 604, par. 3).

Since the cloister in houses of sisters is episcopal and not papal, the canonical penalties and censures provided for by the common law for those who violate the cloister of nuns do not apply to transgressors of the law of enclosure in convents of sisters.

V

DEPARTURE FROM THE CONVENT

209. Departure of Nuns

In monasteries where the **major papal enclosure** is in effect, the nuns may not leave the monastery after profession for any reason, not even for a short time, without a special indult of the Holy See. However, an exception is to be made if the nuns would be in imminent danger of death if they did not leave, or if some other grave evil would befall. If possible, permission for this departure should be obtained in advance in writing from the Ordinary (c. 601, par. 1 and par. 2; cf. *supra*, n. 201).

A nun who unlawfully leaves the cloister after profession is excommunicated, as has been said above (n. 204). If she has solemn vows and leaves the monastery with the intention of not returning she automatically becomes an apostate from religion (c. 644, par. 1; cf. *infra*, n. 274).

The discipline in regard to nuns leaving the monastery where the

minor papal cloister is in force has already been discussed *(supra,* n. 201).

210. DEPARTURE OF SISTERS

Regarding the departure of sisters from the monastery or convent, the Code gives the following rules:

1) Superiors shall take care that the prescriptions of their constitutions are faithfully observed regarding the departure of sisters from the house or their visiting with outsiders (c. 606, par. 1).

2) Superiors and local Ordinaries shall see to it that the religious do not go out singly from the house except in cases of true necessity (c. 607). Another religious or laywoman should always accompany them when possible.

Shall see to it. Hence the Church does not establish any absolute law in this regard; the constitutions, however, can strictly oblige in this matter. Nevertheless, whenever such prescriptions of the constitutions cannot be rigorously observed, it is evident that, in order to dispense from them from time to time, there is no need of an apostolic indult since it is a question of mere constitutional observance.

3) Ordinarily, superiors may not allow a religious to remain outside a house of her own institute for more than six months. Even for a period of less than six months they may not permit a sister to remain outside a house of her own institute, except for a just and grave cause, and for as short a time as possible (c. 606, par. 2).

For an uninterrupted absence of more than six months, the permission of the Holy See is always required, unless the sister is absent from her house in order to follow some special course of studies (c. 606, par. 2). An exception is also made if the constitutions of the institute expressly permit the religious to be absent from houses of the institute for more than six months because the special work of the institute demands it. In this case, however, all the safeguards enjoined by the constitutions must be faithfully followed.

4) A professed sister who unlawfully leaves her monastery or convent without the permission of her superior becomes a *fugitive* if she does so with the intention of returning (c. 644, par. 3; cf. *infra,* n. 278). If she leaves without the intention of returning and she has perpetual

vows, she becomes an apostate (c. 644, par. 1; cf. *infra*, n. 274); in either case she disobeys a grave precept of the particular and common law.

VI

THE PARLOR

The parlor is that part of the monastery outside of the cloister to which the faithful of both sexes may be admitted in order to visit with the religious. The Code tells us that in monasteries the parlor should be as near as possible to the entrance of the monastery (c. 597, par. 2). If possible, it should also be near the entrance in other religious houses too, so that visitors will not need to pass through sections reserved for the sisters.

Those who have the custody of the enclosure shall carefully see to it that during the visits of outsiders the regular discipline and religious spirit are not weakened by useless conversation (c. 605).

In the parlors of nuns, the opening where they speak with outsiders must be closed by two screens. These screens should be about twenty-five inches apart and attached to the wall so that they cannot be opened (S.C.Rel., February 6, 1924). Furthmore, if the constitutions allow it, there may also be a wheel to pass things from one side to the other in the parlor of nuns (Instr. *Circa Clausuram Monialium*, n. 17).

VII

CORRESPONDENCE

In regard to sending and receiving letters, besides the prescriptions of the constitutions of each religious institute, the following rules of the Code must be observed (c. 611):

1) Religious, whether they be nuns or sisters, may freely send letters without any inspection: to the Holy See; to the pontifical legate of the country in which the religious dwells; to the cardinal protector of their religious institute; to their own major superiors; to their local superior, if she is absent; to the local Ordinary; to the major superiors of the Order if the community is subject to the jurisdiction of regulars; and, to the Promoter of the Faith whenever they come to a knowledge of some particular fact which should be made known in causes of beatification and canonization of a servant of God (c. 2025, par. 2). (In this case they may also give the letter to their confessor who must forward it without delay to the Ordinary or the Promotor of the Faith.)

2) Religious may also receive sealed letters from all those persons to whom they can freely send them, and no one save the religious herself has a right to open these letters (c. 611).

266

The Code does not explicitly state that sealed letters sent to the above mentioned persons need not pass through the hands of the superiors. The Code gives this privilege explicitly only to those who have the duty of writing the Promotor of the Faith (c. 2025, par. 2). However, since giving the letter to the superior in order that she may forward it could render the privilege of sending a sealed letter useless or even harmful, it does not seem that a subject need pass a sealed letter through the hands of the superior. She may for example, send it through a friend, her confessor, or some other religious, provided that she does not employ dishonest means.

3) The Code does not grant the right to write sealed letters to confessors or spiritual directors. Hence if the constitutions do not grant this right, the matter is left to the discretion of the superior. Even if a letter has "case of conscience" written on it, the superior would not be strictly bound to send this letter to a confessor, or to give it to the sister concerned. However, superiors should not be too strict in this matter. If a superior does give permission to send or receive a "case of conscience" letter, she should not read it before passing it on since these letters partake to a certain extent in the secrecy of the confessional. Only if such letters are most probably subterfuges may the superior open them; but if the superior sees she made a mistake she must immediately seal the envelope and keep the entire matter a secret.

Even those matters which come from letters not marked "case of conscience" must be kept secret insofar as possible. Although religious give up the right to free and secret correspondence, it does not mean that the superiors have the right to divulge whatever they learn from the letters of their subjects. Prudence and justice demand that the contents of the subjects' letters be revealed only when it is necessary and useful to do so.

VIII

SPIRITUAL EXERCISES

211. The Sacrament of Penance

Superiors must take care that all religious go to confession at least once a week (c. 595, par. 1, n. 3). If subjects are negligent in this regard, the superior never has a right to inquire about the reception of the sacrament, but only whether the subject "went to confession"; that is, whether or not she approached the confessor. In other words, the superior may investigate to see whether the external act of approaching the sacrament is being regularly performed. In case of negligence, she may kindly remind the subject of her obligation to observe this point of the law. The right of the superior to inquire concerning the reception of this sacrament does not extend to those confessions made to the occasional confessor (c. 519; c. 522; cf. *supra*, n. 80, ff.).

Each and every religious has the obligation of presenting herself to the extraordinary confessor, at least to receive a blessing, whenever he comes to the convent to exercise his office (c. 521, par. 1; cf. *supra*, n. 82).

212. HOLY COMMUNION

Superiors should promote the frequent, even daily, reception of Holy Communion among the religious (c. 595, par. 2). Liberty must be given to every properly disposed religious to approach frequently, even daily, the most Holy Eucharist (*loc. cit.*). Superiors should never, therefore, impose abstention from Communion as a penance. However, if a religious has given grave scandal to the community since her last sacramental confession, or has committed a serious external fault, the superior can forbid her to receive Holy Communion until she has approached the sacrament of penance (c. 595, par. 3).

Although frequent, even daily, reception of Holy Communion is recommended, the Code also notes that if the rules or the constitutions or even the calendars of any institute of simple or solemn vows assign or prescribe certain fixed days for the reception of Holy Communion, such regulations are to be regarded as merely directive and they are in no way obligatory (c. 595, par. 4). The religious is to be left perfectly free to abstain from the reception of Communion on any and every day she wishes. An attempt should be made to make it possible for sisters to abstain from Communion without the knowledge of the other sisters in the house.

213. MASS

Religious should daily assist at Mass, unless they are legitimately impeded (c. 595, par. 1, n. 2). To hear Mass daily is not a strict obligation for religious unless the constitutions expressly command it; nevertheless, only a good reason can legitimately dispense a religious from this observance. The manner of hearing Mass, especially the dialogue Mass, will be discussed later (n. 244).

214. MEDITATION

The Code prescribes daily mental prayer or meditation for religious (c. 595, par. 1, n. 2). It does not say when or for how long this daily meditation should be made. By custom, it is usually made for at least half an hour each day, and if possible it should not be interrupted. The constitutions of each institute give further particulars concerning this spiritual exercise which has become common to all forms of religious life.

215. RETREAT

A retreat is that time in which a person, setting aside customary occupations insofar as is possible, collects her thoughts in silence and prayer in order to devote herself in a more perfect way to things of the soul.

The Code prescribes a yearly retreat for all religious (c. 595, par. 1, n. 1). Nothing about the duration of this annual retreat is stated in the Code since the particular constitutions usually contain directives in this regard. At least one week of retreat is required in most institutes since it is difficult to fulfill the end of a retreat in less time.

A retreat of at least eight full days must precede the beginning of the novitiate and the profession of vows (cc. 541; 571, par. 3; cf. *supra*, n. 125, par. 8).

216. OTHER PIOUS PRACTICES

Religious shall also faithfully perform the other exercises of piety prescribed by the rules and constitutions (c. 595, par. 1, n. 2).

IX

ASSESSMENTS FOR DIOCESAN NEEDS

Every religious house, even if exempt, can be obliged by the local Ordinary to pay a tax for the diocesan seminary (c. 1356, par. 1). An exception is made only for the following institutions: (1) those religious houses to which schools are annexed, whether the schools be within or outside of the house; (2) novitiate houses; (3) houses which live solely on alms (*loc. cit.*).

The tax is to be imposed according to the norms prescribed by the Code (c. 1356, par. 2 and par. 3). The tax must never exceed five per cent of the income, and not of the entire income, but only of that part which remains at the end of the year after all obligations and necessary expenses have been paid. Moreover, the offerings of the faithful are not counted as part of the revenue (*ibid.*, par. 3).

It follows, therefore, that if after paying the debts of the monastery or convent, and after deducting the necessary expenditures for the maintenance of the house, no revenue (not counting alms from the

271

faithful) remains, there is no obligation from a strict interpretation of the Code to pay any tax. It is certainly most fitting, however, even for religious who are not obliged to the tax, to be generous in contributing to the needs of the diocese.

X

OBLIGATIONS IN COMMON WITH CLERICS

Religious women are also bound by the obligations for clerics contained in the Code in canons 124 to 142, unless from the context of the law or the nature of the case it appears otherwise (c. 592). Hence religious women are forbidden to do the following:

1) They may not engage in unbecoming arts and professions, and they must abstain from all actions and occupations unbecoming to their state (c. 138).

2) They may not administer property of lay people or accept secular offices which involve rendering an account, without permission of the Ordinary or major superior (c. 139). Thus a nun or sister could not be an executor or an administrator of a will without permission of the Ordinary or major superior.

3) They may not practice medicine or surgery (*loc. cit.*). Caring for the sick in hospitals, however, or even assisting at surgical operations, is not forbidden by this canon.

4) They may not attend public events or shows which are unbecoming to their state or which would involve scandal (c. 140).

5) They may not engage in commercial or mercantile trading, personally or through agents, for their own profit, or the profit of others (c. 142). By this canon, merchandising, money-changing for profit, manufacturing by means of hired labor, and speculation in stocks and bonds, are forbidden to individuals and communities. When these forms of business are practiced habitually and large sums of money are involved, an excommunication specially reserved to the Holy See is automatically incurred. Investments of an economic nature, manufacturing which does not involve hired labor, sale of livestock or produce, and many other forms of business are not forbidden by this canon. In general, canonists agree that it is not forbidden to conduct a book store or cafeteria even if a profit is realized, if the store or cafeteria is also run for the convenience of the pupils or people who attend church or school and the profit is usually very small. If the profit is large and the note of convenience of the faithful is not present, the endeavor could well fall under the prohibition of this canon.

PART NINE

PRIVILEGES OF RELIGIOUS

I

PRIVILEGES IN GENERAL

In the juridical sense, **a privilege is a particular law which confers some favor.**

A law; because a privilege imposes an obligation, not upon the possessor, but upon others, to recognize and respect the privilege.

A particular law; because it does not have reference to everyone, but only to a particular person or a particular category of persons, for example, the members of one family, the members of one confraternity, or of one religious institute.

Which confers some favor; for example, exemption from a tax, the right to exercise certain offices or to demand certain services.

217. KINDS OF PRIVILEGES

Privileges may be **contrary to the law** or **outside the law.** A privilege is *contrary* to the law if it contradicts the common law in favor of some individual; for example, exemption from a common tax, or from some service which all others are obliged to render. A privilege

277

is *outside*, or above the law, if it grants a favor to certain persons but is not contrary to any existing law; for example, the privilege granted by the Holy Father to certain priests to bless rosaries and apply to them the apostolic indulgences.

Privileges may also be **common** or **proper.** Privileges are *common* when they may be participated in by several persons or classes of persons who are in the same state; for example, the privilege which clerics and religious enjoy of being exempt from the jurisdiction of secular courts (cf. *infra*, n. 223). Privileges are *proper* when they are granted only to one person or to a definite class of persons in such a way that others, even those who are in exactly the same state, may not participate in them; for example, the privilege granted to a religious house to reserve the Blessed Sacrament, not only in the main chapel, but also in the novitiate chapel.

218. PRIVILEGES OF RELIGIOUS WOMEN

Since the publication of the Code, religious women possess the following privileges:

1) Those which are expressly contained in the Code as granted to all religious women in general (c. 613, par. 1). We shall point out what these privileges are later on (Part IX, Chap. 2).

2) Those which have been or will be directly granted to them by the Holy See, or by a competent superior (c. 613, par. 1; c. 63).

Directly; that is, granted by name to a definite religious or religious institute.

By the Holy See; that is, by the Holy Father or by one of the Sacred Roman Congregations.

By a competent superior; for example, the bishop who, within the limits of his jurisdiction, may grant certain privileges in regard to diocesan law. If nuns are subject to a regular superior, he too can give them privileges in regard to the laws of the Order.

3) Those which have been introduced by prescription or legitimate custom (c. 63, par. 1). When customs are legitimate, that is, when they fulfill all the conditions required by law (cf. c. 25 ff.), they have the force of law; likewise, the mere fact of having exercised a certain action for a number of years establishes prescription in re-

gard to that action—in other words, this is a sufficient reason for claiming a right to perform this action.

4) Those in which they communicate. Communication of a privilege is its extension to one other than the principal beneficiary. It may be made in two forms: perfect and imperfect. *Perfect communication* means that the one who communicates as a secondary beneficiary enjoys his rights independent of the grant made to the original beneficiary. *Imperfect communication* means that the communicated privilege shares the same fate as the privilege given to the original beneficiary. Thus, if the original privilege is revoked, the imperfectly communicated privilege would be revoked also, but not the perfectly communicated privilege. Today, the communication of privileges is practical for nuns but not for sisters (cf. *infra,* n. 219).

Before the Code, mendicant Orders communicated in each other's privileges in a perfect manner. The Code suppressed all future communication of privileges, but allowed religious institutes to retain the ones that they obtained before the promulgation of the Code (c. 613, par. 1; P.C.I., December 30, 1937).

219. Extension of Privileges

Novices in every religious institute partake of all the privileges and spiritual favors granted to professed religious (c. 613, par. 2; cf. *supra,* n. 133). **Postulants,** on the other hand, very probably do not enjoy these privileges.

The privileges which regulars enjoy belong likewise to the **nuns** of the same Order insofar as they are capable of enjoying them (c. 613, par. 2).

Nuns. Hence this does not hold true for sisters even if they belong to a religious order. Sisters enjoy only those privileges which have been given them and not those privileges which are granted to the Order in general. Nuns, on the contrary, partake of all the privileges of the Order insofar as they are capable of enjoying them, and this is true whether they are exempt, that is, subject to their own regular superior, or whether they are immediately subject to the local Ordinary.

Of the same Order to which they belong; for example, Franciscan nuns in the Franciscan Order or Dominican nuns in the Order of St. Dominic.

Insofar as they are capable. Thus nuns cannot participate in any manner in the privileges conceded to religious men insofar as they are clerics or priests.

220. RENUNCIATION OF PRIVILEGES

Private individuals can renounce only those privileges which have been conceded in their own personal favor (c. 72, par. 2 and par. 3).

Not even a community may always renounce privileges which they possess. The Code determines cases in which they may not do so (c. 72, par. 1).

In all cases, in order that a renunciation of privileges be valid, it must be accepted by the competent superior (c. 72, par. 1).

221. CESSATION OF PRIVILEGES

Privileges are to be considered perpetual unless the contrary is expressly stated (c. 70). Nevertheless, they can cease in various ways:

1) By the revocation of the superior who granted them (c. 71).

2) By a renunciation accepted by the superior (c. 72, par. 1).

3) By the expiration of the time if the privilege was temporary (c. 77).

4) By the death of the one possessing it if the privilege was personal (c. 74).

5) By cessation of the original privilege if the privilege was imperfectly communicated (c. 65).

6) By non-use if it is burdensome to others and the conditions for prescription are fulfilled (c. 76).

II

PRIVILEGES IN PARTICULAR

222. PRIVILEGE OF THE CANON

The privilege of the Canon implies that all the faithful should honor clerics and religious and that the Church punishes with special penalties anyone who dares to inflict real injury upon them. It is called the "privilege of the Canon" because the penalties to be inflicted upon transgressors were formulated for the first time in a canon or article of the Second Lateran Council held in 1139, and are now confirmed in canon 2343, paragraph 4, of the Code.

Anyone who violently and culpably strikes a religious or inflicts other physical injury upon her by this very act incurs excommunication reserved to the Ordinary (c. 2343, par. 4).

Strikes or inflicts other physical injury; that is, materially injures the person of the religious by striking her, imprisoning her, killing her, or in any manner whatsoever injuring her person. The penalty would not be incurred by verbal injury, or injury to one's reputation.

Culpably; that is, sinfully. In order for one to incur excommunica-

281

tion, it is required that the blow or the injury be grave enough to constitute a mortal sin because only grave external sins are punished with ecclesiastical penalties (c. 2242, par. 1).

A religious; even if she is only a novice, not, however, if she is a postulant (cf. *supra,* Part VII, Chap. 4).

The Ordinary may add other penalties to the excommunication if he judges it prudent to do so (c. 2343, par. 4).

Whoever inflicts a real, that is, a physical injury, upon a religious also commits a sacrilege (c. 119; c. 614).

223. PRIVILEGE OF THE FORUM

The privilege of the forum implies that ecclesiastics and religious are exempt from appearing before a lay judge and may be summoned in judgment only before an ecclesiastical tribunal (c. 120).

The end of this privelege is not, as some have declared, that those who are delinquent may go unpunished. Rather, it is because ecclesiastical and religious persons can be tried and punished more fittingly and opportunely by the competent ecclesiastical authority to which they are immediately subject.

The privilege of the forum is very ancient in origin and it was always recognized in Catholic countries up to the time of the French Revolution. Today, however, there are not many nations in which this privilege is respected by the civil authority. In many countries the Church has partially or fully ceded this right in concordats (cf. c. 3).

Religious who belong to a canonically approved institute may not be tried except before ecclesiastical judges, whether the lawsuit be criminal or civil (c. 120; c. 614).

Religious; not only the professed, but also novices (cf. *supra*, n. 133), and also those who live in community after the manner of religious even though they do not profess vows (cf. c. 680).

In order to summon religious before a civil court it is necessary to obtain first the permission of the Ordinary of the place where the case is to be tried (c. 120, par. 2). Exceptions to this law exist in certain countries where the Church, by concordat or other decisions, has stipulated or at least allows another course of action (c. 120, par. 1).

Nevertheless, if religious have already been summoned, to avoid greater evils they may appear in court before secular judges even if the person who has summoned them has not obtained permission. In this case, however, they are obliged to inform as soon as possible the superior from whom permission should have been obtained (c. 120, par. 3).

The local Ordinary should not refuse such permission without a just and serious reason, especially if the plaintiff is a layman and the Ordinary's attempts to bring about a friendly settlement have failed (c. 120, par. 2).

224. COMPETENT JUDGES OF RELIGIOUS WOMEN

The Holy Father as supreme head of the Church, either personally or by means of courts instituted by him or judges delegated by him, can settle any controversy, and all can have recourse to him to obtain justice (c. 1597).

The Ordinary of the place may also act as judge in controversies between religious. But if the decision is not satisfactory, before having recourse to the Sovereign Pontiff, an appeal may be made to the metropolitan (cf. c. 1594, par. 1, par. 2 and par. 3).

Institutes of religious women do not have the power to establish true ecclesiastical courts because the judicial power of the Church can rest only in clerics. Hence in order that a controversy among religious women be *juridically* settled, the presence of an ecclesiastical superior is required, that is, the bishop or regular superior, or one delegated by them or the Sovereign Pontiff.

225. RIGHTS OF RELIGIOUS IN COURT

Religious may not have recourse to the courts, even ecclesiastical, without having first obtained permission from their proper superiors (c. 1652). However, an exception is made in the following cases:

1) When it is a question of obtaining rights which a religious believes she has acquired in her religious institute in virtue of her religious profession (c. 1652).

2) When a religious lives legitimately outside of the monastery and must protect her rights without delay (*loc. cit.*).

3) When a religious wishes to bring action against her proper superior *(loc. cit.)*.

Religious superiors may not appear in a court of justice in the name of their community unless their constitutions permit them to do so, and then they must fulfill all of the conditions prescribed by the constitutions (c. 1653, par. 6).

226. TRANSGRESSIONS OF THIS PRIVILEGE

If anyone summons religious before a lay tribunal without having first obtained permission from the local Ordinary, he shall automatically incur, if he is a cleric, suspension from office, reserved to the Ordinary; if he is a layman, he shall be punished by his proper Ordinary with penalties proportionate to the gravity of his fault (c. 2341).

227. THE PRIVILEGES OF IMMUNITY AND COMPETENCE

The privilege of immunity implies that religious in virtue of this privilege are exempt from certain offices and duties of civil life.

The privilege of competence connotes a certain respect towards ecclesiastical persons, and hence towards religious, when they are burdened by debts. This privilege provides that when religious are heavily burdened with debt, they may not be forced to pay their collectors to the extent that it will deprive them of what is necessary for a decent maintenance. This fitting standard of living is to be determined by the prudent judgment of an ecclesiastical judge. It is understood, however, that the religious are bound to pay their creditors in full as soon as this is possible (c. 122).

228. LOSS OF THE ABOVE PRIVILEGES

These four privileges (Privilege of the Canon, Privileges of the Forum, Immunity, and Competence) cannot be renounced by an individual religious since they pertain to religious as a class, not as individuals (c. 123). However, if a religious leaves the religious life or is any way reduced to the lay state she loses these privileges (c. 123).

229. PRIVILEGE OF EXEMPTION

The privilege of exemption is the privilege by which women reli-

gious, by the will of the Sovereign Pontiff, are removed from the ordinary jurisdiction of the local bishop, and are made immediately subject to the Holy Father or to the superiors of the Order to which they belong, or to other superiors delegated by the Sovereign Pontiff. In a word, this privilege makes them exempt or independent of the jurisdiction of the local Ordinary.

Exemption implies that women religious are removed from the jurisdiction of the local Ordinary with the exception of those cases expressly mentioned in the Code. However, since these exceptions are very numerous, the privilege of exemption of religious women, even in the case of nuns, is very limited in nature (cf. *infra*, n. 231; c. 615).

If the local Ordinary dispenses all of the faithful from a common law (from the law of fast, for example), this dispensation is also valid for exempt religious who reside in his diocese, unless they are bound by special vows or their constitutions rule otherwise (c. 620). Hence if the bishop dispenses the faithful from the law of abstinence from meat on the Wednesdays of Lent, religious who are not bound by special vows or who have no special constitutional obligations in this regard may also make use of this dispensation. The same holds for all other dispensations from the common law granted by the bishop (cf. *supra*, n. 24).

230. Women Religious and Exemption

In virtue of the common law, only **nuns** pertaining to a regular Order and subject to the superiors of that Order are exempt (c. 615).

And subject to the superiors of that Order. Hence, if they are not subject to superiors of an Order, it is evident that although they are nuns they are under the immediate jurisdiction of the local Ordinary. Today, there are not many monasteries of nuns subject to regular religious superiors and hence, like the faithful living within the limits of the same diocese, most nuns are subject to the local Ordinary.

Institutes of **religious women with simple vows** enjoy the privilege of exemption only if it has been granted to them in a special manner by the Sovereign Pontiff (c. 618, par. 1). All others are subject to the local Ordinary. However, if a religious institute, even though nonexempt, is an institute of papal approval, the local Ordinary is not allowed to do the following:

1) He is not allowed to change the constitutions (c. 618, par. 2, n. 1).

2) He is not allowed to be involved in the temporal administration of the institute except in those cases enumerated above (n. 99).

3) He is not allowed to interfere in the internal government and discipline, except in those cases expressly mentioned in the Code (c. 618, par. 2, n. 2).

4) He may and should, on the other hand, inquire whether the religious discipline is observed in accordance with the constitutions, whether the religious are instructed in sound doctrine, and whether the moral virtues are fostered, whether the cloister is observed, and whether the sacraments are received regularly and frequently. If grave abuses are found in these matters, the bishop must make this known to the respective superiors. If these superiors do not take proper steps to correct the abuses, the Ordinary himself shall do so. Whenever a case arises which does not permit of delay, the local Ordinary shall settle it immediately and send to the Holy See to report of the action he has taken (c. 618, par. 2, n. 2).

231. CESSATION OF THE PRIVILEGE

The privilege of exemption ceases in the following cases, even for those who ordinarily enjoy it:

1) When a religious dwells unlawfully outside of the monastery (c. 616, par. 1).

2) If a religious has committed a crime while lawfully outside the house and the legitimate superiors, although informed of the matter, have failed to punish her (c. 616, par. 2).

3) When a religious house is not a formal house (cf. *supra,* n. 17, A). In this case, the religious house does not totally lose its exemption, but it does remain under the special vigilance of the local Ordinary who, if abuses arise which are a source of scandal to the faithful, can take the steps necessary to put an end to them (c. 617, par. 2).

4) If schools, hospitals, orphanages or other works of religious, education or charity are annexed to a monastery. Such institutions are subject to the supervision of the local Ordinary in all matters pertaining to the teaching of religion, moral conduct, exercises of piety and the administration of the sacraments (c. 1491, par. 2). Conse-

quently, the bishop has the right to visitate such institutions (c. 1491, par. 1).

5) If the local Ordinary makes laws which even exempt religious must obey. This could occur in the following cases:

a) When he makes laws whose direct purpose is to prevent abuses in public worship or to exclude superstitious practices among the faithful (c. 1261, par. 2).

b) When the bishop orders that at all Masses said in churches and public oratories a short explanation of the gospel or other religious instruction should be given (c. 1345). This obligation, as is evident, does not directly regard religious women but rather the chaplain or pastor of the church. Religious women, however, must allow the chaplain or pastor to fulfill this obligation, and in case of grave neglect they should notify the Ordinary.

c) When the bishop orders the ringing of bells, or public prayers, or other sacred functions for a public reason.

6) If a religious should commit a fault in some matter in which she lacks exemption, she may be punished by the local Ordinary.

232. PRIVILEGE OF COLLECTING ALMS

The privilege of collecting alms consists in the power or right to freely, publicly and personally collect alms from the faithful.

Freely; that is, without interference from others.

Publicly; that is, by going from door to door, or to public places where the faithful are accustomed to gather or pass by. In order to collect alms privately, there is no need of any special privilege.

Personally. The gathering of alms through letters or notes is not, strictly speaking, the collection of alms in the sense in which we are now using it.

233. RULES TO BE OBSERVED

In order to collect alms, **religious of diocesan approval** must have the written permission of the Ordinary of the place where their house is situated and of the Ordinary of the place where the alms are solicited (c. 622, par. 2).

The Code (c. 622, par. 3) advises local Ordinaries not to give this permission too readily, especially when other religious are already engaged in seeking alms in the diocese. Also, if it is possible to provide for the necessities of the monastery by collecting alms only within the limits of the diocese or district in which the religious reside, bishops should not give more extensive permissions.

Religious of papal approval may not publicly seek alms without a special privilege of the Holy See. They must also have the written permission of the local Ordinary of the place in which they intend to beg, unless the papal privilege expressly dispenses them from obtaining this permission (c. 622, par. 1).

Superiors may confide the collection of alms only to those nuns or sisters who are professed, serious minded and of mature age (c. 623). Moreover, **all of the instructions issued by the Holy See relative to the collecting of alms are to be observed** (c. 624). Some of the principal instructions given by the Holy See and now in force are contained in a decree of the Sacred Congregation of Religious, November 21, 1908, in which it is stated that:

1) Religious seeking alms shall carry with them authentic letters from their superior and local Ordinary authorizing them to do so. They shall show these letters to the pastor or the Ordinary whenever they are requested to do so (n. 6);

2) Religious should travel in pairs (n. 8). The Decree makes an exception to this rule when the alms-seeking is carried on in the same place in which the religious house is located and the person asking alms is publicly known. It is our opinion, however, that this exception applies only to men religious and not to women religious. Since the Code prescribes that religious women should not leave the monastery or convent alone without necessity (c. 607), for all the more reason this law is to be observed when they go about seeking alms.

3) When religious seek alms at a distance from the monastery, they must not stay in hotels, but rather they should request hospitality from the pastor or other priests, or better still, in other religious houses. If, however, they must stay with seculars, let them choose families which are well known for Christian piety and solid virtue (n. 9).

4) They must not remain outside of the monastery for more than a month if the collection of alms takes place within the limits of their own diocese, or for more than two months if alms are sought in other dioceses. Nor may religious who have already made a tour of alms-seeking be sent out again before another period of one or

two months, according as they were absent from the monastery for one or two months, and during their stay in the monastery they must live the regular life in all its fullness (n. 10).

5) They must not spend the night outside of the monastery when they seek alms in the same place in which their monastery is located (n. 11).

6) They must always strive to be outstanding in humility, modesty and cleanliness. They must avoid places which are not in keeping with their state of life, and, although outside of their monastery, they must faithfully carry out their spiritual obligations and the exercises of piety which are customary in the monastery (n. 12).

Superiors shall not fail to give to their religious who go out seeking alms precepts which will protect them from danger (n. 13).

233a. PRIVILEGE OF PRECEDENCE

Within each religious institute, the particular constitutions are to be followed in determining the order of precedence among the various members of the institute. If the constitutions are silent on this point, then legitimate customs are to be followed, and if no lawful customs exist, precedence is to be determined by the common law (c. 106, n. 5; c. 491, par. 1).

Although the Code does not mention the question of precedence among different institutes of women religious, we believe that we may apply to them the following rules set down by the Code for men religious:

1) Religious of whatever kind always take precedence over lay people (c. 491, par. 1).

2) Congregations of papal approval take precedence over those of diocesan approval (c. 491, par. 1).

3) Among congregations of the same kind, that is, either all of papal approval, or all of diocesan approval, that congregation has the right of precedence which has enjoyed undisputed possession of it in a particular place. If this is not certain, then that congregation takes precedence which was first instituted in the particular place (c. 106, n. 5; c. 491, par. 1).

In any controversy which may arise, the decision of the bishop is final (c. 106, n. 6).

PART TEN

DIVINE WORSHIP

I

CHURCHES AND ORATORIES

A church is a sacred edifice dedicated to divine worship for the principal purpose of being used by all the faithful for public worship (cf. c. 1161).

An oratory, on the other hand, is a sacred edifice dedicated to divine worship with the intention that it will be used by a determined group or a determined category of persons (cf. c. 1188).

An oratory is called either public, semi-public or private:

1) It is *public* if it has been erected principally for the convenience of a community or for a group of private persons but in such a way that all of the faithful who wish to do so may enter the oratory, especially during the time of divine services (cf. c. 1188, par. 2, n. 1).

2) It is *semi-public* if it has been erected exclusively for the convenience of a determined community or group of persons, so that it is not open to the unrestricted use of the faithful (cf. c. 1188, par. 2, n. 2).

3) It is *private or domestic* if it has been erected in a private house

293

for the exclusive use of some family or of a private individual (c. 1188, par. 2, n. 3).

234. Erection of a Church or Oratory

Religious may not erect a church, or even a public or semi-public oratory, without the written permission of the local Ordinary. The vicar general may not give this permission without special delegation (c. 1162).

With the permission of the local Ordinary, several semi-public oratories may be erected in the same religious house or school. For example, one oratory may be erected for the aspirants and another for the novices, or one for the sisters and one for the students, if in the judgment of the Ordinary there is need of this. In this case the oratory dedicated to the service of the community is to be considered the principal oratory, and the others are secondary oratories (c. 1192, par. 4; c. 1267).

The consent of the superior is sufficient to erect a private oratory out of simple devotion, but if one wishes to have Mass celebrated there, an apostolic indult is required (c. 1195, par. 1).

235. Care of Sacred Furnishings

The sacred vestments, as well as purificators, palls and corporals, are to be blessed before they are used for Mass.

For the churches of women religious, these sacred furnishings may be blessed by the local Ordinary, the rector of the church, or the pastor in whose parish the religious house is situated. **In churches of nuns** subject to a regular superior, the blessing may be given by the regular superior as well (c. 1304, n. 3 and n. 5).

Purificators, palls and corporals which have been used in the Sacrifice of the Mass are not to be given to lay persons to be washed until they have first been purified by a priest or at least by a cleric in major orders (c. 1306, par. 2). Religious, even nuns, may not make this first purification without the permission of the Holy See (S.C.Rites, September 8, 1857). Today, however, the Holy See readily gives this permission where there is cause for it.

236. REGULATIONS FOR CHURCHES OF RELIGIOUS

In the churches and in the public or semi-public oratories of religious women:

1) Marriages may not take place. Ordinaries should not permit this unless necessity demands it and due precautions are taken (c. 1109, par. 2).

2) Funerals or obsequies of the faithful may not be held (c. 1216), unless a person has expressly chosen such a church for his funeral (c. 1216, par. 1), or unless the deceased is a woman who worked as a servant and lived within the monastery (c. 1221, par. 3).

Funerals or obsequies. This means the usual ceremonies which are carried on in the presence of the body before burial, but not the ceremonies or solemn Masses for the dead which are celebrated on anniversaries or in other circumstances. Such ceremonies and Masses may always be held in the churches of religious women.

3) Confraternities may not be erected (c. 712, par. 3). In the churches of religious women the local Ordinary may allow the erection of associations of women alone, or of pious unions, even mixed, which have for their object only the recitation of certain prayers and the obtaining of spiritual favors *(loc. cit.)*.

4) In semi-public oratories, even those of women religious, all sacred functions in conformity with the rubrics may be performed, unless restrictions are placed on these functions by the local Ordinary (c. 1193). Furthermore, in every church, public or semi-public oratory, even those of women religious, the obligation of hearing Mass may be fulfilled, and not only by the religious but also by all the faithful (c. 1249).

237. SINGING IN CHURCH

Religious women may sing during the sacred functions which are held in their own churches or oratories, provided that their constitutions and the liturgical law permit it, and they have obtained permission of the local Ordinary (c. 1264, par. 2). However, they must always sing from a place where they cannot be seen by the people (c. 1264, par. 2). It is clear that when no lay people are present the permission of the local Ordinary is not needed in order for the sisters or nuns to sing at liturgical functions.

Three very important documents on sacred music have been published in recent times: the Motu Proprio *Tra le Sollecitudini* of St.
Pius X, November 22, 1903; the Apostolic Constitution *Divini Cultus*
of Pope Pius XI, December 20, 1928; and *Musicae Sacrae Disciplina*
of Pope Pius XII, December 25, 1955. The principal sections of these
and other documents pertaining to sacred music and the liturgy have
been set down concisely in a recent special instruction *On Sacred
Music and the Sacred Liturgy"* (S.C.Rites., September 3, 1958). Sisters
and nuns especially engaged in the teaching of music should be fa-
miliar with this document, as should those who select the music to
be sung and played by women religious during liturgical functions.

238. ADMISSION FOR THE CELEBRATION OF MASS

Every priest who has with him authentic and still valid documents,
signed by his Ordinary if he is a secular priest, or by his superior if
he is a religious priest, or by the Sacred Congregation for the Oriental
Church if he is a priest of the Oriental Rite, should be allowed to
say Mass in the Churches of religious women, unless it becomes
known that after receiving the document he has done something
which renders him unworthy to celebrate Mass (c. 804, par. 1). Hence,
every visiting priest who has the proper commendatory letters, or
celebret, cannot be refused permission to say Mass unless it is certain
that he has been guilty of some crime since this letter was issued.
Moreover, the local Ordinary cannot forbid sisters to grant this permission if the above requirements are fulfilled, nor may Ordinaries
make this permission dependent upon letters from their curia.

If a priest does not possess an authentic document he may nevertheless be allowed to say Mass if he is in good standing. If he is unknown, he may still be permitted to say Mass once or twice, provided
he wears the ecclesiastical garb, does not receive any remuneration
under any title for the celebration of Mass, and inscribes in a special
book his name, office and diocese (c. 804, par. 2).

If, however, the Ordinary of the place where the monastery or convent is located makes special regulations concerning the admission of
priests to the celebration of Mass, provided they are not contrary to
what has been said above, these regulations must also be observed by
religious women, even though they are exempt from the jurisdiction
of the Ordinary (c. 804, par. 3).

239. CHRISTMAS MIDNIGHT MASS

In the church of religious women, the conventual Mass can be celebrated at midnight, but not the other two Masses without an Apostolic indult (c. 821, par. 2). However, in the oratories of religious houses in which the Blessed Sacrament is habitually reserved, one priest may say three Masses at midnight on Christmas. Those who assist at these Masses can satisfy their obligation of hearing Mass, and Holy Communion may be distributed to those who wish to receive it (c. 821, par. 3). Bishops in the United States, by reason of the Quinquennial Faculties, have the power to permit the celebration of one or three Masses on Christmas night in churches of religious which are not included in the privilege enunciated in canon 821, paragraph 3.

240. THE LITURGICAL CALENDAR

Congregations of religious women, whether nuns or sisters, **which are affiliated to a religious Order,** should follow the liturgical calendar of that Order. (*Code of Rubrics,* S.C.Rites, July 25, 1960, n. 54, a.). Thus a community of Carmelite nuns should follow the calendar of their Order.

Congregations of religious women that do not pertain to a religious Order may have their own liturgical calendar if they are obliged to say the divine Office in choir by ecclesiastical law *(ibid.,* n. 54, b). Thus, all communities under the one supreme moderator could use the same calendar. They must also follow the diocesan calendar if they are not bound to choral recitation of the divine Office *(ibid.,* n. 54, c). Those congregations who follow this calendar, however, may add some of their own feasts to it. They may celebrate the feast of their title, of their founder if he or she is canonized or beatified, of their principal and secondary patrons, and of their saints and blesseds *(ibid.,* n. 53, c; n. 46).

Every liturgical calendar, whether religious or diocesan, must include the following feasts: the feast of the principal patron of the country, of the region, of the diocese, and of the town or city; and the feast of the anniversary of the dedication of the Cathedral Church *(ibid.,* n. 57).

When any priest celebrates Mass in a church, public oratory, or principal semi-public oratory of a religious house or institution, he should follow the calendar of the place *(ibid.,* n. 275). If Mass is said in a secondary semi-public oratory of a religious house or institution, or at a portable altar outside a sacred place, the priest may use his own calendar or the calendar of the place *(ibid.,* n. 276 and n. 277). The priest, therefore, should always be careful to say the Mass according to the calendar of the church, public oratory, or principal semi-public oratory where he says Mass. A diocesan priest for example, should say Mass according to the Dominican liturgical calendar when he says Mass at a convent of Dominican Sisters.

II

DIVINE OFFICE AND
COMMUNITY MASS

The divine office is that liturgical and public prayer made up of psalms and other prayers, which clerics in major orders and some religious are bound to say each day in the name of the entire Church.

241. RECITING THE DIVINE OFFICE

The recitation of the divine Office may be *choral, in common* or *solitary.* Recitation of the Office is choral if it is done in common by those obliged to say it in common by ecclesiastical law; it is in common if it is recited in common by those who are not bound to choral recitation by ecclesiastical law; it is solitary if an individual says it alone *(Code of Rubrics,* S.C.Rites, July 25, 1960, n. 140). This new division of the Sacred Congregation of Rites does away with the term "private recitation." Perhaps the reason the Congregation has acted in this manner is to stress the fact that the divine Office, even when said "privately," is an integral part of the public worship of the Church.

242. OBLIGATION OF RECITING THE DIVINE OFFICE

Only **choir nuns** who are professed are obliged to recite the divine office (c. 610, par. 3) and they must do so in the following manner:

1) Solemnly professed choir nuns are bound to the choral recitation of the divine office, and the private recitation of it when they are not present for office in choir. If they miss one canonical hour or its equivalent, they are guilty of grave sin.

2) Simply professed choir nuns are only bound to the choral recitation of the divine office. Hence if they cannot be present in choir they have no further obligation to say the office.

3) Nuns who, according to their constitutions, should take solemn vows, but who actually take only simple vows because of an Apostolic Indult, are not bound to the private recitation of the divine office (S. Penitentiary, November 25, 1852).

Lay nuns, even though they are solemnly professed, are not bound to say the divine office (c. 610, par. 3).

The obligation of the private recitation of the divine office begins for choir religious from the moment of their solemn profession (cf. St. Alphonsus, *Theol. Mor.* I, V, n. 140). Hence a solemnly professed religious, on the day of her profession, is held only to that part of the office which corresponds to the hour of her profession and to the other parts which follow it. She has no obligation to recite the preceding portions of the office. The parts of the office correspond to the hours of the day in the following manner: Prime, after sunrise; Terce, about nine o'clock in the morning; Sext, about noon; None, about three o'clock in the afternoon; Vespers and Compline about sunset; Matins, at midnight; Lauds, at three o'clock in the morning.

The time during which the obligation of the private recitation of the divine office can be satisfied is from midnight to midnight of each day. However, Matins for the following day may be anticipated after two o'clock in the afternoon (*Code of Rubrics*, S.C.Rites, July 25, 1960, n. 144).

243. CHORAL RECITATION OF THE OFFICE

In religious communities bound to the choral recitation of the

office, **the office must be recited when four religious who are bound
to the duty and who are not legitimately impeded are present in the
house.** The constitutions may impose the choral recitation even
when there are less than four religious in the community who are
not impeded (c. 610, par. 1).

In communities bound to the choral recitation. Thus the Code
does not impose this choral recitation, but rather it presupposes that
it is obligatory in virtue of the rule, or customs. Only in the event
that this obligation already exists does the Code determine when, by
reason of the number of religious in the monastery, the community
is bound to fulfill it.

Four religious bound to the choir; or even less than four if the
proper constitutions so determine; for example, three, or even two,
since the alternate recitation of the office is possible with just two
present. Even if four religious are available, the obligation to say
Office in choir could still be statisfied by two or three.

Not legitimately impeded; that is, not impeded by a just cause when
it is time to go to choir. The gravity of the cause must be judged in
proportion to the gravity of the obligation. For cloistered religious,
we believe that only illness can be a just reason. We do not see how,
in ordinary circumstances, there could be any other sufficient reason
to dispense a religious from being present in choir when without her
it would be impossible to fulfill the choral recitation of the office.

To satisfy the choral obligation of the office, it must be recited in
church; or if there is no church, in the principal oratory of the community. It is customary to recite the office in the choir, that is, in
that part of the church or principal oratory set aside for the recitation of the prayers which the religious say in common (S.C.Rites,
December 12, 1879); but strictly speaking, the office may be recited
in the church itself.

**The useful time for satisfying the choral obligation of the office
is, strictly speaking, from midnight to midnight.** However, if the
liturgical laws are to be observed (and they must be observed under
pain of at least venial sin), the various parts of the office must be
recited in the order and at the times prescribed by the rubrics, unless
there is a good reason for having them at different times. However,
a recent instruction of the Congregation of Rites allows Compline
to be said as the last prayer of the day even if Matins for the following day has been anticipated (S.C.Rites, July 25, 1960, n. 147).

The choral obligation of the divine office applies both to the entire office taken as a whole, and to the individual parts (c. 135). Hence it would be a sin to omit either the entire office or a notable part of it.

A *notable part* of the office according to moralists, is a part which is equivalent to one small hour.

The Office of the Blessed Virgin, or other offices or daily prayers prescribed in many religious institutes of simple vows in place of the divine office, must be said to fulfill the prescriptions of the rule of the institutes. However, the Code neither mentions this obligation nor increases the obligation of the rule. In fact, the Holy See has several times said that recitation of the Little Office should not be imposed under pain of sin. To omit it, or other specified prayers, therefore, would not in itself be a sin.

244. COMMUNITY MASS

In monasteries of nuns the Mass corresponding to the office of the day must be celebrated whenever possible, and the community should assist at this Mass (c. 610, par. 2).

Whenever possible, because the nuns cannot be strictly obliged to observe a rule whose fulfillment does not depend directly upon them. Sometimes they will not find it possible to assist at community Mass since there will be no priest to say it for them.

A Mass corresponding to the office of the day. The Conventual Mass must correspond to the office of the day, unless a ferial day of the IV Class occurs; then a votive Mass may be said (*Code of Rubrics,* S.C. Rites, July 25, 1960, n. 288).

The community must assist at this Mass. Not every member of the community need be present, but all who are not legitimately impeded should attend the community Mass (cf. *supra,* n. 244). The conventual Mass should be solemn or sung, but if particular law or dispensation permits a low Mass, the community should participate in it by reciting at least the Ordinary of the Mass (*Code of Rubrics,* S.C. Rites, July 25, 1960, n. 288).

In convents of sisters it is certainly praiseworthy to have daily Mass with the community in attendance, but the Code does not impose this as an obligation.

The practice of having a dialogue Mass is not only permitted but strictly encouraged. A recent institution of the Sacred Congregation of Rites, *On Sacred Music and the Sacred Liturgy* (September 3, 1958), states that: "The faithful should be present at low Mass in such a way that they exercise that participation which is demanded by such a great mystery and which yields such abundant fruits." And: "The most perfect manner of participation is had when the faithful give the liturgical responses to the celebrant's words, pronouncing the parts proper to them in a clear voice." *(ibid.,* n. 28 and n. 31). Certainly, it is the mind of the Holy See that religious especially participate in the Mass by giving the liturgical responses.

III

THE HOLY EUCHARIST

245.   RIGHT OF RESERVING THE BLESSED SACRAMENT

Communities of **nuns and exempt sisters** have the right and the duty
to reserve the Holy Eucharist in their own churches (c. 1265, par. 1,
n. 1). **Non-exempt sisters** must have an Apostolic indult to reserve
the Blessed Sacrament in their churches; the bishop, however, may for
a just cause grant this permission temporarily (c. 1265, par. 2).

The churches in which the Blessed Sacrament is reserved must be
left open at least for a few hours each day (c. 1266).

To reserve the Blessed Sacrament in the principal oratory, whether
public or semi-public, of any religious house or pious institute, the
permission of the local Ordinary is required and is sufficient (c. 1265,
par. 1, n. 2).

If a religious house has a church annexed to it and the community
uses it for religious exercises, the Blessed Sacrament may not be reserved simultaneously in the church and in the principal oratory;
but if, on the other hand, the community for some reason does not
use the church for religious exercises, then, with the permission of

the Ordinary, the Blessed Sacrament may be reserved not only in the church but also in the principal oratory for the convenience of the community.

Moreover, when a religious edifice is materially one, although formally distinct communities dwell in it, then each of these communities, if they do not use the church, may, with the permission of the bishop, reserve the Blessed Sacrament in their own principal oratory (P.C.I., June 2, 1918).

The difference between a church and oratory has been pointed out above (Part X, Chap. 1).

The Blessed Sacrament may not be reserved in any place except the church or principal oratory. This prohibition extends to the choir of the nuns or in any other place within the enclosure (c. 1267). Sisters who live in a building with another community can be considered a distinct community relative to the reservation of the Blessed Sacrament. Thus sisters working in a seminary or college could have the right to reserve the Blessed Sacrament in their own oratory with the permission of the local Ordinary. The same would not be true of the novitiate chapel, however, since the novices can hardly be considered a religious community distinct from the rest of the house.

With only the permission of the Ordinary, may the Blessed Sacrament be reserved in the country-house of women religious where either all or a part of the community goes during the year for a more or less prolonged time? This depends on the way in which the country-house is considered.

1) If it is a filial house, the Blessed Sacrament may be reserved because although a filial house depends upon the principal house, it is nevertheless a true religious house (cf. *supra*, n. 17), and hence, regarding the reservation of the Blessed Sacrament, it may make use of the provisions of canon 1265, paragraph 1, number 2 relative to all religious houses.

2) If, on the other hand, the country-house is considered merely as a property of the monastery where the sisters go for a time during the year for reasons of health or rest, without it ever being erected into a filial house or functioning as such, then the answer is no. In other words, to reserve the Blessed Sacrament there habitually, the permission of the bishop of the place is not sufficient. An Apostolic in-

dult is required because the conditions demanded by canon 1265 for the reservation of the Blessed Sacrament are not verified.

An indispensable condition for the reservation of the Blessed Sacrament either in a church or in an oratory is that there is someone to watch over it, and at least once a week a priest celebrates Mass there (c. 1265, par. 1). In the case of a religious community no special guardian of the Blessed Sacrament is required since the entire community fulfills this function.

The pastor may obtain the Blessed Sacrament from any church, even in churches of women religious, to bring Holy Communion to the sick (c. 483, n. 2).

246. MANNER OF RESERVATION

The reservation of the Blessed Sacrament is governed by the following regulations:

1) The Blessed Sacrament must be reserved in an immovable tabernacle placed in the middle of the altar (c. 1269, par. 1).

2) The Blessed Sacrament may be habitually reserved on only one altar of the church, and as a rule, this should be the main altar (c. 1268, par. 1 and par. 2). In churches where perpetual adoration is held, the Blessed Sacrament should be reserved on two altars, on one for adoration, and on the other for distributing Holy Communion.

3) At least one lamp, made of either olive oil or beeswax, must burn day and night before the tabernacle in which the Blessed Sacrament is reserved (c. 1271). Where olive oil cannot be obtained, the local Ordinary may, according to his prudent judgment, permit the use of other oils which, insofar as is possible, should be vegetable oils (c. 1271).

During the last war, because of the scarcity of oil of any kind, Ordinaries were allowed to permit the use of even electric lights. This permission still endures whenever in the judgment of the Ordinary serious reasons exist for its continuance.

4) The key of the tabernacle in which the Blessed Sacrament is reserved must be carefully guarded (c. 1269, par. 4).

Carefully. To this end, an instruction issued by the Sacred Congregation of the Sacraments on March 7, 1938, states that "the key of the tabernacle must never be left on the altar table, or in the door of the tabernacle." As soon as Mass is finished or Holy Communion is distributed "it is to be taken to the sacristy and put in a safe and sacred place, and locked up with a second key."

In the church of nuns or of other religious women, "the key must not be kept within the enclosure of the monastery, but in the sacristy, in a place which is safe, strong and secret, and locked up with two keys, one of which the superior keeps, while the other one is given to the religious sacristan" (*Instr. cit.*)

5) The number of particles which are necessary for the Communion of the sick and of other members of the faithful shall be reserved in the tabernacle (c. 1270), and they must be fresh so that there may be no danger of corruption; the instructions of the local Ordinary in this matter must be observed by all (c. 1272).

The particles must be *fresh*, that is, not only recently consecrated, but also freshly made or newly acquired. The practice of using particles which are two or three months old, and even more so of reserving the consecrated species for this length of time, is absolutely forbidden (S.C. of Sacraments, December 7, 1918). The Second Council of Baltimore declared that the hosts in the ciborium must be renewed at least once a week. This law is still in effect in the United States.

247. EXPOSITION OF THE BLESSED SACRAMENT

Private exposition, that is, exposition with the tabernacle door open while the Blessed Sacrament remains within the tabernacle, may be held for any just reason and without the permission of the Ordinary in churches and oratories in which the Holy Eucharist is habitually reserved. There is no minimum number of persons that must be present in order to have this ceremony, but the *Tantum Ergo* or some other prayer must be sung or at least recited (S.C. Rites, n. 3157).

Public exposition, that is, exposition with the Blessed Sacrament exposed in the ostensorium, may be held on the Feast of Corpus Christi and every day during the octave in all churches during Mass and at Vespers. At other times public exposition may be held only for good and serious reasons, especially a public cause, and with the permission of the local Ordinary (c. 1274, par. 1).

It is not necessary to ask this permission each time; it can be given habitually. A convenient custom of many houses of religious women is to draw up a list of the days on which solemn exposition is desired and to submit it to the local Ordinary for approval once and for all.

According to the liturgical laws, solemn exposition ordinarily may not be held more than once a day in any church or oratory.

248. The Forty Hours Devotion

In all churches where the Blessed Sacrament is habitually reserved, the Forty Hours Devotion shall be celebrated each year with all possible solemnity on the days assigned by the local Ordinary (c. 1275). The manner of conducting the Forty Hours service is explained in the *Instructio Clementina* of Clement XI, January 21, 1705. In the United States, if the exposition is interrupted during the night, the indulgences can still be obtained if the *Instructio* is observed.

If for some special reasons the Forty Hours Devotion cannot be celebrated without grave inconvenience, or if the reverence due to the Blessed Sacrament cannot be observed, the local Ordinary may and should see to it that the Holy Eucharist is solemnly exposed for several hours on certain determined days (c. 1275).

IV

THE LAST SACRAMENTS

The last sacraments are Viaticum and Extreme Unction. They are called the last sacraments because they are administered in danger of death so as to prepare the soul for its passage into eternal life in the best possible manner.

249. ADMINISTRATION TO WOMEN RELIGIOUS

In monasteries of nuns, the ordinary confessor, or one who takes his place, has the right and the duty of administering the last sacraments (c. 514, par. 2). We have treated of the ordinary confessor above (n. 81).

The Code does not expressly state who it is that "may take the place of the ordinary confessor." It is our opinion that it can be the chaplain, or a priest delegated by the confessor; in case of necessity when both the confessor and the chaplain are absent any priest may perform this function.

In houses of sisters, even of papal approval and exempt, the right and duty of administering the last sacraments belongs to the pastor of the place, or to the chaplain whom the Ordinary has assigned in place of the pastor to take care of the spiritual needs of the monastery (c. 514, par. 3).

The pastor of the place; namely, the pastor in whose parish the convent is located. An exception to this rule occurs in the case of sisters who work in seminaries. Since canon 1368 exempts seminaries and "those in them" from parochial jurisdiction, the rector of the seminary has the right to give the last sacraments to sisters dying there.

Or the chaplain whom the Ordinary assigns. The bishop may, for just and grave reasons, exempt pious institutes and religious houses from the jurisdiction of the pastor and confide them, as long as they are not houses of exempt men religious, to the care of a chaplain (c. 464, par. 2; cf. *supra,* n. 92).

250. Administration to Externs

The priests who may administer the last sacraments to women religious, may also administer them to postulants, novices and to all other persons who live day and night in the religious house of nuns as servants, as guests, or for reasons of health or education (c. 514, par. 1 and par. 2). In this case, the confessor, or the one who takes his place, has the same powers as a religious superior, who may also administer the last sacraments to all those persons mentioned above (cf. c. 514, par. 2 and par. 3).

Day and night. Hence, it would not suffice if a person merely called at the monastery for a visit, or went there to work during the day but returned home in the evening.

In the religious house. In our opinion it is not necessary, even in the case of monasteries of nuns, that the persons in question dwell within the cloister. It is sufficient that they live in a building which is under the direction of the religious and that they can be said to form one house and family with the religious.

V

FUNERALS

By the term funeral is meant the interment of the deceased and all the ceremonies in conformity with the liturgy of the Church which precede it. A funeral, therefore, includes three distinct phases: the transfer of the body of the deceased to the Church; the funeral Mass; and the burial of the body of the deceased in a cemetery.

In the religious houses of women, the **rights of the pastor** relative to funerals are regulated in the following manner:

1) When the religious house is exempt from the jurisdiction of the pastor, and the religious has died in the house, it pertains to the chaplain of the religious to accompany the body to the church or oratory of the religious and to conduct the funeral services there (c. 1230, par. 5).

A religious house can be exempt from the jurisdiction of the pastor either by papal privilege or by the disposition of the bishop, in conformity with canon 464 (cf. *supra,* n. 92 and n. 93).

Nuns, even when they are subject to the jurisdiction of the bishop, are exempt from the jurisdiction of the pastor relative to funerals.

311

Consequently, the right of conducting the funerals of nuns belongs to their chaplain (P.C.I., January 31, 1942).

2) When the religious house is under the jurisdiction of the pastor and a religious dies in the house, the right of accompanying the body to the church and of conducting the funeral belongs to the pastor of the parish in which the convent is located (c. 1230, par. 5).

3) When a religious dies outside of the convent, the funeral is to be conducted by the pastor of the place where the religious died, unless the superior wishes to have the body transferred to the deceased religious' house of assignment (c. 1250, par. 5). If this latter course of action is followed, then the rules explained in number 1 and number 2 above are to be followed. If the sister was working in a seminary when she died, it seems that the rector of the seminary has the same rights that the pastor has when a religious dies in her religious house which is in his territory (c. 1368).

4) Novices, in regard to funerals, are to be considered as religious (c. 1221, par. 1; cf. *supra*, Part VII, Chap. 4). Nevertheless, unlike religious, they may if they wish, choose the church for their funeral. The same is true of servants who form part of the religious family and live day and night in the monastery or convent, if they die in the monastery or convent (c. 1221, par. 3). If they die outside the monastery or house, they must be buried according to the norms prescribed for other lay people. Aspirants and postulants, on the other hand, are entirely subject to the jurisdiction of the pastor in this matter, just as ordinary members of the faithful (P.C.I., July 20, 1929).

5) Persons who live in a religious house as guests, or for reasons of education or health, are to be buried according to the regulations governing the ordinary faithful, even if they died in the religious house in which they are living (c. 1222). If they reside within the cloister of a convent of nuns, however, they may choose the monastery church as the church of their funeral (c. 1225).

In all cases, neither the priest nor others may ever enter the cloister because of the funeral services. This is to be especially noted in the case of nuns who are bound by papal cloister. The religious themselves must carry the remains to the limit of the enclosure (c. 1230, par. 5).

VI

THE CEMETERY

A cemetery is that place which is blessed and set apart for the burial of the dead (c. 1205, par. 1).

251. Right to a Private Cemetery

Exempt communities of nuns have the right to have their own cemetery, distinct from the common cemetery of the faithful (c. 1208, par. 2). Communities of sisters may have their own burial ground outside the common cemetery and blessed like a cemetery if they obtain the permission of the local Ordinary (c. 1208, par. 3).

252. The Right to Choose a Cemetery

Professed religious, including superiors, may not choose their place of burial, but when they die they are to be buried in the cemetery of the monastery if there is one, and if not, they are to be buried in the common cemetery (c. 1224, n. 2).

Professed religious. Hence novices, and with greater reason, postulants, retain the right to choose, if they so wish, the place in which they wish to be buried (c. 1221, par. 1).

Religious are strictly forbidden to induce anyone to promise with an oath, a vow, or in any other manner to choose their cemetery for burial. If a promise is made under such circumstances, it is null and void (c. 1227).

VII

INDULGENCES

253. GAINING INDULGENCES

When a visit to a church is prescribed for the gaining of an indulgence, and the church is not designated, then religious, whether they are nuns or sisters, may gain the indulgence, provided they have performed the other prescribed acts, by visiting a chapel of their own house in which they are able to fulfill the obligation of hearing Mass (c. 929).

And the church is not designated. If the church to be visited is named (for example, the parochial church or the church where the confraternity of the Most Holy Rosary is established), what has been said above does not hold true. Thus, another church may not be substituted for gaining the Portiuncula Indulgence because this indulgence can only be gained at a church of the Franciscans.

Not only the religious themselves, but also those who dwell with them day and night as guests, or for reasons of education or work, enjoy the privilege described above.

If confession is prescribed for gaining an indulgence, it may be made within the eight days which precede the day to which the indulgence is attached, the day itself, or on any of the days within the octave. **If Holy Communion is required,** it may be received the day before, on the day itself, or on any of the days within the octave (c. 931, par. 1). For example, to receive a plenary indulgence attached to Christmas, confession may be made from December 17 to January 1, inclusive; Holy Communion may be received from December 24 to January 1, inclusive.

The faithful, including religious, who customarily confess at least twice a month, or who go to communion daily, even though they fail to receive it once or twice a week, can gain all indulgences, except jubilee indulgences, even if they have not gone to confession within the prescribed time (c. 931, par. 3).

Religious who are prevented by sickness or some other reason from performing works prescribed for the gaining of some indulgences, may ask their confessor to substitute other good works (c. 935).

In order to gain an indulgence, a habitual intention suffices provided the proper works are performed at the right time (c. 925, par. 2).

254. PAPAL BLESSING

Religious who have the privilege of receiving the papal blessing at certain times during the year, may not receive it except in their own church and oratory, and never on the same day on which the bishop imparts this blessing in another place in the same city (c. 915). The formula used for this blessing is that found in the *Roman Ritual*, Tit. VIII, Chap. 32.

255. GENERAL ABSOLUTION

General absolution is a special blessing given in religious Orders which carries with it a plenary indulgence. Granted to regulars by Apostolic privilege, it is imparted on certain feast days or in certain circumstances during the year, according to the tenor of the privilege. Nuns and sisters who are affiliated to a religious order enjoy this privilege of general absolution in conformity with the privilege of the Order.

This absolution can be imparted to religious women either public-ly or privately.

Publicly; that is, to the entire community, by the ordinary con-fessor (S.C. Indulg., February 11, 1903), or by another priest dele-gated by the bishop (S.C. Indulg., March 12, 1905). If the religious are Third Order sisters, then any priest approved for confession may give the absolution (S.C. Indulg., December 15, 1910).

Privately; that is, in the confessional, by any confessor, immediate-ly after confession.

After confession. If, however, the penitent is in the state of grace, it is not necessary that the sacramental absolution have first been given; it is sufficient if the general absolution be imparted in the confessional.

The formula to be used is that which is given in the appendix of the *Roman Ritual,* Tit. VIII, n. 33.

PART ELEVEN

SCHOOLS AND MISSIONS

I

SCHOOLS, ORPHANAGES AND HOSPICES

256. The Opening of Schools

When a religious institute whose purpose is the training and instruction of youth has obtained due permission to establish a new house (cf. *supra*, n. 18), it may, in conformity with the rule of the institute, also open a school. It must always, however, observe the conditions contained in the permission to open the new house (c. 497, par. 2). The same is true regarding hospices for the aged, orphanages and other similar institutions (*loc. cit.*).

If, however, the school, hospice or orphanage is to be opened in a building which is separated from the religious house, then, even if the religious house is exempt, that is, even if the existing house is independent of the bishop, the special written permission of the Ordinary is required in order to open the new institution. The permission of the local Ordinary is sufficient; hence it is not necessary to have recourse to the Holy See (c. 497, par. 3).

257. RIGHTS OF THE LOCAL ORDINARY

The bishop of the place has the right and the duty to see to it that nothing is taught or done in the schools which is contrary to faith or good morals (c. 1381, par. 2). The local Ordinaries also have the right to approve religious text books when the good of religion and morals demands this (c. 1381, par. 3), and to approve the teachers of religion, even if they are religious. The Ordinary cannot, however, deprive all religious of the right to teach religion in their schools (S.C.Rel., January 26, 1959).

The local Ordinaries have the right to visitate schools, even when they are conducted by exempt religious, in all that regards religion and morals (c. 1382).

What has been said relative to schools, also applies to oratories, orphanages, hospices and similar charitable or educational institutions.

II

MISSIONS

258. Mission Territories

Mission territories are all those places in the world where the Catholic religion has not yet been propagated, or, if it has been propagated and is being practiced, a place where true ecclesiastical hierarchy has not yet been established (c. 252). Moreover, all mission territories are under the jurisdiction of the Sacred Congregation of the Propagation of the Faith (c. 252).

259. Permission to Establish Missions

All religious, no matter to what Order or congregation they may belong, must have the permission of the Holy See, that is, of the Sacred Congregation for the Propagation of the Faith, to open a house in mission territory (c. 497, par. 1).

Vicars and prefects apostolic have the right and duty to demand of religious who go to mission fields, letters which testify to their assignment to the missions, the scope of their works, and their destination (c. 295, par. 1).

260. JURISDICTION OF VICARS AND PREFECTS APOSTOLIC

Religious missionaries, in all that regards the government of the missions, the direction of the schools confided to them, the gathering of alms, and the fulfillment of bequests given for the missions, are subject to the jurisdiction of the vicars and prefects apostolic who may make visitations and corrections in these matters (c. 296, par. 1). Vicars and prefects apostolic are the local Ordinaries in the territory which they govern (c. 198, par. 1).

Moreover, although vicars and prefects apostolic may not interfere in the internal discipline of the religious except in the cases mentioned above, if a conflict arises between the commands of a vicar or prefect apostolic and those of a religious superior, the orders of the vicar or prefect must be obeyed, saving the right of recourse *in devolutivo* to the Holy See and special statutes approved by the Holy See (c. 296, par. 2).

The meeting of the juridical expression *"in devolutivo"* has been explained above (n. 55).

261. EXPULSION FROM THE MISSIONS

Vicars and prefects apostolic may not expel religious missionaries who have been sent by the Holy See, nor may they allow the religious to leave the vicariate or prefecture permanently, without first consulting the Holy See (c. 307, par. 1). In case of public scandal, however, vicars and prefects apostolic, after consulting their council, and informing the religious superiors if this is possible, may remove the religious immediately, and afterwards inform the Holy See of the removal (c. 307, par. 2).

262. MATERIAL GOODS OF THE MISSION

Any money given to the mission, or to a religious institute for the mission, shall be administered according to the constitutions of each religious institute, the intention of the donor always being observed (c. 532, par. 1).

To invest the money mentioned above, the consent of the local Ordinary is required (c. 533, par. 1, n. 4). The same is true regarding any change in this investment (c. 533, par. 2).

The vicar or the prefect apostolic may demand that an account be given of all offerings made in favor of the mission, and he may inquire into the fulfillment of the will of the donors. If there is need of it, he may also correct and punish any negligence which he discovers (c. 296, par. 1).

263. PARTICIPATION IN THE PROPAGATION OF THE FAITH

Women religious may participate in the indulgences and privileges of the *Pontifical Works of the Propagation of the Faith* in the following manner:

1) If they belong to an Order or congregation which has missions, it is sufficient that they recite the prescribed prayers each day; that is, one Our Father and Hail Mary, with the invocation, "Saint Francis Xavier, pray for us."

2) If they belong to an Order or congregation which does not have missions, they must individually recite the above prayers, and the community to which they belong must make a donation each year to the aforementioned works (S.C. Prop., February 1, 1928).

PART TWELVE

TRANSFER TO ANOTHER
RELIGIOUS INSTITUTE OR CLASS

I

TRANSFER TO ANOTHER CLASS

In religious institutes in which there are two classes of members, for example, choir sisters and lay sisters, a transfer from one class to another is permitted unless the constitutions of the institute expressly forbid it (c. 558).

Unless the constitutions expressly forbid. The constitutions may not allow such a transfer, and in this case the constitutions and not the common law are to be followed.

The novitiate made for one class is not valid for another class (c. 558). Hence the novitiate must be repeated if the transfer is made after the religious has made her profession; it must be recommenced if the transfer is made during the first novitiate. There is never any need to repeat the postulancy since the Code speaks only of the novitiate.

If the transfer is made after the religious has made her profession, the profession must be repeated when the new novitiate is completed. If the vows of the religious expire while she is in the novitiate, they must be renewed because professed religious should not even be one day without vows (cf. *supra,* n. 169). In this case the vows must be renewed until the termination of the novitiate.

II

TRANSFER TO ANOTHER
RELIGIOUS INSTITUTE

Transfer to another institute is that action by which professed members of one religious institute are allowed to leave and join another religious institute. The regulations for transfer, therefore, do not affect novices and postulants. Since novices and postulants are legally free to leave the religious life whenever they choose, they are free to join other institutes without observing the regulations that follow for transfer.

No professed religious may transfer from one religious institute to another, even though it is a stricter one, or from one independent monastery to another, without the special permission of the Holy See (c. 632). This is true even if two institutes of diocesan approval are concerned, since the Code makes no distinction.

No professed religious, no matter who she may be, or what motives she may have for transferring to another institute. If she has good reasons for wishing to transfer, the religious should submit them to the Sacred Congregation of Religious which has competency in these matters.

Even though it is a stricter institute. These words abrogate the pre-Code privilege by which a religious could freely transfer from a less strict institute to a more strict institute.

Is the permission of the Holy See necessary in order to transfer from one institute to another, or from one monastery to another, within the same Order? For example, may one go from one congregation of Dominican Sisters to another, or from one Dominican Monastery to another, without special permission? To answer this question the following distinctions must be made:

1) If the monastery which the religious wishes to leave is an independent one, the apostolic permission is certainly required. For example, if a religious wishes to transfer from an independent monastery in New York to an independent monastery in Rome. In this case, however, the novitiate will be dispensed with since it is a question of two religious institutes which follow the same rule (cf. *infra,* n. 264).

2) If the transfer desired is from one house to another house of the same institute or of the same congregation, then it is clear that no Apostolic authorization is required since the permission or the command of the proper superiors is sufficient.

3) If the desired transfer is between two institutes or congregations of the same Order, which have their own juridic personalities and their own rule, then Apostolic permission is required even though the religious would belong to the same Order after the transfer. For example, if a Franciscan sister belonging to a congregation whose motherhouse is in Chicago should wish to transfer to a congregation whose motherhouse is in New York, she would have to have Apostolic authorization.

The consent of the monastery or institute which is to receive the religious is also required. This consent must be expressed with all the formalities and conditions which are employed in receiving a postulant or a novice. The Code makes no mention of the necessity of acceptance by the new institute, but from the fact that a new novitiate and a new profession are required, it is implied that all of the formalities required for the novitiate and profession are to be observed. It is also the practice of the Sacred Congregation of Religious to demand the opinion of the monastery or institute which the religious intends to leave, before granting permission for the transfer.

264. NEW NOVITIATE AND PROFESSION

When a religious transfers from one religious institute to another
with the permission of the Holy See, she must repeat the novitiate and
profession just as though she had never been a religious (c. 633, par.
1 and par. 2).

The following should be noted, however:

1) During the novitiate the vows endure, and with the vows, all of
the obligations which are common to the religious state. The rights
and particular obligations of the institute which the religious has left
are suspended, but the novice is obliged to obey the superiors of the
new institute and also the mistress of novices in virtue of the vow
of obedience (c. 633, par. 1).

2) Admission to the novitiate must be made according to the norms
referred to above (n. 125 and n. 126). Likewise, the novitiate must be
made in conformity with the regulations explained above (n. 127 ff.).
During the novitiate, the religious, although bound by vows, must
wear the habit of the novices of the new institute (S.C. Rel., May
14, 1923). The postulancy need not be repeated, since the Code speaks
only of the novitiate (c. 633, par. 1 and par. 2).

If a religious transfers from one monastery to another monastery of
the same order (for example, from the cloistered Dominican monastery of Saints Dominic and Sixtus in Rome to the cloistered Dominican monastery of Saint Agnes in New York), it is not necessary to
repeat either the novitiate or profession (c. 633, par. 3).

Of the same Order. In order that the monasteries belong to the
same Order, it is not sufficient that they follow the same rule; they
must also be subject to the same supreme head of the Order. For
example, the different Dominican monasteries which have the Master
General of the Dominican Order as their supreme head, belong to
the same Order, but the Claretian Franciscan nuns and the Cappuchin
Franciscan nuns do not belong to the same Order because the supreme
heads of the orders are different. This is also true in the case of religious congregations which belong to the same Order. Therefore, if
one transfers from one to another, the novitiate must always be repeated in conformity with canon 633, paragraphs 1 and 2.

Even when a transfer to another institute is made, the novitiate
may be prolonged by the legitimate superiors, but not for more than
six months (c. 571, par. 2).

When a religious in solemn or simple perpetual vows transfers to another institute in which solemn or simple perpetual vows are professed, after repeating her novitiate, she must omit temporary profession and either be admitted to solemn or simple perpetual profession, or be sent back to the institute from which she came (c. 634).

In this case, therefore, temporary profession is omitted, but when the novitiate is completed, the superiors have the right to extend the period of probation; not, however, for more than one year (c. 634). The vote of the council or chapter is definitive in this case (P.C.I., July 1, 1922).

The following points apply to a religious who is only in temporary vows when she joins another institute:

1) If she joins an institute in which solemn or simple perpetual vows are professed, when the novitiate is completed, she may be admitted to perpetual profession if she is twenty-one years old and if the three years of temporary vows required before perpetual profession were completed in the former institute. Otherwise, she must profess temporary vows until the time when the three years temporary profession and her twenty-first year are completed.

2) If she joins another institute in which only temporary vows are professed and periodically renewed, after she has completed the novitiate, even if she is in solemn vows, unless she has an Apostolic indult, she must profess only temporary vows as the members of the new institute do, and she must profess their rule (c. 636).

The vote of the chapter and of the council for admission is deliberative because it is truly a case of first profession (c. 575, par. 2).

A religious who transfers from one religious institute to another, and does not make profession in this institute when her novitiate is completed, must return immediately to her former institute, unless in the meantime her vows have expired (c. 633, par. 2). This is true even if the new institute is one in which vows are not pronounced. If the vows were temporary and have expired in the meantime, the religious is no longer obliged to remain in religion, and the religious institute has no obligation to keep her. Thus if she should wish to re-enter her former monastery, a special dispensation from the Holy See would perhaps be necessary, just as for one who has left a religious order and then wishes to return.

265. Effects of Transfer

When a religious transfers from one monastery to another monastery of the same institute, from the very day on which she makes this transfer, or when a religious joins another religious institute, from the day on which she makes her new profession, she loses all the rights and is freed from all the obligations of the former religious institute or monastery, and she assumes all the rights and duties of the new religious institute or monastery (c. 635, n. 1).

All the rights and obligations; that is, those which were based on her membership in the institute which she has left; not the rights and duties which are inherent in the religious state as such; these endure as long as the individual stays in religion.

The vows endure during the novitiate, and only the particular obligations of the institute which the religious has left cease to bind (c. 633, par. 1). Once the profession is renewed, all the rights and obligations implied in the profession in the new institute are assumed. Hence even if a religious was first bound by solemn vows, and the institute where she now makes profession is of simple vows, the solemnity of the vows ceases in virtue of the new profession and the new vows are merely simple unless the Apostolic indult which authorized the transition to the new institute specifies the contrary (c. 636).

In regard to temporal goods:

1) If it is a question of goods over which the former institute or monastery has already acquired ownership, even due to the work of the religious who is departing, the institute or monastery retains ownership of these goods (c. 635, n. 2). For example, if the religious has given to the monastery or congregation, with due permission, all or part of the goods which she possessed over and above her dowry, the monastery retains ownership of these goods because a donation legitimately made and accepted may not be revoked. The same is true of all these goods which are acquired by the monastery thru the work of the religious; for example, through her nursing or teaching (cf. *supra*, n. 173).

2) When it is a question of the dowry, its revenue or other personal goods, if the religious transfers from one monastery to another of the same institute, from the day of the transfer these goods belong to the monastery which she joins. But, on the contrary, if the religious

transfers from one congregation to another congregation, the new institute has a right to the goods only from the day on which profession is made (c. 551, par. 2).

3) During the novitiate, the new religious institute has a right only to that just compensation for food and clothing which has been established by the constitutions or by express agreement (c. 635, n. 2). If such a sum is exacted, it should be deducted from the fruits of the dowry. If no compensation is required, it seems the fruits of the dowry belong to the old institute until profession is made in the new one.

4) A religious who previously professed solemn vows and who will profess only simple vows in the new institute, reacquires on the day of her new profession the capacity of possessing temporal goods (c. 580, par. 1). Before profession, therefore, she should make a will which will be effective on her profession day (c. 569, par. 3), and as soon as she acquires some property she must make a cession of its administration and a disposition of its use and revenue (c. 569, par. 1 and par. 2).

5) On the other hand, a religious who previously professed simple vows and in the new institute will profess solemn vows, retains the capacity of possessing and acquiring temporal goods during the novitiate. Before solemn vows, however, she must make the renunciation of property required of religious at that time (c. 581, par. 1).

6) If a religious professed of simple vows transfers to an institute of simple vows, before her new profession she must renew her cession and disposition, because in virtue of the transfer, the previous cession and disposition are voided (cf. c. 580, par. 3). The wisdom of this is clear when it is considered that many institutes require their members to cede administration of property in favor of the institute. It would be unfitting to have a religious' property administered by one institute while she belongs to another. However, if a will was made, it remains in force and may not be changed except in conformity with canon 583, paragraph 2.

7) When a religious with an annuity or a pension transfers to another institute, the annuity or pension belongs to the new institute after profession. This is true even if a religious in solemn vows had given it to her institute before taking solemn vows. However, if we interpret canon 635, number 2, strictly, there is room for doubt whether the pension, when it has been ceded in favor of the first religious

institute, belongs to the new institute from the day the religious joins the new institute, or only after she makes her profession. It would seem to be more prudent to wait until the religious has made her profession in the new institute before transferring the pension or annuity.

PART THIRTEEN

DEPARTURE FROM THE
RELIGIOUS LIFE

Abandonment of the religious life implies that a religious temporarily or permanently leaves her religious institute without transferring to another. Abandonment of religious life occurs through expiration of vows, exclaustration, secularization, apostasy, flight and dismissal. In the following chapters we will consider these various means of leaving the religious state.

I

DEPARTURE AFTER TEMPORARY VOWS

266. FREEDOM TO LEAVE RELIGION

If one is bound by temporary vows and they expire (for example, if the three year period for which the vows were professed has elapsed), then, a religious may freely leave her religious institute without any dispensation (c. 637).

May freely leave; that is, she is free as far as any juridical obligations contracted by her profession are concerned. Whatever is fitting and obligatory concerning her obligation to persevere in her vocation is something which does not pertain to the common law of the Church. This problem rests in the sphere of conscience and spiritual guidance.

The religious institute may, for just and reasonable motives, exclude a religious from renewing temporary vows or from taking perpetual vows (c. 637).

The religious institute. The superiors who can dismiss the religious at the end of temporary vows are the same ones who can admit them to profession.

For just and reasonable motives. The Code does not say what these motives should or can be; it is left to the prudence and conscience of the superior to decide. But the Code does point out that illness is not a just and reasonable motive for dismissal unless it is clearly proven that the religious had fraudulently concealed or hidden the illness before profession (c. 637).

If a religious becomes afflicted with a mental illness during temporary vows, she may not profess vows when her temporary vows expire, but she must be kept in the institute in the same juridical state in which she was when the malady manifested itself (S.C.Rel., February 5, 1925). If illness has been contracted but there are other reasons which are more than sufficient for dismissing a religious, the superiors may send her away, notwithstanding the fact that she has contracted the illness in the institute and after profession. The Code only forbids the dismissal of a religious solely because of ill-health contracted after profession; it does not wish to exclude other just motives for which it is judged opportune by superiors to deny a renewal of vows. It is understood, however, that superiors must proceed with all prudence and charity.

A professed religious who spontaneously, or because of dismissal, leaves her religious institute, and then wishes to return, must have an Apostolic indult to do so (c. 542, par. 1). If she receives this indult she must repeat her novitiate, but not it seems, her postulancy (cf. c. 640, par. 2).

Is an Apostolic indult of re-entry required if a religious has doubts about her vocation and does not renew her vows on the day they expire, but stays in the monastery or convent, and a few days later, her doubts being dispelled, wishes to renew her vows? Many good canonists agree that in this case an indult of re-entry is not necessary. It is true that the Code, in virtue of canon 577, forbids religious to be without vows for even one day, but it does not say that if a religious does not immediately renew her vows that she automatically ceases to be a religious.

267. Compensation

Religious who leave an institute when their temporary vows have expired, or who are dismissed by their superiors, cannot demand any compensation for the work they have performed for the religious institute (c. 643, par. 1; cf. *supra,* n. 150 and n. 170). Some institutes to avoid future difficulties, have their members sign a document to this effect when they enter religion.

Personal goods should be restored in their entirety to those dismissed or leaving at the expiration of vows, because they retained radical ownership over these goods while they were professed religious. The institute may keep only the revenues which have already matured, if these revenues were given to the institute before profession (c. 580).

Revenues which have already matured, include those which have not yet been received by the institute but to which it has a right.

The **dowry** should also be returned if the religious brought one with her when she entered religious life. If, however, a religious who has been received without a dowry leaves the religious life and has not the means to support herself, out of charity the religious institute must give her what is necessary for a safe and proper return to her home and provide her with the means of a decent livelihood for a reasonable length of time. This should be done in accordance with natural equity and by mutual agreement. In case of disagreement, the matter is to be settled by the local Ordinary (c. 643, par. 2).

By mutual agreement; that is, agreement between the religious who is leaving and the religious institute. If the interested parties cannot reach an agreement, the local Ordinary is to intervene.

II

INDULT OF EXCLAUSTRATION

An indult of exclaustration is the permission by which a religious is allowed to remain temporarily outside the convent and to be exempt for a time from the authority of the superiors of the religious institute to which she belongs (c. 638; c. 639).

Temporarily. This condition differentiates an indult of exclaustration from an indult of secularization, since the latter is a permanent or perpetual departure from religious life, as we shall explain below (Part XIII, Chap. 3).

Exempt for the time from the authority of the superiors of the religious institute to which she belongs. This condition distinguishes an indult of exclaustration from a simple permission to stay for a certain time outside of the convent, for example, in a college, or with one's family (cf. *supra*, n. 210, par. 3).

268. GRANTING OF THE INDULT

An indult of exclaustration: in the case of institutes of papal approval can be granted only by the Apostolic See (c. 638); in institutes

342

of diocesan approval it may be granted by the local Ordinary or the Holy See (c. 638).

Local Ordinary; that is, it can be granted by the bishop of the place where the religious lives and not the bishop of the place where the mother house of the institute is located (P.C.I., July 24, 1939).

269. EFFECTS OF THE INDULT

Six effects oblige one who has obtained an indult of exclaustration:

1) She remains bound by the vows and all the other obligations of her profession which can be observed under the conditions in which she now lives (c. 639). Hence:

   a) The vow of chastity remains unchanged.

   b) The vow of obedience remains, but the competent superior is the local Ordinary (cf. 4, below).

   c) The vow of poverty is still in effect but mitigated so that one may administrate and use her own goods (cf. 5, below).

   d) The obligations of the common life which cannot be observed cease, but certain constitutional obligations which can be continued, such as fasting and reciting certain prayers, should be observed.

   e) The obligations for religious contained in the Code (cf. Part VIII) must be observed insofar as possible.

2) She must put aside the habit of her community, at least in its exterior form (c. 639).

At least in its exterior form. That is, she must put aside that part of the habit which appears externally. She may wear the little scapular which in some institutes is considered a symbol of the religious habit (cf. *supra*, Part VIII, Chap. 3).

3) She loses active and passive voice for the duration of the indult, but she enjoys the purely spiritual privileges of her institute, for example, indulgences (c. 639).

Does she also enjoy the suffrages of her community? It would seem that she does not. Suffrages are not merely a privilege, but they are a right acquired by members of a religious institute in conformity with their particular constitutions. An exclaustrated religious, during the time of the indult, is not subject to her proper superiors, and consequently she cannot be considered, strictly speaking, a member of the institute; at least she cannot be considered an active member.

Therefore, she does not participate in the rights which are proper to these members. This point of view is confirmed by the Code which distinguishes between the purely spiritual favors and suffrages that novices may enjoy. We must admit, however, that this distinction is not repeated in canon 639.

4) She is subject to the Ordinary of the place where she lives, and not only after the manner of the simple faithful, but also in virtue of the vow of obedience (c. 639).

5) She is free while the indult lasts to administrate and to use her own goods, if she has any, insofar as this is necessary for the needs of daily life. Nevertheless, she remains bound by the vow of poverty which she must observe both in letter and in spirit in accordance with the rule of her religious institute. If she earns anything it belongs to the community, which in turn should use this to provide for the support of the religious.

6) She is strictly obliged when her indult of exclaustration has expired to return to her community as soon as possible. If she cannot do this she must petition for an extension of the indult; otherwise, she is liable to become a fugitive or an apostate (cf. *infra*, n. 274 ff.).

When her indult of exclaustration has expired; that is, the religious' obligation to return to the convent begins at this time, but there is nothing to prevent her from returning before the indult expires if she so desires.

Two new forms of exclaustration were recently introduced by the Sacred Congregation of Religious. One, known as *qualified* exclaustration, pertains to religious priests and is therefore not pertinent to our study. The other type, exclaustration *by the will of the Holy See*, is imposed on a religious when she is disturbing the peace of the community but has not committed a crime for which she could be dismissed. The effects of exclaustration *by the will of the Holy See* are substantially the same as those mentioned above. However, this new type of exclaustration is not adopted for any definite period of time and the religious cannot return to the community unless she first obtains permission from the Holy See.

III

INDULT OF SECULARIZATION

An indult of secularization is the permission granted to a religious to live permanently "in the world" without any further connection with the institute in which she has made profession (c. 638; c. 640, par. 1).

Permanently. This differentiates an indult of secularization from an indult of exclaustration which is granted only for a definite period of time (cf. *supra*, Chap. 2).

Without any further connection with the institute in which she has made profession. Hence a secularized religious ceases entirely to be a religious.

270. GRANTING OF THE INDULT

In institutes of papal approval, an indult of secularization is granted only by the Holy See. In institutes of diocesan approval it may be validly and licitly granted by the local Ordinary or the Holy See (c. 638).

The local Ordinary, in this case, is the bishop of the diocese where the religious lives (P.C.I., July 24, 1939).

345

271. ACCEPTANCE OF THE INDULT

An indult of secularization is not effective until the religious who applied for it accepts it. She may refuse to accept it, even if she requested it, and even if the dispensation has been "executed" by the person assigned to do so by the Sacred Congregation of Religious. However, once an indult has been accepted and signed by the religious, the decision is irrevocable (S.C.Rel., August 1, 1922). In order to do away with vacillation on the part of the departing religious in accepting and signing the indult, the Sacred Congregation of Religious adds the following clause to the indult of secularization for religious who are not priests: "If this indult which was requested is not accepted within ten days after the religious has received it, it loses its value."

Superiors are not deprived of the right to dismiss a religious merely because she refuses to accept an indult of secularization. If they have just and serious reasons, they may dismiss her in accordance with the norms prescribed for dismissal, but not merely because she refused to accept the rescript of secularization (cf. *infra,* n. 279).

272. EFFECTS OF THIS INDULT

The following effects oblige a religious who has obtained an indult of secularization:

1) She is separated from her religious institute and no longer has rights or obligations in the community (c. 640, par. 1, n. 1).

2) She is obliged to jut aside her religious habit, at least in its exterior form *(loc. cit.;* cf. *supra,* n. 269).

3) She must be considered as one of the ordinary faithful *(loc. cit.).*

4) She is automatically freed from her vows (c. 640, par. 1, n. 2), even the vow of chastity, and from the obligation of reciting the divine office to which she might be bound in virtue of her religious profession *(loc. cit.).*

5) She is likewise freed from the observance of the rule and constitutions and all obligations of religious *(loc. cit.).*

Therefore, a secularized religious is no longer a religious. If she should wish to return, she would have to obtain an Apostolic indult and repeat her novitiate and profession, and her place among the professed would be determined by the date of her second and not her first profession (c. 640, par. 2).

273. DISPOSITION OF TEMPORAL GOODS

A religious who has obtained an indult of secularization must observe the following in regard to temporal goods:

1) She may not demand any compensation for services rendered in religion (c. 643, par. 1; cf. *supra,* n. 150). Some institutes wisely demand that members sign a document to this affect when they enter religion.

2) If the religious was in *simple vows,* all personal goods to which she retained title of ownership are to be returned to her. If the revenue of her property was disposed of in favor of the institute, then only the revenues that are already due to the institute may be retained. The cession and disposition of property rights cease to have any effect (c. 580, par. 3), and the last testament may be freely changed or nullified (c. 569, par. 3). If the religious was in *solemn vows,* the renunciation she made before solemn vows loses its force, but no one has an obligation in justice to return the goods that they received from her through the renunciation. The validity of such a renunciation is conditioned upon the profession of solemn vows (c. 581, par. 1), not upon the perseverance of the person in the religious life.

3) If she brought a dowry with her when she entered the religious life, it must be returned to her after deducting revenues which have already matured. If she has been received without a dowry and has not the means of support, or she had a dowry but it is insufficient to provide for her support, the religious institute, out of charity, must give her what is necessary for a safe and proper return to her home and should provide her with the means of a decent livelihood for a suitable length of time. This should be done in accordance with natural equity and mutual agreement. In case of disagreement, the matter should be settled by the local Ordinary (c. 643, par. 2; P.C.I., March 2, 1924).

IV

APOSTATE AND FUGITIVE RELIGIOUS

274. APOSTATE RELIGIOUS

An apostate religious is one who, after the profession of solemn or simple perpetual vows, unlawfully departs from her religious house with the intention not to return, or who, after a lawful departure from the religious house, does not return, deciding to withdraw herself from subjection to her religious superiors (c. 644, par. 1).

Apostate religious should not be confused with those who apostatize from the faith. The latter offense is also a grave one, but does not have the same canonical sanctions as apostasy from religious life.

Solemn or simple vows. Hence a religious in temporary vows who unlawfully leaves her religious house before the expiration of her vows sins gravely (cf. *supra,* n. 198, B), but she is not considered an apostate.

With the intention of not returning. A culpable intention of not returning is automatically to be presumed if within one month after

348

her illicit departure, the religious has not returned and has not manifested to her superior her intention of returning (c. 644, par. 3). The culpable intention of not returning can be manifested in other ways before a month expires, for example, if the religious attempts marriage or accepts a position incompatible with religious life.

275. FUGITIVE RELIGIOUS

Fugitive religious are of two kinds:

1) Those who leave the convent or monastery without permission of the superiors, but who have the intention to return to their own or another convent or monastery of the same institute.

2) Those who leave their convent or monastery with the permission of their superiors but do not return to it at the appointed time (c. 644, par. 3).

Those who leave the convent or monastery, whether in temporary or perpetual vows, can be fugitives in the canonical sense. As we have seen, only those in perpetual vows can be classified as apostates in the canonical sense. It seems, therefore, that if one in temporary vows performs actions which would classify her as an apostate were she in perpetual vows, she should be punished as a fugitive.

At the appointed time. Canonists agree that a religious must be absent from her convent two or three days contrary to the will of her superior before she can be classified as a fugitive.

The difference between a fugitive and apostate is that the former, although unlawfully leaving the convent for a certain time, does not intend to leave the religious institute; an apostate from religion, however, leaves the religious institute itself.

In order for a religious to be truly a fugitive, it is not sufficient that she merely leave the convent or monastery without permission. It is also required that she have some intention of withdrawing herself from religious obedience, at least for a short time. Consequently, if a religious leaves the convent against the wishes of her superior to visit her family or to be with a friend, she certainly commits a sin of disobedience, but she cannot be considered a fugitive unless she has the intention of withdrawing herself from the obedience due her superiors. The same is true of a religious who lawfully leaves the convent and then fails to return within the time allotted to her; she commits a sin if she does so without a justifying reason, but she does not, because of this fact alone, become a fugitive.

276. ATTITUDE OF SUPERIORS

In the case of nuns, the local Ordinary has the obligation of solicitously seeking apostates and fugitives and seeing to it that they are readmitted to the convent if he finds them truly penitent (c. 645, par. 2).

If he finds them truly penitent. Hence there is no obligation of readmitting into the convent a fugitive or apostate nun who does not manifest sufficiently sincere signs of repentance. On the contrary, if she persists in her wickedness, steps should be taken to expel her canonically.

If a monastery is exempt, this obligation of seeking apostates and fugitives also devolves upon the regular superior (c. 645, par. 2).

Also. Hence even in this case the obligation of the bishop does not cease, but both the local Ordinary and the regular superior must work simultaneously for the return of the apostate or fugitive nun.

In the case of sisters, it pertains to the respective superiors to seek apostate or fugitive religious with solicitude, and to receive them anew if they are truly penitent (c. 645, par. 2).

If they are truly penitent. An insincere fugitive or apostate need not be readmitted since their illicit departure is sufficient grounds for proceeding to their dismissal.

277. OBLIGATIONS OF APOSTATES AND FUGITIVES

Apostate and fugitive religious are not freed from the obligations which they formerly had, and moreover, they are strictly bound to return to their convents without delay (c. 645, par. 1).

278. CANONICAL PENALTIES

A religious who becomes an **apostate from religion** incurs the following:

1) She automatically incurs excommunication which is reserved to the Ordinary of the place where she resides (c. 2385).

2) She is immediately deprived of all the privileges of her religious institute (c. 2385) and the right to suffrages as well (cf. *supra,* n. 269, par. 3).

3) She is forever deprived of active and passive voice if she returns to her community. Moreover, she should be punished by her superiors with other penalties which are proportionate to the gravity of her guilt, in accordance with the constitutions of her particular institute (c. 2385).

4) She is to be considered automatically dismissed from religion if she not only abandons the religious life but also publicly apostatizes from her Catholic faith, or runs away with a man, or attempts to contracts marriage, even civilly (c. 2385; c. 646; cf. *infra,* n. 279).

A **fugitive religious** incurs the following:

1) She automatically incurs deprivation of any office she may hold in her religious institute (c. 2386).

2) She must be punished in accordance with the constitutions when she returns; if the constitutions do not provide for such punishment, then she must be punished by her major superior in a manner which is proportionate to the gravity of her guilt (c. 2386).

V

IMMEDIATE DISMISSAL OF RELIGIOUS

Dismissal from the religious life implies an authentic declaration made by competent superiors that a religious no longer belongs to the religious institute of which she was a professed member. It implies, therefore, that the religious who is dismissed is bound to leave the religious institute, even against her will.

Sometimes, in order that dismissal be legitimate, it must be preceded by certain formalities and admonitions; at other times it may be immediate. In this chapter we shall treat immediate dismissal, and in Chapters VI and VII we shall consider dismissal which requires legal formalities.

279. CAUSES OF IMMEDIATE DISMISSAL

A religious may be immediately expelled when she has committed one of the following crimes:

1) If she publicly apostatizes from the Catholic faith (c. 646, par. 1, n. 1).

Apostatizes from the Catholic faith; that is, she totally renounces her faith, even though she does not join another religion or sect (c. 1325, par. 2).

From the faith. Hence, it is not sufficient that she merely apostatize from the religious institute in which she made profession (cf. *supra,* n. 274).

Publicly; that is, the fact must already be known by the public, or at least the circumstances must be such that it seems impossible for it not to become public knowledge (c. 2197, n. 1).

2) If she runs away with a man (c. 646, par. 1, n. 2).

A religious; that is, even if she is only in simple vows.

Runs away; that is, she leaves the convent without permission, or even if leaving the convent with permission, instead of returning, runs away with a man. Flight with a man is sufficient reason for immediate dismissal; it is not necessary that the religious be also an apostate.

With a man, no matter who he may be, single or married, or a religious, of age or a minor, with the intention or without the intention of contracting marriage.

3) If she has contracted or attempted to contract marriage, even if only civilly (c. 646, par. 1, n. 3).

Contracted or attempted to contract marriage. A religious in solemn vows can only attempt to contract marriage since her vow is an invalidating impediment to marriage, but a religious in simple vows, although she sins if she contracts marriage during the period she is bound by vows, can contract a valid marriage if there are no other impediments (cf. *supra,* n. 154).

If only civilly. Any kind of marriage, even though it be false, is sufficient reason for expulsion. Concubinage alone would not suffice, or at least it would not suffice in virtue of canon 646, for immediate expulsion. However, if the fact of concubinage were publicly known, it would be sufficient grounds for expulsion on the basis of canon 653, in which it is stated that a religious in such a situation can be immediately dismissed.

4) If she has given grave external scandal or if there is danger that

she will cause very serious injury to the community (c. 653; S.C.Rel., May 16, 1911).

Grave external scandal; that is, scandal which is known outside the convent, so that the faithful are truly and greatly scandalized by the actions of the religious; for example, when she has committed a truly infamous crime, has been guilty of grave public immorality, homicide or public concubinage.

Very serious injury to the community. This could be due to the scandal itself, or because of other grave reasons; for example, if a religious is so evil and vindictive as to seriously threaten to set fire to the convent or injure the superior. In these and similar cases there is sufficient cause for immediate dismissal.

280. Procedure in Immediate Dismissals

In the first three cases mentioned above (n. 279, pars. 1, 2 and 3), it suffices that the major superior, having convoked her council or chapter in accordance with the prescriptions of the constitutions, makes a declaration of the fact of the crime. Once the existence of the crime is thus attested to, the religious is considered by Canon Law as expelled from her religious institute (c. 646, par. 2).

The major superior. Hence the provincial as well as the superior general has the power to declare a sister dismissed from her religious institute.

Makes a declaration. It is not necessary that the crime be declared in order for the religious to be dismissed; for valid immediate dismissal due to the crimes enumerated in canon 646, it is sufficient that the crime actually have been committed. If the superior and her council are negligent in declaring the crime, the religious is nevertheless dismissed (P.C.I., July 30, 1934).

In the fourth case mentioned above, that is, in case of grave public scandal or of great danger to the community, the dismissal may be made not only by the major superior with the consent of her council, but also, if time does not permit recourse to the major superior, by the local superior with the consent of her council and of the local Ordinary (c. 653).

In this case, the matter must be immediately submitted to the Holy See by the local Ordinary whose consent the local superior has asked, or by the major superior, if it is she who has pronounced the sentence of expulsion (c. 653).

A religious who has been dismissed is obliged to lay aside immediately her religious habit, at least in its external form (c. 653). Her vows cease if they were temporary; they continue to exist if they were perpetual (c. 648; c. 669).

Put aside the habit; see number 269, above.

Superiors shall take care to preserve in the archives the documents attesting to the truth of the crime which has been committed by the religious and by reason of which she has been dismissed (c. 646, par. 2).

281. EFFECTS OF DISMISSAL

If the vows are temporary, a religious who is legitimately dismissed is automatically absolved from her vows and returns to the secular state (c. 648). **If the vows are perpetual,** a religious remains bound by them even after dismissal, unless special indults from the Holy See declare otherwise (c. 669, par. 1); but she may no longer wear the religious habit (c. 653; c. 668). Thus another juridical act besides dismissal is necessary to free a dismissed religious in perpetual vows from the obligations of poverty, chastity and obedience.

Whether the religious is in temporary or perpetual vows, the religious institute is bound to return the dowry to the religious who has been dismissed if she brought a dowry with her when she entered religious life. If she was received without a dowry, the institute must at least give her the assistance of which we have spoken above (n. 267).

Is a religious institute of women obliged to readmit a penitent sister or nun who has been dismissed, just as a clerical institute must readmit a penitent cleric (c. 672, par. 1)? It seems that if she was dismissed for one of the crimes mentioned in c. 646, there is certainly no need to readmit her (P.C.I., July 30, 1934). Even if she was dismissed for other reasons, it seems probable that there is no need on the part of the institute to take her back.

VI

DISMISSAL OF RELIGIOUS IN TEMPORARY VOWS

282. CAUSES OF DISMISSAL

Besides the urgent cases which demand the immediate dismissal of religious, there are ordinary cases which may lead to dismissal of religious in temporary vows. There can be various reasons for such a dismissal but they must always be grave. The reason can arise on the part of the religious or on the part of the religious institute (c. 647, par. 2); in other words, a religious may be expelled either because her presence is harmful to the community or because for this particular religious, remaining in religion is a greater evil than good.

The Code does not indicate what constitutes a grave reason for ordinary dismissal of those in temporary vows, but we may note two things in this regard:

1) A lack of religious spirit which is a source of scandal to others, if repeated admonitions accomplish nothing, is a sufficient reason for dismissal (c. 647, par. 2, n. 2).

2) Illness or poor health is not a sufficient reason for a dismissal, unless it is known with certainty that such a state of health existed before profession and that it was culpably concealed or disguised (c. 647, par. 2, n. 2), or unless there are other grave and just reasons for the dismissal of the religious accompanying the serious illness (cf. *supra,* n. 266).

The reasons for dismissal of a religious must be known with certitude by the superior who authorizes or orders the expulsion, but it is not necessary that the reasons be proven by a formal trial (c. 647, par. 2, n. 3).

283. SUPERIORS COMPETENT TO DISMISS

In the case of **nuns,** a religious in temporary vows may be dismissed or expelled before the expiration of her vows by the local Ordinary; and when the monastery is subject to regulars, by the regular superior, provided that the superior of the monastery together with her council have attested in writing to the reasons for dismissal (c. 647, par. 1). It is not clear from canon 647, paragraph 1, how the Ordinary and major superior should proceed, but in such a grave matter it would seem best that they act together.

In the case of **sisters belonging to institutes of pontifical approval,** the superior general, or even the local superior, if the monastery is *sui juris,* that is, independent, may dismiss a professed religious in temporary vows, with the consent of her council, which is to be expressed by secret vote (c. 647, par. 1). The consent of the council is required under pain of invalidity (c. 105, n. 1).

If the **sisters belong to institutes of diocesan approval,** then it pertains to the Ordinary of the place in which the religious resides to dismiss a religious who is in temporary vows; but the Ordinary must not make use of this right if he does not first advise the superiors of the religious congregation of his action, or if the superiors have good reasons for disagreeing with his decision (c. 647, par. 1). If the superiors do not agree and the Ordinary acts contrary to their opinion, the superiors have the right and duty to appeal to the Holy See.

284. MANNER OF PROCEDURE

Besides the necessity of obtaining the consent of the council or chapter (cf. *supra*, n. 283), when dismissing a religious in temporary vows, the following must be observed:

1) The reasons for the dismissal must be made known to her and she must be given full freedom to answer the charges (c. 647, par. 2, n. 3). Moreover, before proceeding with the dismissal, through counsel, correction and penances, every effort must be made to induce her to amend her ways (c. 647, par. 2, n. 2). If a religious is to be dismissed for offences contrary to the rule and constitutions, or for lack of the proper religious spirit, at least two warnings must precede the dismissal. Usually, these warnings should be made in writing or before witnesses, in such a way that the religious cannot deny later on that they were given.

2) The answer of the religious who is to be dismissed to the reasons set forth for her dismissal must be faithfully transmitted to the superior who shall have to approve the dismissal, if there is need for approval (c. 647, par. 2, n. 3).

3) If a religious who is dismissed had no dowry when she was received into the community and has no means of supporting herself, the religious institute is obliged in charity to furnish her for a time with the means necessary for living in a fitting manner (c. 643, par. 1 and par. 2; c. 647, par. 2, n. 5; cf. *supra*, n. 273, par. 3).

4) Finally, in the process of expulsion or dismissal, all the other rules and prescriptions made by the Church for similar cases must be observed, and the fulfillment of these requirements is a grave obligation for superiors (c. 647, par. 2). Moreover, the religious has the right to have recourse to the Holy See against a decree of dismissal, and while the appeal is pending, the dismissal has no juridical effect and may not be enforced (c. 647, par. 2). The useful time for making an appeal to a decree of dismissal is ten days from the moment in which the decree is conveyed to the dismissed religious, providing she knows she has the right of appeal and is able to exercise it (S.C.Rel., July 20, 1923). If she is ignorant of this right, or cannot institute the proceeding necessary for the appeal, then the useful time for appeal is not computed. The superior should always inform the religious of her right to appeal and the way to institute it at the same time that she informs her of the decree of dismissal.

285. EFFECTS OF DISMISSAL

A religious in simple temporary vows who has been legitimately dismissed: (1) is automatically freed from her religious vows (c. 648), and consequently, from all the obligations of the religious life; and, (2) must immediately lay aside the religious habit (c. 668; cf. *supra*, n. 280).

The religious institute has no other obligations than to restore the personal goods of the religious, if it has any, and to return the dowry, if the religious had one when she entered religious life. If she had no dowry, the charitable assistance spoken of above should be given her if it is necessary (n. 273).

VII

DISMISSAL OF RELIGIOUS IN PERPETUAL VOWS

286. CAUSES FOR DISMISSAL

With the exception of the extraordinary crimes spoken of above (cf. *supra*, n. 279), for which a religious may be immediately dismissed, the following conditions must be fulfilled in order that a professed religious in solemn or simple perpetual vows may be lawfully dismissed:

1) The reasons for dismissal must be grave and external, that is, the crime must be committed in such a way that they can be proven in a juridical process (c. 651, par. 1).

External. It is not necessary, however, that the crimes be committed publicly, whether outside or inside the monastery; it is sufficient that they be external acts and done in such a way that they can be proven in the process of dismissal.

Grave. Hence the cause for dismissal may not be venial sins.

2) It must be proven that the religious is incorrigible (*loc. cit.*).

3) This incorrigibility must be established by a sufficient number of

360

attempts to correct the religious, so that in the judgment of the superiors there is no hope of amendment *(loc. cit.).*

Before incorrigibility can be established, the religious must be admonished at least twice. The Code does not say how these attempts to
correct the religious are to be carried out. Certainly the admonitions
in strict canonical form which are prescribed for dismissing men religious are not required. However, at least two or three admonitions
under threat of dismissal should be made by the superiors, because
the Sacred Congregation usually demands these before confirming
a dismissal.

287. MANNER OF PROCEDURE

In the case of **sisters who belong to institutes of diocesan approval,**
the Ordinary of the place where the convent of the religious in question is situated, must examine the case submitted by the superiors and
issue the decree of dismissal or expulsion (c. 652, par. 1).

When it is a question of **sisters who are members of institutes of
pontifical approval,** but who are not nuns, the superior general must
refer the matter to the Sacred Congregation of Religious, submitting
to it all of the acts and documents, and the Sacred Congregation will
decide what action is most opportune in the case (c. 652, par. 3).

In the case of nuns, the local Ordinary must send to the Sacred
Congregation of Religious all of the acts and documents, together with
his own opinion and that of the regular superior if the monastery is
subject to regulars (c. 652, par. 2), and the Sacred Congregation will
determine what is the most opportune course of action in the case (c.
652, par. 3).

In every case, and no matter what type of religious institute is
involved, if the religious who is expelled was received without a dowry, and does not have the means to provide for herself, the institute
is obliged in charity to give her what is necessary to return to her
home in a safe and fitting manner, and to provide her, for a certain
period of time, with the means of a decent livelihood. This should be
done in accordance with natural equity and by mutual agreement (c.
643, par. 2; c. 653, par. 3). In case of disagreement the matter is to
be settled by the local Ordinary (c. 643, par. 2; cf. *supra,* n. 273).

Finally, a religious who is being expelled has the right to present her reasons for her conduct and these reasons must be faithfully entered in the acts of the proceedings (c. 650, par. 2; c. 651, par. 2). If the decree of dismissal was issued by the local Ordinary, the dismissed religious may always appeal to the Holy See (c. 1569). In the case of the religious whose case was decided by the Sacred Congregation of Religious, there is no appeal, although sending the documents to the Holy See implicitly includes an appeal.

288. EFFECTS OF DISMISSAL

When a religious in perpetual vows is dismissed, she is obliged to lay aside her habit immediately, at least in its external form (c. 653).

At least in its external form; see number 193, above.

Nevertheless, she remains bound by her vows (c. 669, par. 1). There are two exceptions to this rule:

1) If the constitutions expressly determine otherwise, that is, if the particular constitutions state that the profession will be made under the condition that if the religious should be expelled for any reason the vows will cease (c. 669, par. 1).

2) If the Holy See declares in the rescript of dismissal that the religious is dispensed from her vows (c. 669, par. 1).

When a religious has been dismissed and has not been absolved from her vows, she must do what is possible to return to her religious institute (c. 672, par. 1).

Do what is possible; that is, by manifesting repentence, by reforming her life, and by making all the reparations which are necessary in order that she can be received again into religion. If her return to religion is impossible, she must at least seek a dispensation from her vows as soon as possible in order to avoid sin and scandal.

The religious institute from which a religious in perpetual vows is dismissed, must restore her dowry if she brought one with her, or in charity give her the assistance of which we have spoken of above (n. 287) if she was received without a dowry.

PART FOURTEEN

NON-RELIGIOUS STATES OF PERFECTION

I

PIOUS SOCIETIES OR CONGREGATIONS WITHOUT VOWS

The societies or congregations now under consideration are associations of women leading a community life after the manner of religious, under the government of superiors and according to duly approved constitutions, but without the usual public vows of religion (c. 673, par. 1).

Public; that is, accepted by legitimate ecclesiastical authority in the name of the Church (c. 1308, par. 1). There is no reason, however, why the three vows of poverty, chastity and obedience, cannot be taken privately, and many members of these pious associations do this. But their vows remain private, just like those taken by any ordinary member of the faithful (cf. *supra*, n. 143).

These associations may be of papal or diocesan approval, according as they are approved by the bishop of the Sovereign Pontiff (c.

673, par. 2; cf. *supra,* n. 3, B). These associations are not true religious institutes nor are their members true religious in the strict sense of the term (c. 673, par. 1). Although they may wear habits resembling those worn by true religious, and though they live a community life, still, since they lack one of the essential elements of the religious state (cf. *supra,* n. 2), they belong to a canonical category all their own.

289. FOUNDING AND SUPPRESSION

The founding and suppression of these societies and of their provinces and houses is governed by the laws for the founding and suppression of religious institutes properly so-called (c. 674; cf. *supra,* n. 11 ff.).

290. GOVERNMENT OF THESE SOCIETIES

The government of these associations is determined by their individual constitutions, but they must observe, insofar as the nature of the society allows, all of the prescriptions of Canon Law regarding religious (c. 675).

291. ADMINISTRATION OF TEMPORAL GOODS

These societies and their provinces and houses, if they are legitimately established, are capable of acquiring and possessing temporal goods (c. 676, par. 1). The administration of the temporal goods of these associations must be regulated in the same manner as the temporal goods of religious (cf. *supra,* n. 94, ff.), keeping in mind, however, the special nature of these associations (c. 676, par. 2).

Everything a member acquires as a member of the association belongs to the association (c. 676, par. 3). They may acquire, retain, and administer other goods according to the prescriptions of their particular constitutions (c. 676, par. 3). Goods which are acquired by a member of an association by means of his own industry, may or may not belong to the individual depending upon the constitutions.

292. ADMISSION OF POSTULANTS AND NOVICES

In admitting postulants, the constitutions of each association are to be followed (c. 677). In admitting novices, all that has been said above regarding the requirements for the valid and licit admission of postulants to the novitiate is to be followed (c. 677; cf. *supra,* n. 114, n. 115, n. 125 ff.).

293. THE CLOISTER

The cloister must be observed in accordance with the constitutions of each association, and under the supervision of the local Ordinary (c. 679, par. 2). In such institutes, therefore, the enclosure may never be papal; at most it may be episcopal.

294. OBLIGATIONS

The members of these associations are obliged: (1) to observe all the prescriptions of their regularly approved constitutions (c. 679, par. 1); and, (2) to fulfill all of the obligations prescribed by the Code for religious properly so-called in regard to pious exercises, wearing the religious habit, correspondence, and subjection to the local Ordinary, unless their constitutions expressly state the contrary, or the nature of the association will not permit this (c. 679, par. 1).

295. PRIVILEGES

Members of these associations enjoy the following privileges (c. 680): (1) the privilege of the canon; (2) the privilege of the forum; and, (3) the privileges of immunity and competence (cf. *supra,* Part IX, Chap. 2).

Neither the individual members nor the association itself may renounce these privileges (c. 123); but the members lose the privileges as soon as they are perpetually deprived of the right to wear their religious habit or are dismissed from the association. However, they regain the right to these privileges if they are readmitted to the association (cc. 123; 680).

Members of these associations also enjoy all of the privileges directly granted to their association (c. 680).

They may, if they wish, belong to a Third Order, even as individuals (cf. c. 704, par. 1).

They do not, however, enjoy the privileges of religious properly so called, unless they have received a special indult (c. 680).

296. TRANSFER TO ANOTHER SOCIETY

A transition from one of these associations to another, or from one of these societies to a true religious institute, must be done according to the rules prescribed above for a transfer from one religious institute to another religious institute (c. 681; cf. *supra*, n. 265).

297. DEPARTURE OR DISMISSAL

Regarding the departure of a member from an association, everything said above relative to a voluntary departure from a religious institute is to be observed, taking into account, however, the special nature of the association (c. 681; cf. *supra*, n. 264 ff.).

Regarding the dismissal of a member of an association, everything said (cf. *supra*, n. 282 ff.) relative to the dismissal of religious in temporary vows is to be observed (c. 681).

298. PENALTIES

We have pointed out above that the common law which regulates true religious institutes is to be applied to the government of these associations, taking into account their special characteristics. Hence, regarding penalties, the common law for religious is to be applied unless the contrary is expressly stated in the particular constitutions.

II

SECULAR INSTITUTES

Secular Institutes are societies, whether clerical or lay, whose members, moved by the desire of acquiring Christian perfection and of engaging in the apostolate, profess the evangelical counsels, even though they remain in the world (Apostolic Constitution, *Provida Mater Ecclesia*, February 2, 1947; unless otherwise noted, all references in this section will be to this Apostolic Constitution).

Profess the evangelical counsels, especially the counsel of perfect chastity. Consequently, as we shall see, those who are married may not become full fledged members of these secular institutes. The commitment to a life of evangelical perfection differs from one institute to another. It can be accomplished by a private vow, a consecration, a promise or an oath.

Moved by the desire of Christian perfection. As we have pointed out (cf. *supra*, n. 2), the pursuit of Christian perfection is obligatory for religious properly so-called, but may also be pursued by all good Catholics even while remaining in the world.

And of engaging in the apostolate. Consequently, secular institutes of a purely contemplative nature may not be founded. The apostolate is an essential requisite of these institutes, but the manner of engaging in it will differ from one institute to another.

While remaining in the world. Members of secular institutes do not wear a special type of clothing, and ordinarily they do not have the obligation of leading a community life.

299. EVOLUTION OF SECULAR INSTITUTES

The origin of secular institutes was briefly summed up by His Holiness, Pope Pius XII, in the following manner:

> Our most kind Lord, who without respect of persons, again and again has invited all the faithful to seek perfection everywhere, has arranged in the wonderful plan of his divine providence, that even in a world which especially in our days is depraved by so many vices, there are many chosen souls who not only burn with a desire for individual perfection, but by a special vocation from God, remain in the world where they can become members of splendid new forms of associations which are admirably suited to the needs of our times and in which these souls can lead a life which is well adapted to the attainment of Christian perfection (*op. cit.,* Introduction).

The Holy Father also stated that these associations which were established here and there in the last century, in order to practice the works of charity which were almost forbidden to religious due to the wickedness of the times, have been extraordinarily multiplied in varied forms in our own day. The Church, however, had never authoritatively regulated these associations in any special manner.

Consequently, on February 2, 1947, by the Apostolic Constitution *Provida Mater Ecclesia,* the Sovereign Pontiff considered it opportune to intervene and to regulate authoritatively the establishment and functioning of these secular institutes which today have entered into the life of the Church as a new and legitimately approved type of organization, for the good of souls and the furthering of the Christian Apostolate.

300. ESSENTIAL ELEMENTS

Secular institutes may be composed of men alone or of women alone; and if they are societies of men, they may be clerical or lay (cf. *supra,*

n. 3, D). In all cases however, in order that a society be a true secular institute, at least the three following elements must be present:

1) The practice of Christian perfection with some form of consecration to God; according to the Apostolic Constitution cited above, this must be effected:

   a) By profession of celibacy and perfect chastity with a vow, oath or consecration, according to the constitutions of the particular institute (art. III).

   b) By profession of obedience so that the members depend upon their superiors in all things, in conformity with the constitutions. Through this vow or promise the members dedicate themselves to the works of charity and the apostolate in a stable manner (*loc. cit.*).

   c) By profession of poverty which limits the free use of temporal goods in a manner determined by the constitutions (*loc. cit.*). The effects of this vow or promise differ greatly from one institute to another depending upon the work in which the institute is engaged.

2) A promise, or bond, of stability, which is perpetual or periodically renewable, in virtue of which the member is bound to give herself completely to the institute at the time that the institute assumes responsibility for her must be present (*loc. cit.*).

3) Common life is not required, but there must be one or several houses in which those who have supreme authority in the institute may reside, and to which the members may come to receive their spiritual and religious formation, and where they may retire whenever they are no longer able to support themselves because of ill health or old age (*loc. cit.*).

Whenever one of the three elements enumerated above fails to be verified, the association ceases to be a secular institute in the sense and in the juridical form referred to in the Apostolic Constitution *Provida Mater,* and reverts to the category of ordinary associations of the faithful which are governed by canon 684 ff., and which are subject to the Sacred Congregation of the Council (art. 4).

Hence **secular institutes differ from:**

1) Religious institutes properly so called, because no public vows are taken in secular institutes.

2) Societies or pious unions in which the members do not take vows but live in community after the manner of religious. Secular insti-

tutes do not necessarily have a community life, or at least, not the type required for societies living in common in conformity with canon 594.

3) Ordinary associations and sodalities of the faithful, because membership in these does not involve a stable incorporation but only an inscription. In addition, many ordinary associations of the faithful are subject to the Sacred Congregation of the Council while secular institutes depend upon the Sacred Congregation of Religious.

301. ERECTION OF SECULAR INSTITUTES

Local Ordinaries, but not vicars capitular or vicars general, can erect a secular institute, whether of men or women (art. 5, par. 1). Even bishops, however, may not erect these institutes or permit them to be erected without consulting the Sacred Congregation for Religious according to the norm of canon 492, paragraph 1 (art. 5, par. 2).

When the permission, or better, the *nihil obstat,* has been obtained from the Sacred Congregation of Religious, the bishop can proceed in his own right with the canonical erection of the institute. The institute, in virtue of this erection, becomes a juridical or moral person according to the norm of canon 100, paragraphs 1 and 2. When the erection has taken place, the bishop must notify the Sacred Congregation of Religious (art. 6, par. 2).

To proceed further, that is, to obtain a laudatory decree or definitive approbation from the Holy See, the procedure outlined above for the approbation by the Holy See of any new religious congregation must be followed (*supra,* n. 10). The Sacred Congregation of Religious recommends that bishops try out new institutes before they request approval for them; thus it is wise to have these new institutes function as unofficial associations for a while before legal approval is sought for them (S.C.Rel., March 19, 1948, n. 6).

When a secular institute obtains approval or a decree of praise from the Holy See, it becomes an institute of papal approval (art. 7, n. 1).

A secular institute, before or after its canonical erection, may become affiliated with a religious order, according to the norms of canon 492, paragraph 1, in the same way as a religious congregation or society of the common life. However, a close form of dependence which would detract from the autonomy of government of secular institutes is very rarely granted (S.C.Rel., March 19, 1948, n. 9, b).

302. LAWS FOR SECULAR INSTITUTES

Besides the general laws of the Church which concern all the faithful, secular institutes are governed by the following regulations which are proper to them:

1) The general norms for secular institutes contained in the Apostolic Constitution, *Provida Mater Ecclesia* (art. 2, par. 2).

2) The norms which the Sacred Congregation of Religious has issued or will issue relative to the Apostolic Constitution referred to above (*loc. cit.*). Besides the Apostolic Constitution, *Provida Mater Ecclesia,* the Holy See has issued the following documents which pertain to all secular institutes: Motu Proprio, *De Institutorum Saecularium Laude atque Confirmatione,* March 12, 1948; Instruction of the Sacred Congregation of Religious, *De Institutis Secularibus,* March 19, 1948.

3) By the particular constitutions of each institute, when these constitutions have been legitimately approved (art. 2, n. 3). The laws of the Church regarding the discipline of the religious life are not applicable, for the most part, to secular institutes, but the particular constitutions of any institute may be conformed to these laws and prescriptions as long as this does not impede the principal end of the institute (Motu Proprio, March 12, 1948, n. 3).

303. GOVERNMENT

The internal form of government may follow the usual form of government found in religious institutes or societies of common life, but due allowances must be made for the purpose, nature, and circumstances of each particular institute (art. 9).

Ordinarily, secular institutes are subject to the bishops in the same way as non-exempt religious institutes (art. 8), but the Holy See has given some secular institutes special privileges of exemption.

A secular institute may be given a diocesan or a universal form of government, and it may even be established as a federation, just as any other association which is organized as a moral person (Motu Proprio, March 12, 1948, n. 4).

304. ADMISSION, NOVITIATE AND PROFESSION

The laws for religious, governing admission, postulancy and the novitiate, do not apply to secular institutes. Therefore, until the Church prescribes special norms in this matter, the duly approved constitutions of each institute are to be followed. In forming the constitutions of any secular institute, the rules for religious institutes in regard to admission, postulancy and novitiate may be used as a guide.

INDICES

CANONICAL INDEX

The number or numbers following the colon after each canon (c.) or canon and paragraph (p.) refer to the numbered paragraphs of this book, or to a specific Part and Chapter.

377

ALPHABETICAL INDEX